Sarah Beattie's fresh, inventive approach to meatless cooking has earned her national recognition in numerous cookery competitions. She was named *Food and Drink/ Radio Times* Mastercook 1990, National Cheese Challenge Champion 1990 and Masterchef of the North 1991. She now writes regularly for magazines and newspapers and has guested on television and radio programmes.

She lives in North Yorkshire with writer Michael Gray, her three children and a fox terrier. She looks forward to warmer weather.

either
cook for love
or
love the cook

Neither Fish Nor Fowl

Meat-free Eating for Pleasure

SARAH BEATTIE

Photographs by Patrick McLeavey

O P T I M A

An OPTIMA book

Copyright © Sarah Beattie 1993
Photographs copyright © Patrick McLeavey 1993

First published in Great Britain in 1993 by Optima

The moral right of the author has been asserted.

ISBN 0 356 20764 1

Typeset in Sabon by Leaper & Gard Ltd, Bristol
Printed and bound in Great Britain by
BPCC Hazell Books Ltd
Member of BPCC Ltd

Optima
A Division of
Little, Brown and Company (UK) Limited
165 Great Dover Street
London SE1 4YA

Contents

List of Illustrations

Photographs by Patrick McLeavey
Food cooked and arranged by the author

(*location of recipes given in brackets)

Acknowledgements

Love and thanks for help, encouragement and quiet faith to:

Jessamyn Beattie; Dylan Beattie; Magdalena Gray; Wendy Coslett; Kathleen Tibbitt; Valerie Lowe; Caroline Ambler; Mick & Nadine Douch; Peter & Vivienne Hellens; Patrick McLeavey; Lynda Sunderland; Peter Harrison; Linda Thomas & Andrew Darke; all other family and friends;

and to Alan Samson, for his early support; Helga Houghton and Sheila McIlwraith for their professional expertise;

but most of all to

Michael Gray, who saw me through.

Note:

Generally, each recipe serves 4–6 people.

Within each recipe you should adhere to using only one system of measurement (either imperial *or* metric) as they are not exact equivalents.

Introduction

*N*either *Fish nor Fowl* is a cookery book for people who love food. A meat-free diet need not be one of hardship or denial, of abstinence and foregoing of pleasure; rather it should be a celebration of life and an affirmation of the joy in eating. The following recipes shun the wholemeal-everything approach and revel in lightness or indulge in richness of cooking; in colour, in flavour and in texture.

This book contains original recipes, classic dishes and carefully explained basic techniques. It is a complete cookery book for novice and expert cook alike. It covers a terrain scarcely charted by the august Vegetarian Society, which is still trying to foist tofuburgers and vegebangers on an unwilling public. The attitude of the *Vegetarian Good Food Guide* typifies the unhappy state of meat-free eating. Stringent standards of worthiness, as in its big sister publication, simply cannot be applied. It would probably end up the size of a pamphlet if they were. Vegetarian choices in restaurants are almost invariably sloppy, fibrous masses and although entitled variously moussaka, lasagne, or whatever, they are homogenetical. This book gives these recipes definition and distinction.

Vegetarianism has been around for a long time in one form or another. In the beginning there was Man the Gatherer as opposed to Man the Hunter. Devout Buddhists and Hindus have always been vegetarians and many of the best Chinese and Indian dishes have their origins in temple foods. John Gummer, who regularly pontificates on the 'unnaturalness' of avoiding meat, would not take kindly to the idea that Jesus may have been a vegetarian. He was an Essene and they eschewed meat. The 'faddists', as Mr Gummer has dubbed them, include Lord Weatherill, the venerable former Speaker of the

House, George Bernard Shaw, Pythagoras, da Vinci and Shelley to name but a few. Of the progressive thinkers in Britain in the 1880s and 90s a large proportion were vegetarians. Statistically speaking the point at which a person in the West is most likely to be vegetarian is when they are a student, perhaps when they are most likely to question an accepted order. Many former vegetarians of the 1960s and 70s, now Grumpies in adman's parlance (grown-up, mature professionals) have glimmers of guilt in their self-acknowledged recidivism. Often they have turned away from vegetarianism out of boredom or from pressure of social convention. They are aware of the issues and would like to be able to enjoy good food without guilt. By responding to the new awareness of Green eating and also by accommodating the revival in the pleasures of eating *real* food, this book seeks to illustrate how you can have your Wensleydale, Garlic and Herb Cheesecake and eat it too.

Unlike the typical vegetarian restaurant, these recipes pay attention to the details of serving and presentation, to daintiness and to pleasing the eye and soul as well as the palate. Vegetarian cookery is here rewritten: clear soups; savoury ice creams; light, crisp pastries enfolding rich pâtés; mousses; terrines; soufflés; will-o'-the-wisp batter puddings cradling Ravigote-sauced vegetables; novel juxtapositions of flavours.

Each recipe is prefaced with a description, and where appropriate a suggestion for a wine is given. I do not claim to be any sort of wine expert; the recommendation is purely a personal one based on my own experience of trial and error.

Inspiration has been garnered from the world's great cuisines. Acknowledgements must be made to Eliza Acton, Mrs Beeton, Julia Child, Elizabeth David, Dorothy Hartley, *Larousse Gastronomique*, Claudia Roden, Irma Rombauer and Marion Becker and Anne Willan for information and confirmation. Thanks, too, to all those nameless cooks who unwittingly triggered further happy culinary experimentation. Ideas for new recipes come from everywhere and this book seeks to communicate an enthusiasm for the creative processes and an understanding of *good* food without meat.

I have consciously ignored the old divisions of starters/main courses/desserts, as a less rigid structure is possible when freed from the yoke of 'meat and two veg'. Our eating patterns are shifting, we are more often informal in our habits. This has tended to mean snacking on junk foods but it need not be so. Many recipes can be used as one-dish meals or 'food to go'. I hope, though, that you will take the time to enjoy cooking, eating and sharing the food in this book. Cooking, although a deeply satisfying creative activity, is also a performance art with instant feedback. One may be fun, but cooking for friends and lovers is more rewarding.

Cooking makes an art out of a necessity. In the affluent West we are privileged to be able to make choices about how and when we eat (even those of us on social security benefits). I chose some seventeen years ago not to eat meat. I did this because I knew I would be unable to kill an animal to eat it and it felt wrong to delegate this task to someone else. I was also concerned with the condition of many farmed animals. I am not evangelical, believing that the decision is a purely personal one. I do care, however, about the irrational vitriolic prejudice of government ministers, certain restaurateurs and uninformed Joe Public. I have written this book to illustrate the scope and quality of food without meat. It is for everyone who appreciates good food: vegetarian or omnivore.

The planet will not support total populations of meateaters; the resources required to produce sufficient meat, especially with humane, unhormone-boosted stock, are too great. Reappraisals of attitudes will be required. In the meantime, you could just eat this food because you like it.

1
Setting Up

The myth, propounded by those who would keep cooking a rarified art form, is that to produce good food you need lots of expensive equipment and a large kitchen. Not so. My own almost subterranean kitchen is quite small, had seven doorways and boasts only two cupboard units. When we arrived here, due to a calamitous relationship with the builder (why did I never notice his spurs?), it was damp with crumbling stonework, no electricity and only a cold tap sticking out of the wall. Our new neighbours kindly lent us a camping gas ring. We ate, not *haute cuisine* perhaps, but well. We needed to, it was the only pleasure then.

The bare essentials are somewhere to work, a source of heat, a pan, a knife and a spoon. Everything else is an extra. How many extras you want is up to you and, of course, your budget. Most of my *batterie de cuisine* has accumulated gradually, and specialist shops and department stores have had little of my money.

Local auction rooms are one of the best hunting grounds for kitchen trivia, the extra extras that you seldom use but might like to have: butter curlers or pats (good for garganelli), dariole and brioche tins, cocktail cutters, cream horn moulds, coeur à la crème dishes, Kitchamajigs and Taste-T-Toasts, grape scissors, bean stringers, shortbread moulds or cherry stoners. These treasures lie undiscovered in anonymous brown cardboard boxes, a lifetime's collection of culinary ephemera, part of a house clearance. I like to think the dear-departed would be pleased to know someone appreciates that springy whisk with the wooden handle. The whole boxful can be yours for a couple of pounds. It is not just the financial incentive that sends me to the salerooms; the quality of the utensils is much higher than all but the most expensive available today. They are classics made to last, not fashion accessories to be replaced every few years. This direct recycling is cost-effective and very satisfying. There's no adrenalin rush in the check-out queue at Habitat; there is bidding against Mr 'Anything for a Quid' Reilly.

Baking trays and tins, heavy-gauge and already seasoned, are also a good buy. You have to be more cautious over saucepans. I avoid aluminium altogether. Many have thin, uneven bases, loose handles and ill-fitting lids. It just is not worth skimping on pans. Casseroles, large bowls and enamelware are bargains.

Whatever your taste in china and glassware you should be able to find something. Style is such a cyclical thing – Deco can look Modern or Retro. Cakestands, by raising the position of a dish on the table, affect how people feel about that food. Soup tureens, large and steaming, somehow give off an aura of Victorian plenty. Tiered glass dishes, originally designed for bonbons, can be used to give a fountain-like delicacy to a translucent salad. Presentation is important to the ambience of a good meal and having various different serving dishes and platters allows you to set the mood. Although you are unlikely to find any of today's colour co-ordinates, you will find classic napery – white damask, heavy linen or chenille table cloths.

Cutlery is another must, with Grandma's good plate often fetching much less than a decent set of new stainless steel. It is harder to find a good knife. Bread knives, palette knives, serrated knives, cheese knives and peelers are all to be had but you will have to seek elsewhere for your essential blade.

A good knife is steel, the handle being an integral part of the blade. You will see this as a spine the length of the handle, which should be comfortable to hold. The knife should feel balanced – this is difficult to explain but if you try various knives in the shop you will get a feel for it. Weigh it up in your hand. The size of the blade is up to you. Some people like long knives, others quite small ones, but if you are going to buy just one good knife I would suggest 6–8 in/15–20 cm. Swiss, German, French and Sheffield knives all have their fans but they all have their cheap imitators too, so beware. A good knife is not cheap but should last your lifetime if you look after it and keep it sharp. *The Joy of Cooking* admonishes, 'a dull knife is a lazy servant'.

Servants these days are likely to be attached to a flex and a three-pin plug. Microwave ovens were bought in their millions, mostly to cope with that other time-saver, the freezer. Taste, flavour and texture have been sacrificed to minute-miserly technology; but what are we saving the time for? How much more of a chore is the drudgery of washing-up, yet comparatively few people in Britain have dishwashers. Dishwashers, perhaps surprisingly, can be 'greener' than washing up by hand. I would much rather spend an hour creatively pottering around the kitchen cooking, with the prospect of a good meal to relax over and enjoy than rush something from freezer to microwave to table to sink and spend a quarter of an hour or more, morning, noon and night washing dishes. Of all the machines in my kitchen, the dishwasher is the one I would be most sorry to lose.

I would not give a microwave kitchen-room. I am unconvinced by the microwave in many areas. Whilst they may be useful for reheating, artifice and subterfuge have to be employed to cover up their shortcomings in other areas – even to achieve simple things. I used to have a Tirolia central-heating cooker. It was able to bake six potatoes faster than a microwave and the difference in flavour was extraordinary. If an oven is used to its capacity it will be far more efficient than a microwave that takes one dish at a time. Amtrak, the US railways, make tea by placing a teabag into a beaker of cold water and zapping it in the microwave. This must be the only occasion on which you would feel the need for instant tea granules! Now the technology exists it is used, even when not appropriate.

The two machines in my kitchen besides the dishwasher are a mixer and a food processor. One was a wedding present and the other a prize. The mixer, despite its years, can do lots of things the processor can't, and more of it. I do not trust either of them to make dough, not pastry (I find the texture inferior) nor kneaded doughs (I enjoy the tactile pleasures of handling these). The mixer is good as a workhorse, for beating and whipping large quantities particularly, and the food processor is an extra pair of hands for grating, mincing or, more rarely, fine-slicing. I do use it occasionally for puréeing but more of that later.

When the day comes for old Ken Wood's departure I want a Kitchen Aid – their styling reminds me of those big beautiful Fifties American cars, all curves and fins. After that I want an ice-cream maker and … hmm, rather too much consumerism – perhaps I had better return to the essentials.

The almost essential extras are the things you find you want constantly. Whilst an empty bottle will suffice for occasional pastry rolling, if you intend to do it often get a good pin. Some like glass, some marble, some even choose Tupperware, but I like a hefty straight-ended wooden one (by now you won't be surprised to know I picked mine up in an architectural antiques emporium in a Victorian warehouse). One of my essential extras is rather an unusual recommendation – a set of four or six crumpet rings. I bought them new, when Elizabeth David had a kitchenware shop, and I use them a lot. They are ideal for making individual flans and quiches, small sponges, cheesecake bases, neat potato galettes, jellied salad, mini-omelettes, regular-shaped blinis, drop scones or fried eggs, as a form for arranging vegetables on a plate, for puddling sauces and I *have* made crumpets with them.

One of my favourite implements is the Kitchamajig which not only lifts and separates but also folds, crushes, strains, mashes and whips. It is a very simple metal tool, almost elegant, and can be tossed into the dishwasher. I do not know if they are still being manufactured.

A sieve, a bowl, scales and a measure, a baking tin and dish, a loose-bottomed cake tin, a whisk and a grater will give you the basic wherewithal to make most of the things in this book. There is little point in buying a pasta roller if you are only going to make pasta biennially. You can roll it out by hand.

Hands, since the dawning of the Science Age, have been only barely tolerated in the kitchen. Formerly, as illustrated by Ruth Mott in *The Victorian Kitchen*, hands were used for beating batters and cake mixtures and for folding in. This practice has been rather frowned upon; a certain squeamishness exists, a prudery. But it is very satisfying to make a cake like this. You really do get a feel for the whole process; each stage is more graphically apparent when in such close contact with the ingredients. Although things are changing, from the 'untouched by human hand' boasts of the Fifties and Sixties to the 'handmade' claims of the Nineties, the anxieties still exist. The furore over Marco Pierre White poking his fingers into pots and pies was a classic example.

Improvisation in the kitchen is a handy skill; my asparagus cooks standing upright in the four-sided grater with a second saucepan over the top. And yet every year I do admit to a sneaky longing for a nice shiny new asparagus kettle. The acquisition of kitchen gadgets is habit-forming.

Not all devices actually save time if you include the cleaning of all the fiddly bits. Use machines in the kitchen, don't be used by them. A quick rubbing-in of fat to flour can be done in the scales pan in a couple of minutes; how long to get out the food processor or mixer and then clean it afterwards?

We have busy lives – we spend time trying to create activities to fill our time. Bring back slow food and conversation. There are recipes in this book which can be prepared in advance, so are ready to eat when needed; others can be partially prepared with a minimum of pre-meal cooking, and some could be frozen if you must.

When cooking is too much of a chore – don't cook. Get somebody else to do it (children, partner, flatmate or Indian take-away) or eat raw fruit, or fast! Hunger can be good for stimulating the digestive and creative juices. Nutritionally there is no reason why you should be contracted to a hot square meal every day. Relax about routines and schedules. This is not an impossibly romantic view, I have a frantic houseful of my own. Most people who say they hate cooking actually mean they resent being the one expected to take responsibility for feeding everyone. One of the nicest meals I have had recently consisted of dark chewy maltmeal bread, soft fresh goat's cheese, a ripe melon dressed with raspberry vinegar and various salad leaves; I shared it with my three children and all of us enjoyed it. Better simple real food than a fraught cook or something fancy out of a packet that disappoints.

2
The Ingredients

To be a good cook you need to be a successful shopper. As a nation, despite the fact that shopping seems to be one of our most popular leisure activities (you can even indulge in shopping holidays), we are not very good at it. It is a cliché, but true, that our Euro-counterparts are far more skilled. One of the great pleasures of trips to the Continent is an excursion to the local market. However small the town it seems that much better quality produce is available. Elizabeth David and Peter Mayle, in their different ways, both evoke vivid memories of French markets. A great deal of haggling goes on in markets all over the world but not in Britain. We take what we are given and we pay for it. Is it a hangover from post-war rationing – that streak of make-do-and-mend – or a lack of interest in quality, or is it British reserve? Supermarket greengrocery would seem to prove the last of these. When customers serve themselves and take responsibility for the choice of fruit or vegetables, they require a higher standard. Unfortunately they do not always know what they are looking for. The British are as embarrassed by a wholehearted enjoyment of food as they are by sex and therefore unlikely to ask questions. Whether this is due to Puritanism or the weather I do not know. People with an intellectual interest in the table are dubbed 'food pseuds', the French are sneered at for wanting to teach their schoolchildren about gastronomy and we are supposed to applaud when fast food makes it to Russia. My heart sinks as I watch TV images of Muscovites queuing around Red Square to spend a week's wages on a Big Mac.

Being interested in food means paying attention to its constituent parts. Good quality ingredients are the essentials for good cooking. Drew Smith, former editor of *The Good*

Food Guide and now editing *Taste*, asserts, '... good food does not have to be expensive, bad food always is.' Big is not always beautiful and small, despite the current obsession with 'baby' everything, is not always sweeter. The embryonic sweetcorn-on-the-cob now available were bred specifically for decoration and in my view that is all they should be used for. Harvesting too early to obtain a miniature can be a mistake. Grapes and gooseberries need to grow and mature before their true flavours emerge. Young peas are delicious but so, cooked a different way, are the larger, older peas. To only buy immature fruit and vegetables is to miss out on a whole range of flavours.

It is wonderful to be able to *choose*. The variety of the potato is supposed, by law, to be displayed at the point of sale but locally I have little choice so that legislation is of little use to me. Often they are merely marked red or white, like cheap house wine. To know the variety of any fruit or vegetable is important – the flavour and texture vary dramatically. There are signs of change. Some old varieties of fruit are tentatively staging a comeback. New ones are constantly being developed but, until recently, almost never with flavour as primary consideration. As a gardener it is possible to order any one of two thousand varieties of apple trees from the National Collection, but most people accept garden centre reluctance to offer little more than Golden Delicious clones, unaware that this rich gene bank not only exists but is open for withdrawals. If this is possible for apples, it must be feasible for other fruits and vegetables too.

Unfortunately at the same time, bureaucracy seeks to standardise size and shape. Lack of funds means many of the collections are under threat. Big business concerns have bought copyrights to certain gene patterns. Already it is illegal to sell some 'unapproved' seed varieties. As the prophetic Bob Dylan wrote, 'I can see the day coming when even your home garden is gonna be against the law.' Concern expressed by environmentalists on this issue does not seem to have been taken up by cooks, although variety may be more than just the spice of life – dependence on one variety of one crop can be disastrous, as the historical example of Ireland and many economies in the developing world testify. *Vive les différences.*

My larder normally contains three or four different flours, the same number of pulses, rices and grains. There are five oils lined up next to assorted vinegars. Olive oil and balsamic vinegar probably take centre stage. Flavoured vinegars are very useful but fairly expensive to buy. They are easy to make – see Chapter Ten. Sugars – icing, golden granulated and caster, and dark and light muscovado – sit on another shelf. A screwtopped jar contains caster sugar with a couple of vanilla pods. A separate set of shelves holds mysterious pots and jars containing spices, seeds and some dried herbs. I use mainly fresh herbs from my garden. You don't have to be a gardener to grow herbs – a pot on the windowsill will do, or an old sink by the back door or a windowbox or hanging basket.

Most herbs are not fastidious and require minimal care. Your salads especially will benefit from having quantities of green herbs to hand. If you do have space, even a balcony, grow edible flowers (calendula, nasturtium, borage and sweet violet), or beans and lettuce in the back and front of the flower borders. However, you do not have to grow it all yourself: the countryside is too generous. Autumn particularly provides delicious freebies. Recent rambles have yielded baskets of delicately-flavoured mushrooms, deep purple pearls of elderberries, rich blackberries, bloomy sloes and glorious red hips. They can be used immediately or be dried, jellied, bottled, vinegared, jammed or syruped.

The sight of various gluts that have been processed into chutneys, jams, marmalades or pickles is very satisfying. And here is genuine timesaving – a good homemade jam can be turned into a delicious sauce in seconds with a little heat and alcohol. Even with the bottles and jars, space in the larder is not much of a problem because there aren't rows of tinned goods on standby filling up the shelves. A few choice delicacies come in cans, but not many.

There are few recipes in this book which do not call for fresh ingredients. If the fruit stipulated in a particular recipe is unavailable consider what you could substitute, altering the flavourings if necessary. For example, if you want to make the brandied peach ring and fresh peaches are not to hand, avoid tinned ones; try rhubarb poached in ginger wine. Think creatively around the problems – you may end up with a recipe as much your own as it is mine. (Sometimes substitution is inappropriate or reductive. Using ordinary plain flour when strong has been specified can spoil the dough; using sunflower oil where sesame or hazelnut is called for will impair the flavour of the dish. Rice comes in a variety of forms, not all interchangeable. Risotto will lack its classic creaminess if made with basmati in place of arborio – it simply won't be risotto.)

By having this attitude to freshness you will end up cooking *au marché*, checking out what is in season before you decide what to make. This will save you money, keep you in tune with the passing year and improve the quality of what you buy. Importation and new varieties mean that fruits and vegetables are in season for much longer now than they ever were. The diversity of produce available has increased even in the gastro-wastelands of the rural North where I live and cook – but greengrocers and delicatessens need supporting if they are not to be squeezed out by supermarkets. The small supplier can respond to individual needs far more easily than the retail giants. This not to say that they will: you must nurture them. However, if the community in which you live is not interested in much more than fish and chips, pie and chips or sausage and chips, things will not be easy. In the short time we have lived here three delis have come, struggled against entrenched attitudes, then gone under. We are in the small minority that mourns them. The likelihood of having good suppliers close at hand seems to have as much to do with luck as population density, economic conditions, social attitudes or racial mix. I know several rural areas that are really excellent places to buy food.

When organic vegetables first came to be marketed under that banner, the quality was variable. Too often the produce was wizened and pockmarked and very expensive. It was available only in a few obscure places. Attention to distribution and marketing has solved many problems. The realisation that organic crops still need looking after in terms of pest control and fertilisation has meant that standards have risen dramatically. Faced with a choice now between organic and non-organic I almost invariably choose the former. The global good has no longer to be balanced against inferior quality. The flavour of organic produce, unplumped by artificial additives, is often markedly better. If you are fortunate enough to be able to purchase from the farm gate, do – the closer you are to the producer the fresher and better your eggs, milk, cheese, fruit and vegetables are going to be. You will know if the eggs are *really* free range and you will get advance warning of a coming glut or shortage. Friendly relations between you and your suppliers do pay off.

When buying fresh produce not only should the senses of sight and touch be used but also, more importantly I would say, the sense of smell. Clues to how well-flavoured or how ripe a tomato, pineapple or melon is, are there for the inhaling. Using your nose as a pointer in the kitchen will allow you to tell when the cake is baked, the sugar caramelised under the grill or when the butter reaches 'the point of fragrance' as it heats up.

To be able to use this undervalued sensory organ you must not abuse it. I was once told never to trust a thin cook – more appropriate not to trust a scented one. Those who splash it on all over are unlikely to appreciate the subtleties of fragrant basmati cooked to perfection. Although we have little direct control over the air we breathe and the odours that assail us outside our front doors, we can to a large extent affect the quality of our domestic environment. A recipe book is an odd place to encourage people to consider their toilet cleaners, but these powerful chemicals are highly charged with noxious perfumes that impair our sense of smell. The olfactory organ is sensitive, with a delicate balance, and too many overblown airfresheners and membrane-searing 'lemon' or 'pine'forest' polishes and cleaners will desensitise it. A scented geranium will gently take care of those natural but unpleasant odours in the toilet. (Gently crushing a leaf releases the plant's pleasant fragrance.) The truly more eco-friendly cleaning products have natural fruit and flower oils and extracts which do not offend. As with organic produce, the green choice no longer means sacrificing high standards – quality and performance have improved noticeably over the past five years.

It has taken Britons a long time to become aware of the problems posed by detergents. As a twelve-year-old in Canada at the beginning of the Seventies I became involved with a petition to reduce phosphates in washing powders. Someone told me then that the amount of clingfilm sold annually was enough to go around the globe 'n' times, and the vivid imagery this induced has stayed with me. I still see the planet suffocated under a plastic blanket. The scares about the possible carcinogenic properties of this material have increased my dislike of it. Regrettably, supermarkets universally use it. Paper, available as recycled and unchlorine-bleached greaseproof or waxed or siliconed, can be used instead for wrapping cheese or pastry. Lids can be improvised with plates, saucers or baking tins. I rarely use aluminium foil and never allow it to touch the food. If I do have to cover a dish with it I always line with a double thickness of paper first. A taint is detectable whenever either foil or film has been in direct contact with food; for this reason alone I would avoid using them. This is very obvious with soft cheese and fruit.

Packaging, or rather the lack of it, often partly determines which goods I purchase – oil must not only be high quality, it must also come in a *glass* bottle or tin which can be recycled. There are disturbing trends to repackage staples such as butter and flour in plastics when previously they came in nice biodegradable paper.

Artificial flavourings have the same effect on the tastebuds as perfumes on the nose. Monosodium glutamate has been around a long time as a 'flavour enhancer' – the Chinese developed it centuries ago. This fact does not endear it to me. In the same way as over-exposure to violence brutalises, many people have lost the ability to appreciate complex flavours due to mass consumption of MSG and similar substances. Delicate flavours are perceived as bland, and a cycle of need is built up. Real food eaters who turn vegetarian gradually become more aware of the 'low notes', as Paul Levy terms them, in vegetable foods. Because in meat cookery these are more aggressively present, it takes time for the palate to start registering them in this new, more subtle way – they *are* there. And while controversy still rages about the effects of the additives in our foods, it is simpler to avoid processed food almost entirely.

Whether to use butter or lower fat margarine is one of the dilemmas of the age. Ambrose Heath, in his *Kitchen Table Talk* of 1953, had little choice. Synthetic cream and margarine had to be used, as butter and cream were still in short supply. We have a choice and I choose butter. The flavour is so much better and often the margarines give a poor texture to the finished dish. I use monosaturated and polyunsaturated oils as well and it should be remembered that I never use lard or animal fats other than dairy ones. The choice is, of course, yours. You can easily substitute a vegetable margarine for the butter. A healthy diet is more to do with balance and variety, though. Giving up the pleasures of butter, eggs, cheese and cream will not necessarily help you to live longer. I recently read a newspaper report of a study of a group of men, half of whom had had their cholesterol level significantly lowered. Researchers were surprised to find that the death rate had not decreased – the incidence of suicide had increased. Is this proof that a little bit of what you fancy does you good? Can it be confirmed too by the news that moderate drinkers live longer than teetotallers?

The power of advertising is awesome. Its ability to persuade people that they are incapable of wielding a breadknife efficiently, or that struggling to open a welded pack of sweaty slices is quicker and more convenient than cutting a piece of cheese off the block, is mind-boggling. The admen deal in insecurities; they tell the housewife she cannot make a lump-free cheese sauce – better stir the milk into the powder from the packet. To make pancake batter, just add an egg and milk to the contents of the packet – wait a minute, you only add egg and milk to flour, what else is in the packet? Instant meringues (just whisk for ten minutes on high speed), tinned porridge, frozen bubble-and-squeak, micro(wave) chips: is this what we all want or is it what we are being duped into believing we *need*, undermined as we are by the subtext of the advertisements? Who put the con into convenience, and who is banking on all those time-savers? Good cooking need not be difficult or time-consuming. A worrying trend in the ready meals market in the USA has been the development of children's complete microwave meals including kiddy directions and a notecard: 'from Mommy – have a nice day, Son'. An unthinkable idea here? I fear not.

Smaller producers, concerned with the state of our food, are springing up all over these islands. Seek them out and support them. This book is a salvo in the side of those in the food industry who seek to distance us from the pleasures of the fresh.

3
Soups

Soup can be a wondrous thing: spicy or piquant, creamy or clear, hearty or delicate. It can fill you up, appetise or cleanse the palate. It can be eaten or drunk, hot or cold, at the beginning, end or in the middle of a meal.

Soup of the day on many restaurant menus is so often a misnomer; it is more likely 'soup of yesterday's leftovers'. In rather too many other establishments, reliance on powdered stocks or indeed powdered soups, is normal. I was shocked to find huge barrel-like cartons of instant lobster bisque and asparagus à la crème in the catering section of the cash and carry. This begs the question, what sort of restaurants are conning their customers in this way? These flavours are not on offer in *cheap* cafés. Condensing, freeze-drying and dehydrolising have all damaged soup's reputation. There is *nothing* like a good homemade soup made with fresh ingredients.

The food processor or liquidiser has been a mixed blessing in the soup kitchen. Formerly, puréeing was a drag; scullery maids were employed to pound and push through sieves. Now, at the touch of a button ultra-sharp blades will chop it all to bits in seconds. But stop and think before you whizz; glubbiness is not necessarily in the nature of soup. Too many otherwise delicious soups have been ruined by a babyfood texture. Clear soups have been neglected. Chunky soups have been puréed out of existence. This is not to say that the liquidiser should *never* be used; sometimes it is exactly what is called for, as in the Sweetcorn Chowder (p. 36), but its constant use should be checked.

Try to find the time for a stock pot. If you simply can't, make sure that the concentrate or cube you use contains no harsh MSG or other additives. Offcuts, clean peelings and extra vegetables can all be used for stock; don't waste them. This is not to say that your stockpot is a bin for all the ordures. Stocks should have definition. Celery, carrots, leeks, garlic and onions, especially shallots, are the basics in a good vegetable stock. Dried mushrooms or mushroom peelings can be used for the very savoury deep notes. Various pot herbs such as Hamburg parsley, with its roots, give aromatic highlights. Do not use too many different vegetables in the same stock – it will be an anonymous hotch-potch. This is acceptable in a homely mixed vegetable soup, but look for more refinement for delicate soups. For a full-flavoured dark stock, brown but do not burn the vegetables in a little fat – butter or olive oil add flavour – before adding the water. An excellent white stock can be made with leeks, fennel and lemon – do not brown the vegetables in this case. If you are in a hurry, mince the vegetables before braising and/or boiling. Potatoes are not always welcome in the stock pot. They cloud the stock as they break down in cooking. This can be useful for thickening in heavier soups but avoid them in clear soups. It is possible to make stock in large quantities and freeze it in ice-cube trays for later use.

The extras when serving soup are important – remember the bread or grissini or croutons, but every so often try something different. Mini-dumplings or gnocchi, won tons or ravioli or noodles, poached or just-hardboiled quail's eggs, tiny tartlets or vol au vents or choux puffs, bruschetta or focaccia are all possibilities.

Swirls of cream, yoghurt or smetana are accepted practice but nonetheless effective. Try, too, swirls of a complimentary soup or place two soups in yin and yang positions in the same soup plate. This cannot work for all soups, of course, but try it with the Curried Parsnip and the English Onion for example.

Sprigs of parsley are a bit clichéd, but why not deep fry them, or other herbs? Try also finely shredded spinach or spring greens dunked in boiling oil until crisp but still bright green. Crunchy garlic or onion rings are especially good on creamy soups. Give chilled soups a garnish of herbs or herb flowers frozen in ice cubes.

If you have a large freezer and a set of small nesting basins you can even make ice bowls to serve the soup in. Pour water into the largest bowl to about halfway. Add the next size down bowl, weighing it down slightly (not so much that it sits on the base of the larger one) so that the rims of the basins are level and the water has come up the sides. Add a little more water if necessary. Freeze until solid then remove the inside basin. Violets or herbs could be dipped in water and arranged against the ice if liked. A further layer of ice can be added by using the smallest bowl in the same way as before. If there is difficulty removing the bowl just run in a little warm water and it will slide out easily. Repeat the process to make as many bowls as needed. They can be stacked, with interleaved silicone paper, wrapped and stored in the freezer until needed. Pour in the chilled soup immediately before serving: delay could be messy! Alternatively stand glass dishes in bowls full of cracked ice.

As in the rest of the book, feel free to experiment and deviate from the recipes, but give thought to presentation and accompaniments. If it is supposed to be hot, ensure it isn't lukewarm and if it should be cold, then don't let it be tepid. Be subtle but not bland. Be definite but not strident. Be confident and you will have the best soup kitchen around.

Apricot Soup

This is a simple dessert soup, lovely, light and slightly tart in the summer months, made with fresh apricots, but welcomingly fruity in the wintertime, richer and sweeter made with the dried. When buying dried fruit, look for unsulphured ones. The ready-plumped varieties may look more enticing but it really is better to soak your own.

A swirl of good vanilla custard and a few toasted flaked almonds on top are good accompaniments, as is a small well-chilled glass of amaretto.

*1 lb/500 g fresh apricots and 2
    large oranges*
or
*8 oz/250 g dried apricots and 1
    orange and 1 lemon*
1 vanilla pod
2 cardamom pods
7 oz/200 g caster sugar
7 fl oz/200 ml water

Scald and peel the fresh apricots and halve to remove the stones. Pour boiling water onto dried apricots, then simmer covered until soft. Allow liquid to cool for 30 minutes, then strain into a measuring jug. It can be used to make the syrup. Finely grate the rind of half an orange and sprinkle over the apricots. Squeeze the orange (and lemon) juice over them and leave to stand.

Put the vanilla, cardamom, sugar and water into a small pan and bring slowly to the boil, allowing the sugar to dissolve properly. Boil hard for 5 minutes then strain over the apricots.

Cool and then liquidise the apricots and syrup. Strain, then chill thoroughly.

Beetroot and Cranberry Consommé

Deep, rich and clear, this soup was made to begin a Christmas feast. The jewel-like colour shimmering in white china, reflecting the light of festive candles, sets the mood wonderfully. Tart but not sharp and aromatic to an almost musky point, it stimulates the most jaded of palates.

With many clear soups, wine is somewhat superfluous – I would dispense with it here, or serve champagne or similar cocktails immediately prior to the soup and carry them through if necessary.

If you must serve something in the soup, make tiny, very light cottage cheese dumplings. Poach them separately and float them in the soup at the table. Or use tiny piroshki or ravioli filled with dark mushrooms and hardboiled eggs for a more Russian feel.

1½lb/750g raw beetroots
8oz/225g fresh cranberries
2 large onions
a few celery leaves
a little oil
1¾pt/1l water
allspice
cinnamon sticks
celery salt
pinch muscovado sugar
black pepper

Wash the beets and coarsely grate or chop. A food processor will stop you staining your hands. Peel and grate or chop the onions. Finely chop the celery leaves. Heat a little oil in a large pan and gently fry the roughly crushed allspice and cinnamon sticks and the celery leaves for a couple of minutes. Add the beetroot and onion and fry for 10 minutes, stirring. Add the water and all but a small handful of the cranberries. Bring to the boil then cover and simmer for 30 minutes.

Remove lid and turn up the heat. Boil hard to reduce by a quarter then strain into a clean pan. Press the pulp with the back of a wooden spoon to extract as much liquid as possible but do not work through the sieve. Season with the celery salt, black pepper and a pinch of sugar. Add the reserved cranberries and heat until the soup is steaming and the cranberries have just popped.

Carrot, Orange and Ginger Soup

This clear soup with its beautiful colour is refreshing and stimulates the palate. An excellent starter, it would also be ideal following a particularly rich first course or entrée. After making this soup for some years, I was startled to find similarly named soups appearing on menus and supermarket shelves. Closer inspection has revealed that thus far the others are all puréed, the carrots tending towards unpleasant glubbiness.

The success of the soup depends on the sweetness of the oranges and the flavour of the carrots. The so-called dirty carrots often seem to be better: perhaps the washing process leaches out the flavour. If it is not nectar the first time you attempt it, don't give up. Search out really good carrots and try again.

2 lb/1 kg carrots
1 large Spanish onion
4 sweet oranges – blood oranges
*   give a fabulous colour*
1 in/2.5 cm fresh ginger
1 oz/30 g butter
2 pt/1 l medium vegetable stock
pinch brown sugar
salt, black pepper

Scrub the carrots and grate them. Peel the onion and either grate or chop it. Over a gentle heat cook the carrot and onion in the butter for 5 minutes. Grate the ginger and add to the carrots and onion, stirring over the heat for a couple of minutes. Add the stock and simmer for 20 minutes. Strain through a fine sieve into a clean pan. Peel a small amount of zest from the oranges, then squeeze their juice into the pan. Season to taste with a pinch of brown sugar, salt and black pepper.

Reheat gently but do not boil. Serve it straight, or swirl a tablespoon of yoghurt or soured cream through the soup, top with a sprig of greenery (parsley, chervil, coriander or savory according to season and taste) and some fine strips of the orange zest (see also Fennel and Ricotta Ravioli, p. 119). Alternatively, season more strongly and serve well chilled in hollowed-out oranges surrounded in ice.

Cauliflower Cheese Soup

An old favourite in a new style, useful for the bargain caulies whose curds are not quite as white as the greengrocer thinks they ought to be. Broccoli (calabrese) is very good too, but cook the reserved florets separately in a little water to preserve their colour. Try the soup with a higher proportion of cream or with Stilton instead of Cheddar.

Good with a glass of cider, or one of the Riesling Ausleses, and a warm walnut loaf.

1 very large or 2 medium
   cauliflower
1 large onion
1 large potato – a white variety is
   best
¹/₂pt/300 ml light vegetable stock
1 pt/600 ml milk
¹/₄pt/150 ml double cream
1 oz/30 g butter
4 oz/125 g mature farmhouse
   cheddar
nutmeg
salt, pepper
paprika

Peel and chop the onion and potato, divide the cauliflower into individual florets. In a large pan, melt the butter and add the prepared vegetables and cook over a low heat for 10 minutes, tightly covered. Shake the pan from time to time to prevent sticking. Remove a few florets and put to one side. Add the stock and bring to the boil. Simmer until all the vegetables are very tender. Reduce liquid by half. Place in a blender or processor with the milk and liquidise until smooth. Return the soup to the pan through a sieve. Add the reserved florets. Season with plenty of black pepper, nutmeg and a little salt. Reheat and barely simmer for 10 minutes. Add the cream, off the heat.

Cut the cheese into small cubes. Ladle the soup into individual heatproof bowls. Divide the cheese evenly between the bowls, scattering the cubes over the surface. Sprinkle with a dusting of paprika and place under a hot grill until the tops are lightly browned.

Celery, Apple and Calvados Soup

The forced local celery has a much better flavour than the all-green Israeli types when used in this soup. It will invariably need washing; the imported is so hygienically spotless it makes me wonder if it is grown hydroponically. Don't discard the wonderfully peppery leaves; reserve the smaller ones for decoration and chop the rest with the stalks.

Serve with warm, malty brown bread rolls fresh from the oven.

1 large head of celery or 2 smaller ones
2 large Bramley apples
1 lb/500 g yellow onions
6 oz/185 g White Stilton
1 pt/600 ml stock or water
1 oz/30 g butter
1 tbs chopped lovage, if available
1 wine glass Calvados, to finish

Wash and chop the celery. Peel and chop the onions. Quarter the apples and remove the cores but do not peel. Cut into rough dice. Heat the butter in a heavy-bottomed pan until it bubbles, stir in the celery, onions, apples and lovage. Season with a little freshly grated nutmeg and a generous grind of black pepper. Cover and cook very slowly for 20 minutes, stirring occasionally. Add the water or stock and simmer, covered, for a further 40 minutes.

Strain into a clean pan, pressing gently on the pulp in the sieve. Finely grate the Stilton and stir through the soup with the Calvados. Check seasonings, reheat but do not boil. Serve with a swirl of cream, if desired, for an extra flourish.

Curried Parsnip Soup

A thick, fragrant, spicy soup of Van Gogh yellow which will warm to the soul. Serve very hot, in small bowls, with nan breads or papadums.

1 lb/500 g parsnips
2 large onions
1 clove garlic
1 tsp turmeric
1 tsp black mustard seeds
1/2 tsp cayenne pepper
1/2 tsp ground coriander
1 cardamom pod
1–2 tsp garam masala
oil
1 pt/600 ml stock or water

Scrub the parsnips and chop roughly. Peel and chop the onion and garlic. Pour a little oil into a large saucepan. Fry the mustard seeds until they pop. Scrape out the seeds from the cardamom pod and crush. Add to the oil with the turmeric, cayenne and coriander. Fry gently for a minute, then add the onion, garlic and parsnips. Continue frying, stirring to avoid sticking and to cover the vegetables in the spices, for another couple of minutes. Add the stock or water, cover and simmer for 30 minutes, until very tender.

Either liquidise or push through a fine sieve. Stir in the garam masala and adjust the seasoning to taste with salt and pepper. Reheat before serving garnished with sprigs of fresh coriander leaves if available or a little parsley.

Clear Mushroom Soups

This isn't one recipe but two. The first is for when Autumn is at her mellowest and bags of mushrooms can be gathered in the dewy cool of the morning. (They can be picked all day if the weather is overcast, but remember that the early bird catches the fungi. The sun can rapidly turn the creamy smooth caps of field mushrooms leathery. When they first arrive, the only thing to do with them is to rush them to a pan with a knob of unsalted butter and fry briefly until the juices run. Immediately pile on toast and devour. When you become a little more blasé add some chopped herbs or a dash of cream.)

The second recipe is a broth which can be used to float won tons in. It contains miso, a paste of fermented soy beans which resembles something unmentionable. Both dried and fresh shiitake mushrooms are used, giving an excellent breadth of flavour.

I

about 3 lbs/1.5 kg freshly picked field mushrooms; a few horse mushrooms or blewits can be added if available
1 lb/500 g shallots
3 cloves garlic
parsley
chives
1 oz/30 g butter
1½ pt/1 l water
little dry sherry or cognac

Clean and trim the mushrooms, check for maggots and weevils – dark brown traces of tunnels will give them away. Discard any affected mushrooms. Peel and finely chop the shallots and garlic. Fry in a large pan with the butter. Slice the mushrooms and add to the shallots when they are just beginning to colour. Gently stir around, taking care not to break up the mushrooms. Fry for 5 minutes then add the sherry or cognac. Cook covered for another 5 minutes. Chop the herbs and add with the water. Season and bring to the boil and simmer very gently for 1–2 hours. Strain, check seasoning and serve very hot with a few slices of mushroom in each bowl and a good pinch of freshly chopped chives.

II

2 bunches spring onions
2 cloves garlic
½ in/1.5 cm fresh root ginger
1 oz/30 g dried shiitake
    mushrooms
8 oz/250 g fresh shiitake
    mushrooms
2 tbs toasted sesame oil
2 tsp tamari soy sauce
1 tbs miso
1¾ pt/1 l water

Boil the water and pour on to the dried mushrooms. Peel and finely chop the spring onions. Squeeze the garlic through a press and grate the ginger. Heat the sesame oil with the soy sauce and add the onions, garlic and ginger. Cook slowly over a low flame. Trim and thinly slice the fresh mushrooms. Add to the pan, shaking to prevent sticking. Cook for a further 5 minutes, shaking or stirring, and then add the dried mushrooms and their soaking liquor. Simmer for 30 minutes then stir in the miso, off the heat. Stir until dissolved completely, reheat and serve with or without straining, as desired.

A typical garnish would be a flower cut from a spring onion. This is not difficult but requires patience. Cut a 2 in/5 cm piece of spring onion, not including the base. Make a lengthwise cut from one end towards the middle, about ⅞ in/2.25 cm. Give a quarter turn and repeat. Now do the same on the opposite end. Set in a bowl of iced water and the cut ends will open out. The more cuts you make the finer the petals.

English Onion Soup

A seasonable soup for after wintery walks. Leave the onions baking whilst you go out in the crisp air, and return to a warm, fragrant kitchen, appetite sharpened by the exercise and the cold.

Drink a farm cider or perry or a well-brewed local ale with the soup and collapse in front of a log fire oozing contentment!

1½lb/750g English onions
cloves
2 bay leaves
nutmeg
white peppercorns
2 cloves garlic
2 big red carrots
2 small turnips
small bunch of parsley, sage and
    thyme, tied together
or
sprig of winter savory, if available
tiny amount of dried rosemary
2 sticks celery, including leaves
2oz/60g fresh white breadcrumbs
½pt/300ml single cream
oil
unsalted butter
water

Peel the onions and stud with cloves, using a total of 15 cloves. Put a thin film of oil in the base of a deep casserole dish. Wash and roughly chop the carrots, celery and turnips. Place on the oil. Put the onions on top. Lay the herbs over them. Season with nutmeg and about 7 crushed white peppercorns. Sprinkle with a little salt. Pour in water to a depth of 2in/5cm. Cover and place in a hot oven, (gas mark 6/400°F/200°C) for 15 minutes, then reduce heat to gas mark 1/275°F/140°C for 3–5 hours. If you have an S setting or an Aga just leave to cook all day.

When the onions are very soft lift out with a slotted spoon. Remove the cloves and put the onions in a food processor or work through a mouli. Strain the cooking liquor into the processor bowl. Add the breadcrumbs and the single cream. Blend until smooth. Check seasonings. Reheat gently, stirring, until piping hot, but don't boil. Serve with a dusting of freshly grated nutmeg and a sliver of cold butter on top.

Celeriac Bouillon

The broth is rich and dark and the sharp tang of lemon vinegar wakes up a jaded palate. If you prefer, use balsamic instead of lemon vinegar, or try dry sherry as a softer alternative.

1 very large celeriac,
  1–2 lbs/500 g–1 kg
1 lb/500 g carrots
1 lb/500 g strong English onions
4 cloves garlic
2–3 tsps alcool de citron vinegar
1¼ pt/1 l water or stock
olive oil
bouquet garni
salt, pepper

Cut a thick slice from the centre of the celeriac, then cut this into julienne strips. Place in a small bowl and cover with the lemon vinegar and sprinkle with the salt and pepper. Put on one side and allow to stand.

Peel the onions and garlic and chop roughly. In a large, heavy-bottomed pan with a good lid, gently heat a couple of tablespoons of olive oil, add the onions and garlic and cover tightly, shaking the pan from time to time. Chop the remaining celeriac and the carrots. Add to the pan, turn up the heat and stir over a medium flame until everything is nicely browned. Pour over the water or stock, add the bouquet garni and simmer, covered, for 1 hour. Strain into a clean pan, tip in the marinating strips of celeriac and check seasonings. Simmer for a further 8–10 minutes and serve steaming hot.

Fennel and Torte di Dolcelatte Soup

This delectable soup can be used hot or cold, accompanied by generous hunks of ciabatta or a hot focaccia. It is a rich, substantial, yet delicately complex soup.

2 large bulbs Florence fennel
3 cloves garlic
1 large sweet onion
1 pt/600 ml vegetable stock
1/4 pt/150 ml soured cream
8 oz/250 g Torta di Dolcelatte
olive oil
seasonings

Reserving some of the feathery tops, roughly chop the fennel, onion and garlic. Place in a large, heavy-bottomed pan with a tight-fitting lid. Add a little olive oil and cook over a low heat, with the lid on, until the vegetables are soft and beginning to colour. Add the stock and simmer for 30 minutes. Tip into a food processor or blender with the Torta di Dolcelatte and most of the soured cream (reserve 2 tbs). Process until fairly smooth. Season to taste.

To serve hot, reheat gently, do not boil. Place in warmed dishes, top with a swirl of soured cream and a wisp of fennel leaf.

To serve cold, chill well, freeze some fennel foliage in small ice cubes and pop into the bowl just before serving.

French Garlic Soup

This is like the classic French onion soup, complete with bubbling cheese topping, but made with garlic. In quantity, simmered like this, the garlic looses its pungency.
Serve with a good plonk from the south of France – a Côtes du Roussillon or a Corbières.

3 bulbs garlic
1¾pt/1 l stock or water
small bunch of sage
2 cloves
6 white peppercorns
1 tsp salt
1 baguette
Gruyère or Raclette

Divide the garlic into cloves and peel. Place in a saucepan with the sage, cloves, crushed peppercorns, salt and stock or water. Bring to the boil. Cover and simmer for 40 minutes.

Cut the loaf into oblique slices ½in/1 cm thick. Toast lightly on both sides. Grate or thinly slice the cheese. Lay on the toast. Strain the soup, squeezing the pulp but not pressing it through the sieve.

Pour the soup into a heatproof tureen or individual bowls. Preheat grill. Float the toast slices on top of the soup and place under the grill until cheese is nicely browned. Serve immediately.

Lettuce Soup

The answer to Mr McGregor's summer surplus; not so appealing to Peter Rabbit perhaps. This delicately flavoured soup needs to be made with the floppy cabbage-type lettuces, the crisp varieties don't work.

A Tokay-Pinot Gris, from Alsace, will not swamp the soup. I prefer to drink it at room temperature, not chilled.

2 lettuces
1 large Spanish onion
1/2 pt/300 ml single cream
1/2 pt/300 ml vegetable stock
1 oz/30 g butter
1 oz/30 g plain flour
a few sorrel leaves (optional – they add a slight piquancy to the creamy soup)
nutmeg (essential)
salt, pepper

Peel and thinly slice the onion. Sauté gently until transparent in the butter. Wash the lettuce, shaking off as much as possible of the water. Tear the leaves into fairly small pieces and add to the onion with the sorrel leaves if using. Stir well, cover tightly and cook over a low heat for 15 minutes. Sprinkle the flour over the lettuce and stir, on the heat, for a further 2 minutes. Blend in a liquidiser or processor with the cream and stock and then pass through a sieve. Return to the pan and season with a good grating of fresh nutmeg and salt and pepper. Reheat gently, allow barely to simmer for 5 minutes, stirring constantly, and serve.

Sweet Potato Soup

West Indian cousin to the Curried Parsnip soup? Sweet potatoes have either white, yellow or orange flesh and a pink skin. Some are enormous, like cassava roots; others are like overgrown carrots. This soup can be made with any of them but I would recommend the smaller, deep orangey ones. Jamaican allspice is a berry that resembles a peppercorn. It smells and tastes like a mixture of cinnamon, nutmeg, cloves, juniper and black pepper. The berries are gathered when green – it loses its aromatic properties as it ripens – then dried and ground.

If you have the good fortune to find callaloo, Jamaican spinach, cut the leaves cross-wise into thin strips and deep fry for a pretty garnish.

1½–2 lbs/750g–1 kg sweet
   potatoes
1 lb/500g shallots
3 cloves garlic
3 sticks celery including the leaves
groundnut oil
2 pt/1 l water
3 tsp ground allspice
white peppercorns
1 bay leaf
1 blade of mace
a little whipped cream to finish

Peel and roughly chop the shallots and garlic. Slice the celery stalks. Crush a teaspoon of white peppercorns. Heat enough oil in a large pan to cover its base. Tip in the shallots, garlic, celery, and peppercorns. Fry until lightly browned; stir or shake to prevent sticking. Pour over the water, add the bay leaf and mace and bring to the boil. Simmer for 1 hour.

Peel and slice the sweet potatoes. Heat 1 tbs oil in a clean pan. Stir in the sweet potato and the allspice. Cook over a gentle heat for 8 minutes, stirring frequently. Strain the water from the shallots over the sweet potatoes. Boil until they are soft. Pass through a sieve and check seasonings. Add a little salt and more allspice if necessary before reheating. Serve in soup plates with a dollop of whipped cream lightly dusted with allspice in the centre.

Sugarcane brandy could be added to the mixture prior to reheating.

Cream of Watercress Soup

A swirl of cream or yoghurt and a small sprig of perfect watercress leaves set this pretty pale green soup off beautifully.

2 bunches watercress – ensure
   they are fresh with no
   yellowing leaves
1 large potato – preferably a white
   variety
1 large onion
1 clove garlic
¼ pt/150 ml milk
¼ pt/150 ml vegetable stock
½ pt/300 ml single cream
1 oz/30 g butter
nutmeg
black pepper, salt

Scrub the potato well and cut into ½ in/1 cm cubes. Chop the onion and garlic. Sauté potato, onion and garlic in the butter in a heavy-bottomed saucepan over a low heat until softened.

Wash the watercress, reserve a few leaves for garnishing and roughly chop the rest. Add to the cooked vegetables and continue cooking a further 5 minutes. Blend in a liquidiser or food processor with the stock, milk and cream. Turn into a clean pan, and season with a little freshly grated nutmeg, black pepper and salt.

Reheat gently but do not allow to boil. Ladle into dishes, swirl cream or yoghurt over the back of a spoon and garnish with the reserved leaves. Delicious with freshly baked, still-warm onion bread.

Gnocchi Verdi in Zuppa di Pomodoro

This rich vegetable soup is an elegant meal in itself. The gnocchi can be made large or daintily small, depending on the occasion.

I would serve a Santa Maddalena from Bolzano at the meal – a soft, well-balanced red wine. Hemingway named his daughter after great wine (that's why she is Margaux, not Margot!), but I have 'found' two because of *my* daughter's name: this one and the St Emilion, Château Magdelaine. A trite reason for choosing the bottle perhaps but after all one cannot taste all the wines in the shop at once.

1 lb/50 g fresh Italian plum
  tomatoes
2 cloves garlic
1 lb/500 g red onions or shallots
2 tbs dried porcini, soaked
  overnight
olive oil
8 oz/250 g Ricotta
2 oz/50 g butter, unsalted
4 tbs freshly grated Parmesan or
  other grana
2 eggs
3 tbs plain flour
good handful sorrel
1 pt/600 ml good vegetable stock
salt, black pepper
nutmeg
fresh oregano
1 bay leaf

Wash the sorrel, shake off the excess water and tear into small pieces. Heat a little olive oil and soften a crushed clove of garlic in it. Add the sorrel, turning it all together well. Cover tightly and cook over a low heat until soft, then allow to cool. Either chop and combine with the Ricotta, butter, Parmesan, eggs and flour and beat well, or place all of these in a food processor and process in short bursts on the pulse button until just combined. Season with plenty of freshly grated nutmeg, a little salt and a grind of black pepper. Refrigerate, overnight if possible as the mixture becomes stiffer and easier to handle.

In a large pan, gently fry until soft and just beginning to colour, the chopped red onion or shallots and the other clove of garlic. Add the porcini and cook a little longer. Chop the tomatoes and stir into the pan. Add ½ tsp chopped oregano and a bay leaf. Season with salt, pepper and a pinch of brown sugar. Turn to low and simmer for 20 minutes.

Turn the gnocchi paste onto a floured board. Using two floured spoons form the mixture into regular cork-shaped dumplings. Heat the stock to a trembling simmer and poach the gnocchi a few at a time, keeping the others warm in the oven or in a dish over hot water. Strain the stock into the tomatoes and stir well. Reduce quickly by a quarter.

To serve, arrange the gnocchi on the base of soup plates like flower petals, ladle over the *zuppa* (soup) and hand around more freshly grated cheese.

Three Green Soup

An out-of-the-ordinary soup, and really seasonal, as green tomatoes cannot normally be bought. It is well worth trying, and a godsend to anyone with a superfluity of garden tomatoes that just will not ripen. One can only use so much chutney. The colour is just beautiful, how pea soup ought to look but doesn't – pale emerald and translucent. The flavour is hauntingly delicate; I find it difficult to describe, it is so unlike anything else. Please do not leave out the salting stage, it does remove the bitterness and is not just chi-chi.

I would be inclined to avoid wine with the soup and to match it to the next course, but if you must, a soft white, not sweet and not dry would be preferable. A German Hock or an Australian Colombard Chardonnay could fit the bill.

1¹/₂lbs/750g green tomatoes
2 large green apples, such as Grenadier
¹/₂in/1.5cm root (green) ginger
8oz/250g yellow onions (or Spanish)
white pepper, salt
sugar
1pt/600ml light stock or water
1oz/30g unsalted butter

Roughly chop the tomatoes and thickly cover with salt. Leave to stand for at least 30 minutes. Wash and drain. Peel and chop the onions, core and cut up the apples and grate the ginger. Melt the butter in a large pan. Add the tomatoes, apples, onions and ginger and fry, turning about, for 10 minutes. Season with plenty of freshly ground white pepper, a pinch of sugar and a little salt. Pour over the water or stock and simmer until all is very tender, about 30 minutes. Pass through a sieve, check seasoning then reheat and serve.

Raspberry Soup

Fruit soups are not unusual in Scandinavia and Germany. Røt Grøt, Rote Grütze or Kissel are mixed berry fruit or cherries in a soup thickened with farina or tapioca. Use at the beginning or end of the meal. A splash of raspberry vinegar is good in a starter version.

Serve with sweet dumplings, yoghurt, cream, meringues or langue de chat biscuits. A honeyed wine, such as the Beaumes de Venise, would be very good. A glassful can be added to the cold soup instead of vinegar.

1 lb/500 g raspberries
4 oz/125 g redcurrants
1 stick cinnamon or 2 lemon
*   verbena leaves*
sugar or honey
small strip orange peel
1 pt/600 ml water

Place the redcurrants, cinnamon or verbena and peel into a pan with the water. Add about 4 oz/125 g sugar, more or less according to taste. Bring slowly to the boil and simmer, covered, for 20 minutes. Strain into a clean pan and add the raspberries. Check sweetness. Heat until the raspberries are hot through and serve.

To serve cold, cook a little longer until the raspberries begin to break up. Strain, extracting as much juice as possible. Chill well.

If you want a Kissel, thicken the soup with 2 tbs potato flour or tapioca and cook it until it thickens, in the top of a double boiler. Pour into small dishes and chill well.

Sweetcorn Chowder

This warming creamy soup is ideal for lunch after a crisp autumnal walk. A glass of dry cider and some malted wholemeal bread complete the homely spread.

Scraping corncobs is easy given a sharp knife. In North America where corn is more widely appreciated special tools are available to strip the ears. The French on the whole regard maize merely as animal fodder. Some corn *is* only fit for the pigsty, tough and fairly tasteless. Freshness is essential. For best flavour use two white, very sweet cobs and two with large yellow kernels. New cultivars bred for tenderness and sweetness are very good. Corn is good roasted over the embers of a bonfire. To do this, pull back the husks (leaves) but do not tear off. Remove the fine thread-like silks. Replace the leaves and run water through them. Twist the leaves together over the top. Keep in a bucket of water in the garden but for not longer than an hour or two.

4 sweetcorn on the cob
2 large onions
1 large potato
2 cloves garlic
¾ pt / 500 ml milk
¾ pt / 500 ml vegetable stock (some can be the water the corn was boiled in)
1 bay leaf
2 oz / 50 g unsalted butter
pinch cayenne pepper

Husk the corns and place in boiling *unsalted* water for 8 minutes. Cool, and scrape the kernels from the cob. Hold the stalk, resting the pointed end on a plate. Use a sharp knife to cut off the kernels, working from top to bottom in a strip. Rotate the cob and repeat. Do not cut too deeply; you do not want any of the cob. Ensure none of the juice is left on the scraped ear by pressing down the cob with the back of a small spoon.

While the corn is cooking, peel and roughly chop the potato, onion and garlic. Melt half the butter in a heavy-bottomed saucepan. Add the chopped vegetables. Cover tightly and cook slowly over a low heat for 15 minutes.

Add the sweetcorn and cook a further 5 to 10 minutes until all is soft. Liquidise the contents of the saucepan with the milk and stock. Return to the pan, add the bay leaf and season with the cayenne pepper, white pepper and a little salt. Allow to simmer very gently for 10 minutes. For added richness melt the remaining butter and serve the soup with a small golden puddle of it in the centre.

Chestnut, Mushroom and Red Wine Soup

Velvety rich and very warming, an excellent start to a winter dinner party or as a meal in itself accompanied by lots of good bread. I adapted this recipe from a sauce one I found on a sticky label on a tin of chestnuts.

Drink the same wine as you used for the soup. Do not be tempted to use an undrinkable wine in the cooking – you will spoil the soup.

8 oz/250 g flat black mushrooms
8 oz/250 g chestnut purée
    (available tinned in most large
    supermarkets)
3 large sticks celery, including the
    leaves
8 oz/250 g red onions
1/4 pt/150 ml red wine (a Bergerac
    or Bordeaux is recommended)
1 pt/600 ml vegetable stock made
    using some dried mushrooms
1 oz/30 g butter
2 cloves garlic
salt, pepper
nutmeg

Chop onions, garlic and celery very finely and sauté in a large heavy pan until soft. Chop mushrooms into chunky pieces, add to the sautéed vegetables and continue cooking over a low heat for 10 minutes. Blend together the chestnut purée, vegetable stock and red wine, then add to the vegetables. Season with a little salt, plenty of freshly ground black pepper and a small grating of nutmeg and allow to simmer for 20 minutes.

This soup improves with reheating, so is best made in advance and reheated before serving. Croûtons made with a sprinkling of sage are particularly good.

Clear Tomato Soup

Tomato soup, maybe thanks to Warhol, is linked to canned, condensed, carroty Campbells. This is a clear consommé – the very essence of tomatoes: sweet but acid, the unmistakeable savoury tang that makes them a vegetable as well as a fruit.

Either have it very hot or very cold with no garnish or accompaniment as a palate cleanser between courses, or swirl spiced yoghurt through for a slightly more substantial starter with warm cheese or olive bread.

I make the soup with Gardeners' Delight tomatoes. These are the sweet, tiny ones now available in supermarkets. Most other commercially available varieties are tasteless. Things are starting to change, with major retailers deciding to bring in 'tomatoes with flavour' as a new, optional, more expensive range. Designer fruit and veg? Why or how we ever got to the stage where flavour became an extra is a mystery to me but not, I suppose, to agrobusiness. There is, tellingly, a tomato variety called Moneymaker.

I would not choose a wine to go with the soup; better to wait until the next course.

2 lbs/1 kg cherry tomatoes
1 small lime
2 cloves garlic
small handful of flat parsley or
     chervil
pinch brown sugar
1/2 pt/300 ml water
salt, pepper

Quarter the tomatoes and place in a stainless steel, enamel or toughened-glass pan. Squeeze over the lime juice. Tie the parsley into a bunch with a thread and lay it on top of the tomatoes with the garlic cloves, unpeeled but bruised. Pour over the water and sprinkle with the sugar and generous grindings of salt and black pepper. Cover tightly and cook over a low flame for 45 minutes. By this time the tomatoes should have broken down. Pour into a jelly bag or a sieve lined with cheesecloth. Coax the liquor only through, very gently – no purée is wanted. Check seasoning. Chill or reheat to serve. Use small white china bowls for maximum impact. A shot of tequila or vodka can be added at the table to each bowl.

If you wish to swirl yoghurt through the hot soup add a teaspoon of arrowroot to a 1/4 pt/150 ml pot of yoghurt first. This prevents the yoghurt from curdling.

The tomato pulp can be pushed through a sieve and used for flavouring other soups or stews.

Avocado Soup

This recipe started life as a chilled soup, but one day I discovered how good it was hot. Do not make it too far in advance, as the colour deteriorates very rapidly. If making the hot version, reheat as little as possible – to boil it would cause a rapid onset of bitterness. Some people like the astringent taste of an avocado subjected to a high heat but I find it most unpleasant. If serving the soup cold, chill the bowls, too. The rims could be decoratively frosted by brushing with egg white and dipping in a mixture of crushed peppercorns (pink, white, black) and sea-salt crystals or finely chopped herbs.

The buttery foil of the avocado with its citrus tang is well complemented by a Sancerre.

1 head celery – smell it, it should
*   be peppery*
2 large carrots
1 large leek
8 oz/250 g shallots
3–5 cloves garlic
2 large or 4 small avocados
1 pt/600 ml water
1 lime
olive oil
salt, pepper
cayenne

Wash and scrub the carrots, celery and leek. Peel the shallots and garlic. Roughly chop them and put into a pan with 2–3 tbs olive oil. Braise over a medium heat, allowing them to begin to change colour. Add the water, bring to the boil and season with salt and pepper. Cover tightly and simmer for 1 hour.

Immediately before the meal, peel and roughly chop the avocado and toss it in the juice of the lime. Place in a food processor or liquidiser. If serving hot, strain the hot vegetable cooking liquor directly over the avocado, process until smooth, add a pinch of cayenne, check the other seasonings and serve straightaway.

To eat cold, strain the liquid, cool, then chill well. Ensure that all the bowls and the avocados are also quite cold. Process as above just before serving.

Although it is possible to see it as lily-gilding, marbling the soup with soured cream, hot or cold, is delicious.

Rhubarb Soup

Rhubarb, strictly speaking, is a vegetable. This is not a savoury soup, though. It could be used to begin a meal or to separate a rich main course from an eggy pudding. It could be dressed up with Floating Islands of poached meringue or tiny crisp profiteroles for the pudding course. Although it is acceptable to make it later in the year, its optimum season is March and April when the forced, cerise stalks no thicker than your fingers are available.

A non-cloying sweet wine, light but not insubstantial, is needed at the end of the meal. I would suggest a Monbazillac or a Côtes de Montravel, both from near Bergerac in the Dordogne. The Monbazillac, formerly a great château wine to rival the Sauternes, is produced by the local co-op and available in Sainsbury's. The Montravel is less easily found but is well worth the hunt. I would avoid a wine altogether with the soup at the beginning of a meal. Rhubarb and (grape) wine are not easy bedfellows – though rhubarb can be turned into quite acceptable wine itself.

2 lb/1 kg sweet pink rhubarb
1–2 in/2.5–5 cm root ginger
powdered ginger
1 pt/600 ml water
8 oz/250 g caster sugar
1 sweet orange

Reserve two stalks of rhubarb; cut the rest into small pieces. Bruise the root ginger, bashing it with a rolling pin or wooden mallet, then place it in a large bowl and cover with layers of rhubarb sprinkled with sugar. Cover with a tea cloth and allow to stand overnight.

Tip into a large pan, preferably enamel or stainless steel. Add the water. Pare the zest from the orange and reserve. Add the juice to the pan and bring to the boil. Cover and simmer until soft. Strain into a clean pan. Taste and add more sugar or powdered ginger as desired. Cut the remaining two stalks into neat ½ in/1 cm pieces and briefly poach in the soup (do not boil hard). Cut the zest into very fine strips and add to the soup before serving.

If liked, on one of those unseasonably hot days around Easter, try chilling the soup very well and serving with a generous dollop of strained Greek sheep's yoghurt.

4
Salads

Mixed Salad Greens

Green salads are beginning their renaissance at last. The health food salad bars of the Seventies and Eighties largely shunned green leaves. Rice salad, lentil salad and mutant coleslaws pushed out lettuce and its fellow greenery. Things have changed and more choice of leaves is available – at a price, of course. The plus is, however, that almost anyone can grow their own salad. Little space is required and the seeds are cheap – about the cost of one packet of supermarket designer mixed lettuce salad. Loose-headed lettuce grows fast and can be cropped continuously for a season. Lettuce thinnings are a treat, very tender and delicate, and less trouble than sprouting seeds. A quick flip through a seed catalogue will give you some idea of what is available.

Herbs should not be ignored – some of the finest green salads contain quantities of fresh garden herbs. Care needs to be taken with certain herbs, coriander particularly; they should not dominate, but accentuate.

The following lists of ingredients are only rough blueprints. Experiment with the greenery around you. Blanch the dandelions you did not get round to digging out properly. Various wild plants can be used judiciously – chickweed, daisy leaves, fat hen (goosefoots) ground elder, lady's smock and purslane all have their uses in the salad bowl. Misticanza is the Italian word for such a wild salad. Mix shop-bought with home-picked for a huge range of flavours.

A melange, a misticanza, a medley, a mixed salad or whatever you choose to call it, a good green salad is always welcome. As a side dish, it makes a good foil for something rich and eggy. It makes a splendid palate cleanser between a main course and a sumptuous pud. A light lunch with cheese or an inviting starter – the green salad can be either of these too, with distinction.

I

1 large iceberg lettuce
2 handfuls salad burnet
8 sorrel leaves
handful of feuilles de chêne
  (oak-leaf) red cut-and-come
  again, looseleaf lettuce

Wash, dry and tear up into small pieces before tossing all together. A squeeze of lemon juice is all it requires before going to the table.

II

1 endive frisée
1 butterhead lettuce
several sprigs pineapple mint
3 handfuls large lovage leaves
borage leaves and flowers

Wash and dry the endive and the butterhead. Separate into individual leaves but do not tear up. Line a large bowl with the largest leaves from the butterhead, with the base of the leaves in the bottom of the bowl. Finely chop the mint, lovage and borage leaves and sprinkle a little over the lettuce in the bowl. Layer the biggest endive leaves inside. Continue layering inwards with alternate rings of butterhead and endive, scattering herbs between each layer. When you reach the centre of the bowl use the tiny leaves from the hearts. The dish will now look like a giant lettuce with alternating frilly and flat leaves. Before serving, using a teaspoon drizzle hazlenut or walnut oil all over the salad and decorate with the borage flowers.

III

2 bunches rocket (arugula)
1 bunch mâche (lamb's lettuce or
  corn salad)
2 Little Gem lettuces
10 sorrel leaves
small bunch chives
1 lemon
2 oz/60 g unsalted butter
2 cloves garlic

Rinse the whole Little Gems under the tap, invert to drain on a clean towel. Clean the rocket, sorrel and mâche. Tear into equal-sized pieces. Cut the bases off the lettuce. Slice the lettuce crosswise, ¼in/0.5 cm thick – Little Gem is such a compact variety that it will stay in nice, neat little rosettes of yellowy green. Combine the rocket, mâche, sorrel and lettuce on a large platter.

With the flat of a knife, crush but do not chop the garlic. Place in a small pan with the butter. Heat gently. Snip the chives with scissors over the pan. Add the juice of half the lemon, allow to bubble up and then remove the garlic. Drip the lemony butter all over the salad and serve immediately. If liked, the butter can be seasoned with some crushed or ground peppercorns too.

IV

small bunch purslane (portulaca oleracea)
2 Tom Thumb lettuces
1 large dark cos (romaine) lettuce

Use the large washed leaves of the cos as 'barquettes' to hold the simple mixture of torn purslane and Tom Thumb leaves. Sprinkle with toasted pine kernels and a very little olive oil.

V

1 Red Oak Leaf lettuce
1 Lollo Rosso
2 handfuls red Salad Bowl lettuce

Not really a *green* salad, just varying shades of red. The Oak Leaf is the darkest, almost a maroon. The red Salad Bowl is lightly flushed with colour on its extremities. Lollo Rosso, a stronger-tasting and tougher leaf, is between the two. The leaves should be washed and gently dried before tossing together with a little sprinkling of sea salt. The perfect topping is a $3\frac{1}{2}$-minute egg, still warm, carefully broken over the salad. I discovered this after a misunderstanding with some hardboiled eggs. I later found out that the triumph snatched from the jaws of failure was already established culinary practice chez Grigson.

Worcester, Walnut and Lovage Salad

Worcester Pearmain is *the* storybook apple, a good bright red with a little green. It is crisp and sweet, great in a salad. Lovage is a herb much like celery in appearance but a darker green. It grows easily in the English climate, dying back in the winter and rising with red streaks in the new shoots every spring. The flavour of the leaves was once described to me as being like Marmite. I would not agree with that although I do appreciate the connection. They are savoury, with a slight bite, but not strong or salty. I use a lot of lovage in plain green salads, especially to wake up bought, glasshouse, floppy lettuces. If you cannot get any, use celery leaves.

This salad would go well with a wedge of true Farmhouse Cheddar, fresh bread and a glass of cider.

3 Worcester Pearmain apples or
*   Spartans*
1 large cos-type lettuce – a
*   Lobjoits is excellent, failing*
*   this, an outdoor-grown, i.e.*
*   dark green, Webbs will do*
good handful lovage
4 oz/125 g shelled walnuts
1 small head celery
¼ pt/150 ml walnut oil
⅛ pt/75 ml unpasteurised apple
*   juice – the pale, cloudy sort*
or 3 tbs cider vinegar
1 tbs clear honey
salt, black pepper

Make the salad just before serving. Wash the lettuce, dry and tear up into manageable pieces. Put in a large bowl. Shred the lovage and cut the celery into ¼ in/0.5 cm slices. Add to the lettuce. Roughly break up the walnut pieces; don't chop, you want them in bits. Scatter over the lettuce. Core the apples and cut in small chunks. Mix with the salad stuffs.

Pour the oil, juice or cider vinegar and honey into a jar. Add a little salt and some black pepper. Shake together very well. Drizzle over the salad before tossing – hands are quick and, I think, best.

Winter Salad

Winter salad, when I was at school, meant partly cooked macedoine vegetables coated in salad cream. Coleslaw, in a cooked vinegar dressing, was not much of an improvement and floppy lettuce and pallid tomatoes were tasteless and expensive. Iceberg lettuces, which keep a long time in proper storage, are now available as a winter substitute for the Webbs Wonder. They are variable, but a good one has flavour and is crisp and refreshing. I welcome it, post-Christmas, as the antithesis of the rich festive fare so recently (over)indulged in. By January I crave light, summery food so I make this and other citrus-based salads as my antidote to winter gloom.

The wine doesn't have to be light, though. In fact if any Christmas Marsala or Madeira remains, it could be chilled and served with the salad and a warm nutty loaf.

1 iceberg lettuce
4 Winter Nellis pears
8 oz/250 g black grapes
1 bunch mâche (lamb's lettuce) or,
*   if unavailable, watercress – the*
*   flavour won't be the same but*
*   it works in a different way*
walnut oil
2 blood oranges

Break up the lettuce with your hands, tearing it into 50 pence pieces. This is therapeutic in retributive January. Place it in a bowl with the grapes. If you like, halve and pip the grapes, but I would rather crunch the seeds so I leave them whole. Quarter and core the pears, peeling if preferred. Cut into ½ in/1.5 cm chunks. Add to the lettuce. Pare a little of the zest of the oranges, cut into fine strips and reserve. Using a serrated knife, remove all the pith and slice quite thinly. Tear up the mâche or watercress and add to the salad with the oranges. Gently combine; hands are probably the best tool for this task. Drizzle all over with walnut oil and scatter the orange shreds on top.

If you are not serving the salad with a nut bread try also incorporating 2 oz/60 g chopped walnuts.

Tomato and Sorrel Salad

One of *the* classic salads is tomato with basil. Delicious as that is (I do make it quite often through the summer, with or without Mozzarella), I am also very fond of sorrel instead of basil. Sorrel can be found wild all over the British Isles, but cultivated in the garden the leaves are larger and more tender. It has a pleasant tang and its colour is bright emerald. Constant picking encourages the plant to produce more. Left to its own devices it will go to seed. If it does, cut right back and the plant will soon regenerate. If you can't find sorrel, tiny new spinach leaves can be substituted or use basil – it won't be the same but it will be good.

Italian wines seem to have an affinity with the tomato – I suppose that is just conditioning, but a good Chianti will work well here too.

1½ lb/750 g good red tomatoes –
there is little else in this dish,
so seek out really excellent
ones
4 cloves garlic
8 medium sorrel leaves
good pinch muscovado sugar
2 pinches sea salt
black pepper
extra virgin olive oil

Horizontally slice the tomatoes quite thinly and lay on a large plate like roof tiles, overlapping in all directions. Place all the sorrel leaves one on top of the other and slice across the leaves into ⅛ in/0.25 cm strips. Scatter evenly over the tomatoes. Peel and finely chop the garlic. Combine the garlic with the salt, sugar and a generous grinding of black pepper. Strew over the tomatoes. Pour olive oil in a thin stream over the salad – be generous but do not drown it. Crusty bread, either a baguette or ciabatta, is a must to mop up the oil on the plate. A handful of black olives is an optional extra.

Sunray Salad

If you are looking for a stunning centrepiece for a cold table, this is the salad. Although instructions are given for a red and green colour scheme there are other possibilities. Try orange with carrots, raisins and cinnamon for example.

Radiccio is available as a small iceberg-looking red lettuce and, as required here, in tight spears like chicory. If you cannot find it, settle for only the pale green or white Belgian endive but retain the two coloured fillings.

2 or 3 large 'chicory' radiccio
2 or 3 large pale green chicory
    spears
2 large ripe avocados
2 oz/60 g roasted, salted pistachios
1 lime
1 tbs olive oil
1 clove garlic
few sprigs red basil
3 medium cooked beetroots
1 large Spartan apple
2 oz/60 g walnuts
¼ pt/150 ml strained Greek
    yoghurt
1 celery heart

Separate the leaves of the radiccio and the Belgian endive and arrange on a plate, bases to the centre, radiating out in sunray pattern or twisted slightly to make it Catherine-wheel style. Alternate the red and green spears. Prepare the two fillings.

Red: peel and cut the beets into julienne strips. Quarter and core the apple. Roughly chop the apple and the walnuts and combine with the beetroot. Add the yoghurt and fold through. Season with salt and a little pepper. Allow to stand to let the colour bleed into the yoghurt.

Green: quarter and peel the avocados. Cut lengthwise into thin strips, about 1½ in/3 cm long. Squeeze the lime all over the avocado and add the pistachios, oil and the pressed garlic. Gently combine, seasoning with black pepper.

Decide whether to match or contrast the filling with the spear and spoon the relevant mixtures into the radiccio and chicory. Use the tiny celery leaves to decorate the endive spears and the red basil for the radiccio.

Strawberry and Avocado Salad

The strawberry season is longer these days, long enough now to do something other than just eat them with cream, delicious as that is. Strawberries are very good in salads, both this one and the Cucumber and Strawberry Salad (p. 55). The vinegar is crucial – please, no palate-stripping malt varieties. The fruity and delicate strawberry or raspberry vinegars now easily available are more than fashion's fancy; they add to the salad without swamping. Fruit vinegars are quite simple to make (see Chapter 10) and can also be used for thirst-quenching summer drinks.

A pleasant, only mildly alcoholic fizz is a German strawberry wine. The colour of pink champagne, it also comes in a similar bottle. It is not like champagne though, more like grown-ups' pop. Not for an Occasion but costing less than a couple of pounds, quite nice to sip in the sun. Beware, the blackcurrant twin is foul, more like mouthwash with soapy bubbles!

If fruit wines don't take your fancy, try an Anjou Rouge – Domaine du Petit Clocher is a drinkable, cheap wine with a hint of the berry fruit.

2–3 Tom Thumb lettuces, depending on size, or 1 large butterhead
2 ripe avocados – the large, almost spherical, bright green ones are best
8 oz–1 lb/250–500 g small strawberries
small handful lemon balm (Melissa) – pick the tiny leaves from the tops
If you can't get lemon balm use mint – apple or pineapple varieties for preference
2–3 tbs strawberry or raspberry vinegar
pinch sugar
salt, dried pink peppercorns

Hull the strawberries, halve or quarter them if you have been unable to find the small ones, and put into a bowl. Chop the lemon balm finely and sprinkle all over the strawberries with a pinch of salt and sugar and some well-crushed pink peppercorns. Pour over the vinegar and gently mix together. Allow to stand for at least half an hour, but no more than two.

Wash, dry and shred the lettuce. Chop the chives and combine with the lettuce. Place, nestlike, around the edge of a white or glass salad bowl or platter.

Peel and cut the avocado into ³⁄₄in/2 cm chunks. Stir gently into the strawberries and pile in the centre of the lettuce border.

Potato and Marigold Salad

T he Jersey Royal potato is with us for much longer these days. It still commands a high price early in the season but by the time the marigolds are ready the price is quite low. They will have disappeared before the end of the summer so try the lovely finger-shaped Italian yellow potatoes instead then.

Mayonnaise is nowhere as difficult to make as most people think. Liquidisers and processors make acceptable substitutes when pushed for time or feeling fainthearted, but if you have never tried making it by hand, have a go. You may never return to bottled or machined again! A birch whisk really comes into its own in mayonnaise making. For this salad it is made with balsamic vinegar, giving a deep, unusual colour. It also contains a smidgen of wholegrain mustard.

A wine of some body is needed with the richness of eggs and oil, the edge of the vinegar and the potatoes. Cahors produces a dark, red wine from the Malbec grape; in fact some, that are casked for many years, are so dark they are termed 'black'. The best bottle I have had was in a Greek restaurant in Périgueux where it coped brilliantly, partnered with spinach and cheese.

3 egg yolks
pinch of salt, white pepper
½ tsp crushed wholegrain mustard
1 tbs balsamic vinegar
7 fl oz/200 ml light olive oil
3 or 4 large open marigolds
*   (calendula) – try to use a*
*   mixture of oranges and yellow*
small bunch chives
1–2 cloves garlic
2–3 lb/1–1.5 kg small potatoes

Wash and scrub the potatoes. Cook in boiling water until *just* tender. Drain, and whilst hot season with a little salt and the crushed garlic. Allow to cool a little.

Lightly whisk the egg yolks, salt, a little freshly ground white pepper, mustard and vinegar until amalgamated and creamy. Start to add the oil, drop by drop, whisking hard. By the time you have added 3–4 oz/150 ml oil, it will be thickening and you can dare to add the oil a little faster, *but* continue to whisk vigorously. Go on adding the oil until the mayonnaise is very stiff. Chop the chives and pull all the petals from the flowerheads. Reserving a heaped teaspoon of petals and chives, gently fold the rest through the mayonnaise.

Whilst the potatoes are still just warm, spoon over the mayonnaise and carefully mix together. Sprinkle the top with the remaining marigold petals and chives before serving immediately.

Williams Salad

Ordinary pears, like the avocado pear, are difficult to purchase perfectly ripe. The grower picks them whilst rock hard and then they are allowed to ripen. A softening around the stalk will tell you that the fruit is almost ready. Indigenous to western Asia and Europe, the pear has been cultivated for centuries. Almost 250 varieties were available by the sixteenth century. How many of those remain is unknown. The William's Bon Chretien is one of the best pears now available. A ripe pear has beautifully tender creamy flesh and an aromatic perfume. The flavour should be light but full and rich. It should be very juicy. Pears discolour quickly, so make this salad at the very last minute – it is so easy this should not present a problem.

If Little Gem lettuce are unobtainable, use Salad Bowl (loosehead) or Tom Thumb (cabbage-type miniature) lettuce, *not* the full-sized cos. These varieties have a sweetness and butteriness about their leaves which is very appealing in this salad.

If the salad is the main part of a lunch or supper – grilled goat's cheese could augment it – a Moscato di Asti or similar would be a superb partner for it.

3–4 ripe William's pears
1 small lime
2 heads Little Gem cos lettuces
1 thick slice day-old maltmeal or
    granary bread
2 tbs toasted sesame oil
few leaves lemon balm (optional)
1 clove garlic
white pepper, salt

Remove the base of the lettuces and slice leaves lengthwise. Place flat and cut crosswise in 1/2 in/1 cm strips. Put into a bowl. Quarter and core the pears. Peel if preferred and slice lengthwise, 1/4 in/0.5 cm thick. Lay on top of the lettuce. Squeeze the lime juice all over. Shred the lemon balm, if using.

Split the garlic in half, top to bottom, and rub the cut side over both sides of the piece of bread. Heat the oil in a small frying pan whilst pulling the bread roughly into crumbs with your fingers or two forks. Throw the crumbs into the hot oil and brown quickly. Sprinkle with a little salt and some freshly ground white pepper. Tip straight over the pears – hear it sizzle – toss the salad, scatter with the lemon balm and serve.

Stuffed Nasturtium Salad

A prettier salad it would be hard to find. The nasturtium is from the same genus as watercress. It is otherwise known as Indian cress. Not only can it be grown for its showy flowers, which range from pale lemon through gold, orange and scarlet to a dark rust, its leaves and seeds are edible too. The seeds, ribbed, fleshy and pale green, appear in twos and threes. They can be simply pickled in small jars with green peppercorn vinegar and are a good substitute for capers. Capers themselves are flowerbuds, not seeds, from a prickly shrub – they could not be further from the smooth succulence of the tender nasturtium. New forms have been developed to climb, trail and bush. Variegated leaves are possible but I find the pepperiness is lacking in those cultivars.

Add a Côtes du Rhône, one with body but no bitterness such as the lesser known *red* from Beaumes de Venise, and some toasted brioche and you have a very pleasurable light meal, best taken *al fresco*.

at least 12 freshly picked
    nasturtium blooms
12 large nasturtium leaves
1 large cucumber
8 oz/250 g full fat cream cheese –
    deep yellow and rich
1 tbs capers or pickled nasturtium
    seeds
2 tsp white mustard seeds
1 small bunch apple mint – use
    ordinary mint if you have no
    choice
1 bunch watercress
olive oil
balsamic vinegar
white pepper, salt
pinch sugar

Chop the capers. Beat the cream cheese and fold in the capers. Chill. Peel the cucumber and slice thinly. Strip the stalks from the watercress. Lay the nasturtium leaves around the rim of a large plate. Slightly overlapping them, lay concentric rings of cucumber slices. Fill the centre of the plate with the watercress leaves. In a small pan heat the mustard seeds until they pop. Scatter all over the plate. Sprinkle with a pinch of sugar and a dusting of freshly ground white pepper. Stuff the nasturtium flowers with the cream cheese mixture. It is probably easiest to divide the mixture into 12 balls and push the balls into the centre of each flower. Layer the stuffed flowers on the watercress leaves.

Just before serving, add one part balsamic vinegar to three parts olive oil in a screw-top jar. Chop the mint very finely and put in the jar. Shake very well until an emulsion is formed. Drizzle all over the salad, to taste. Some people like a well-dressed salad, other prefer a scantily clad one.

Greek Salad

When I was in Corfu I almost lived on salads. Everyone who has been anywhere near Greece has their own idea of what constitutes a classic Greek salad – this is mine. The brininess of the feta and olives reminds me of the Mediterranean which was an incredibly clear azure. The tomatoes were invariably red *and* green and rather meaty. The onions were sweet and mild. The lettuce was coarse but good, and I have not yet found a comparable British one. A compromise is to use a cos, not the Little Gem variety but a large, dark green sort, with some fresh spinach leaves.

The 'correct' wine, I suppose, would be Demestica, but it was not my favourite. Maybe there are superior vintages but the ones I tried had much in common with a similarly named bleach. I would plump instead for a soft Merlot from nextdoor neighbours Bulgaria or Yugoslavia.

1 large cos lettuce
8 oz/250 g feta cheese
4 oz/125 g Greek olives (ones that
    are purply black and have been
    marinated)
2 yellow onions
1 lb/500 g Marmande tomatoes
small bunch of small spinach leaves
several sprigs of rigani – wild
    marjoram – oregano
a little thyme
black pepper
extra virgin Greek olive oil
1 small thin-skinned lemon

Wash the lettuce, separating the leaves, and tear the biggest roughly so they are all about the size of a £5 note and no larger. Cover a large plate with the lettuce. Shred the spinach leaves and toss them onto the lettuce. Slice the tomatoes, horizontally, $\frac{1}{4}$in/0.5 cm thick, and lay over the lettuce. Peel and finely slice the onion, so finely that you can almost see through it. Spread the onion slivers all over the tomatoes. Cut the feta into $\frac{1}{2}$–1 in/ 2 cm cubes. Scatter the cheese and the olives over the plate. Grate about half a teaspoon of lemon rind. Mix it with the finely chopped herbs and some freshly ground black pepper and then strew the mixture over the salad. Avoid adding more salt as the cheese and olives are already quite salty. I like to squeeze half the lemon over the salad and then pour on copious amounts of olive oil but this is a moot point. Some prefer just the olive oil. Warm pitta breads or, better I think, the very crusty but fragrant and chewy white peasant loaves are required to complete the meal in true Greek fashion: and clear blue skies, of course.

Mediterranean Salad

The other taste of Greece that lingers is aniseed – of ouzo and fennel. This salad reminds me of that holiday. It can be made mid-winter and will set you dreaming of balmy days.

Drink it with a well-chilled bottle of Retsina, if you like it. It is rather an acquired taste but an evocative one. Otherwise try it with a very cold amontillado.

2 good heads Florence fennel
2 large mild Spanish onions
5 small Moroccan oranges –
   thin-skinned and sweet
4 oz/125 g black olives
pinch of sugar
salt, pepper
olive oil

This salad is very easy to make. Trim the root base from the fennel and then slice, 1/4 in/0.5 cm thick, including any feathery tops. Peel and slice the onions and the oranges the same way. Put them all in a bowl with the olives. Season with sugar, salt and pepper and toss all together with olive oil. Allow to stand 15 minutes before serving.

Glazed Pear with Elderberry and Port

Unpromising, rock-hard pears are transformed by baking and then glazing with elderberries and port. A rich paste of Blue Brie and finely chopped pecans is hidden within the base of each pear, which stands on a bed of buttery lettuce. A Red Oak Leaf lettuce could be used to carry through the deep colour of the pears if preferred.

Blue Brie may be a bit of a hybrid but change must not always be shunned – and unlike the English attempt, Lymeswold, I think it works. Roquefort and Stilton could be used instead but their flavours are rather more insistent. Perhaps Dolcelatte would be a better alternative. You may prefer to avoid a blue cheese altogether, just use an ordinary Brie, marginally underripe.

The New Zealander, Montana's Lindauer Brut is elegant and as good as many of the better champagnes but less than half the price. It does not fight the elder or port flavours but complements them. The pears *make* the meal an occasion so I make no apology for the bubbly choice.

4 firm, unripe Doyenné du Comice pears
12 oz/275 g elderberries (could be bottled if fresh no longer available)
7 fl oz/275 ml ruby port
7 oz/210 g golden granulated sugar
1 stick cinnamon bark
1 whole dried red chilli
a few juniper berries
a few black peppercorns
8 oz/250 g Blue Brie
2 oz/60 g shelled pecans
2 Tom Thumb lettuces

In a deep flameproof casserole dish, heat the elderberries until they pop. Stir in the sugar, port, cinnamon, chilli, juniper berries and peppercorns. Warm gently, stirring until the sugar dissolves. Peel the pears, retaining the stalks and keeping whole. Place upright in the casserole dish, covering with the berries and liquid. Cook in a slow oven, basting occasionally if necessary, until tender. Remove pears and allow to cool. Strain the liquor into a clean pan.

Chop the pecans. Pare the rind from the Brie and mash the cheese with the nuts. Using a small teaspoon or a parisian baller, scoop the cores of the pears out through the flower ends. Fill the cavities with the nuts and Brie paste. Shred the lettuce and stand the pears upright on it. Reduce the cooking liquor until thick. Immediately use to paint the pears with. Give each pear one coat, then repaint for a lovely deep sheen.

Cucumber and Strawberry Salad

I was first served a salad of fruit and cucumber in Greece; it was so refreshing and welcome in the bright heat. Smaller cucumbers often have a better flavour. If you can grow your own or otherwise obtain cucumbers not grown hydroponically, so much the better. Was it the muck on the old hot beds that gave cucumbers more of a flavour, or is it down to commercial varieties more interested in the long and the straight of it? Large deep red strawberries provide the ideal contrast to the delicate pale green of the cucumber. Balsamic vinegar, mellow and rich, is wonderful with strawberres, not just in this salad. Try it sprinkled on whole fruit with a drizzle of acacia honey. Allow to stand for half an hour before eating with a good dollop of Mascarpone.

For a light meal, serve the salad around a mound of fresh, loose goat's cheese or good Ricotta and accompany with warm lavender- or rosemary-flavoured flat bread – focaccia (see p. 303).

A good wine for this simple repast would be a chilled Beaujolais.

1 large Red Oak Leaf lettuce
3 or 4 small cucumbers
1 lb/500 g strawberries
white pepper
balsamic vinegar

Wash, dry and line a large plate with the Oak Leaf lettuce. Peel the cucumber and slice finely. *Cut* off the strawberries' green tops and slice vertically. Discard, or eat as you go along, the first and last slice of each strawberry. The beautiful markings of the internal slices are important to the look of the salad.

Lay concentric rings of the slices, alternating rings of cucumbers and rings of strawberries, overlapping each ring with the other and each slice with its neighbour. Start with the outside rim and work down to a strawberry five-pointed 'flower' in the middle – a small circle of cucumber peel could be cut for its centre. Dust lightly with ground white pepper. I would avoid using salt as this will cause the cucumber particularly to weep and I prefer this salad without it. However, if required add salt immediately before serving. Sprinkle or, using a pastry brush, very lightly paint the cucumber and strawberries with balsamic vinegar. Stand 10 minutes before serving.

Kiwi fruit can be used out of strawberry season for a lovely winter version, all green and glowing.

Chinese Salad

Chinese in its similarity to stir-fry and its flavours – I make no claims for its authenticity. It is good with a simple omelette or can be used to stuff pitta breads.

Accompany such a light meal with an Australian Sémillon, quite mellow but never sweet.

4 oz/125 g mangetouts
4 oz/125 g fine green beans
8 oz/250 g beansprouts
2 large carrots
1 small cucumber
or 3 in/7.5 cm mooli
2 large nuggets of preserved stem
  ginger
2 star anise clusters
2 oz/60 g cashew nuts
tamari soy sauce
toasted sesame oil

Top and tail the beans and mangetouts. Blanch them in boiling water for 1 minute then add the beansprouts, drain and refresh under cold running water. Stand in a colander to drain whilst preparing the remaining vegetables. Peel the carrots, cucumber or mooli and cut into thin strips, 1½ in/3.75 cm long. A vegetable peeler with a swivel blade enables you to make them *very* thin.

Rinse the ginger and chop finely. Remove the seeds from the star anise and grind in a pestle and mortar. Combine all the vegetables and the ginger and anise in a large bowl. Heat 2 tbs tamari soy sauce in a small frying pan. Add the cashews and cook, shaking until the soy has evaporated and the nuts are coated. Immediately throw the nuts into the salad (sizzle, sizzle), pour on 2–3 tbs sesame oil mixed with another tablespoon of soy, toss together and serve.

Black and White Salad

Another of those fruity, juicy salads for winter. Central heating and stuffy, overheated cars, buses and trains are really dehydrating. One of the cardinal rules for getting over 'flu or colds is to take plenty of liquid. This is a delightful adjunct to that 'cure'.

Pitahaya or cactus fruit is one of the newer imports; it has more flavour than the grenadillo or the carambola (starfruit) and is very refreshing. Its knobbly exterior is fleshy and succulent like the aloe but it is a brilliant yellow. The inside is a translucent, marbled jelly with black flecks of tiny edible seeds. I hope it won't put you off if I tell you it looks like compressed frog's spawn! Barbary Fig, Prickly Pear or Tsabar are all names given to a similar cactus-like fruit. It is not white but either greenish yellow or yellowy orange.

If you are recovering from a winter affliction perhaps you should avoid alcohol and have a restorative lhassi – a yoghurt drink, flavoured, if you like, with mango or mint. Otherwise, try a Jurançon, a sweet wine with hints of lemon and spice, from the foothills of the Pyrenees.

1 large iceberg lettuce, the paler the
    better
2 chicons of well blanched chicory
    (Belgian endive)
2 pitahayas
½ a sweet mild onion
6 oz/200 g black grapes
1 oz/30 g blanched, slivered
    almonds
1 tbs tapenade of black olives,
    thinned with 1 tbs light olive oil

Stand the separated leaves of the chicons around the edge of a deep dish or radiating around the rim of a large plate. Roughly chop up the iceberg; the chunks should be a little larger than an inch (about 3 cms). Place in another bowl. Thinly slice the onion and add to the lettuce with the almonds and the grapes, halved or not according to preference. Cut the pitahayas, lengthways, into quarters. Slide a knife under the jelly-like flesh to remove each quarter in one piece. Slice crosswise, ¼ in/0.5 cm thick. Add to the lettuce and toss all together. Pile into the middle of the dish or plate. Drip the tapenade over all and serve.

Kiwi and Avocado Salad

A simple pale green delicate salad, this works beautifully with a light egg dish for an elegant lunch.

Kiwi fruit, which originated in southern China, are now being rather sneered at. They have gone too downmarket for many fancy establishments, which have moved on to pastures new. The carambola or starfruit, like the kiwi, is very pretty when cut transversely but, unlike the kiwi, it tastes of little – bubblegum is about the best description. A good kiwi fruit can be tangy and sweet and almost fizzle on your tongue. The hairy skin should peel off a properly ripe fruit. If it pulls part of the flesh away it is overripe, if it needs a knife it is underripe.

Avocados are difficult to buy at optimum ripeness. Better to purchase slightly firm and await the right moment at home. Wrapping in brown paper and placing in a dark room will ripen them but it is simpler and more efficient to place them in a fruit bowl with apples or bananas.

Avocados are not a slimmer's food as they have a high oil content – so high that it is claimed Mexicans use them for axle grease – but they do contain eleven different vitamins. I once heard their flavour described as 'eating Vaseline' and most avofficionados would recognise the awful truth in that; a poor avocado is not very pleasant.

My father returned from a business trip in Zambia with several huge bright green orbs concealed in his dirty shirts. The skins were very thin, the flesh was yellowy green and almost sweet. They had an untypical juiciness about them. He told me they could be fatal. The tree overhung the poolside patio and when ripe the bowling-ball fruit plummeted on to unsuspecting sunbathers. The stones from these fruit were larger than the fruit available in my local suppliers. I grew a lovely treelet from one of them which flourished for several years before the cat took a fancy to it.

2 ripe avocados, for preference the black, knobbly-skinned Mexican ones
2 kiwi fruit
1 large cabbage-type lettuce
1 tbs lemon juice
1 tsp clear honey
2 tbs walnut oil

Wash the lettuce, shake dry and tear into pieces. Lay on a large serving plate. Peel the kiwi fruits and quarter lengthways. Slice these quarters crosswise about 1/4 in/0.5 cm thick. Repeat with the avocados. Gently combine the kiwi and avocado slices and then scatter over the lettuce. In a small screw-top jar mix together the lemon juice, honey and oil. If it is cold you may have to warm them slightly. Shake well then drizzle over the salad. Sprinkle very lightly with freshly ground sea salt and black pepper and serve.

Avocado, Tomato and Orange Salad

Colourful and flavourful, seasonal at any time. Make double quantities and serve with warm French bread and/or soft goat's cheese as a complete meal. The almost sweet English white, Barkham Manor, makes a surprising but extremely palatable choice to accompany it.

Do not be tempted to skimp on the oil – extra virgin olive oil is what's required, dark green and very fruity.

Be a discerning consumer, use your nose when marketing. The smell of a good tomato is unmistakeable. Don't be deceived by a good colour, the *only* reliable indicator is the olfactory organ.

2 large ripe avocados – the thin-skinned varieties are best here
2 large oranges
4 medium tomatoes
2 cloves garlic
sprig of mint
a little fresh fennel – the herb or the feathery top from Florence fennel
pinch brown sugar
salt, black pepper
4 tbs olive oil

Peel the avocado and cut into ½in/1 cm chunks. Place in a bowl. Using a serrated knife remove the peel and pith from the oranges. Roughly chop them and add to the avocados. Similarly dice the tomatoes and add to the bowl. Crush the garlic and add to the bowl with the finely chopped mint and fennel. Sprinkle with a little salt, coarsely ground black pepper and the sugar. Carefully mix all together and then drizzle over the olive oil. Gently toss the salad and serve.

5
Pastries

What an extraordinary number of wonderful confections begin with the conjunction of fat and flour. Crisp, melting, flaky, crumbly, rich, plain: pastry is all of these and more. From the fine art of patisserie as glimpsed through the vitrines of smart Paris shops to the consummate skill of the filo maker in a souk, and from massive architectural constructions, gilded and glazed, to humble snap-tin pasties: pastry-making is a diverse skill.

'But I can't make pastry' is a common complaint even from the most competent cooks. Whilst it must be admitted that the easiest way to learn the basic techniques of rubbing in or rolling out is to watch somebody perform them, the following recipes explain in detail the steps involved and advise against common pitfalls. Read them carefully; minimal handling is required in some whereas others *need* kneading. Practice really does make perfect. The more familiar you are with each step, the easier the process becomes. Take notice of the way the dough feels at each stage, look at the texture. If at first it is hard or leathery or greasy, don't despair. Check back, find out where you went wrong – experience is a good teacher. Do try again; homemade pastry is so superior to commercially available pastes.

To begin with, measure everything meticulously; in time, with the simpler doughs, this won't be so crucial. When I make a shortcrust for an everyday family meal, in a rush, as usual, I rarely weigh anything. A handful or two of flour looks about the right amount in the bowl; a couple of large knobs of fat are rubbed in – but this is when experience counts. I *know* what the right proportions of fat to flour should look and feel like at this point and can adjust accordingly. The amount of water that needs to be added can never be accurately given in a recipe as some flours are more absorbent than others. This is not a matter for panic. Proceed with caution and pay attention to the texture of the dough and you will soon find this too is easy. Once you have 'got your eye in' you will wonder why you ever feared the flour bin.

Pastry can be used to enclose or to display. It is particularly useful in vegetarian cooking, giving a focus or centrepiece to a plate or table that may otherwise be lacking. It lends itself to decoration and ornament, giving free rein to individual taste and expression. Whatever your style – classical, popart, deco, nouveau, whimsy, kitsch or peasant – you can make a statement in the presentation. Trimmings can be cut to suit the mood, or shapes altered – a pie doesn't have to be round or square; try a parallelogram or a hexagon.

Some fillings can be used without the crusts, as stews. I have not given any recipe for egg quiches, but the savoury custard recipes could be used as fillings for shortcrust pie shells. Other vegetable recipes could be taken and used similarly. Scraps of puff paste, rolled and cut into strips, could be turned into savoury palmiers, brushed with egg white and sprinkled with salt and seeds. Sandwich them then with the Celeriac Purée (p. 187), enriched with an egg yolk. Serve with glazed shallots and gingered peas or broccoli or use, made tiny, as an entrée or canapé.

Perhaps as a child you had one of those picture books cut into three. By turning over different sections all manner of magical creatures could be created: tops, tummies and tails were all interchangeable. Many of the following recipes can be treated in a similar way. Swap the top of one for the middle of another and so on. Don't always slavishly follow the recipes; experiment by mixing and matching. Be creative – take the idea of one recipe, the sense of another and give birth to something altogether different.

Torta di Torta

Torta di Dolcelatte is a combination of the creamy Italian blue Dolcelatte and the whipped textured cream cheese, Mascarpone. Looking rather like wide striped ticking, it is much less strong than Danish Blue, which should not be substituted. If you cannot find the Torta di Dolcellate try St Agur or Bleu d'Auverge and cream cheese; this will give a rough approximation.

Rich, buttery shortbread encloses mimicking layers of rich Torta di Dolcelatte, calabrese, mushrooms, tomatoes, onions, garlic and herbs. This pie is similar in its construction to the Sablé (p. 74). I had devised and been making them both for quite some time before someone told me this was the form of a traditional Italian recipe using spinach and cheese.

An exceptional picnic treat, cold, with Verdicchio dei Castelli di Jesi and try it, hot, with a Barolo – a wine from the opposite end of the Italian spectrum. It is extraordinary that two such different wines go so very well with the same dish, but they do.

12 oz/375 g Torta di Dolcelatte
1 lb/500 g calabrese (broccoli), broken into florets
1 large sweet onion
6 cloves garlic
8 oz/250 g dark flat mushrooms
12 oz/375 g fresh Italian plum tomatoes (supermarkets have started stocking these; if unobtainable use other well-coloured ones)
4 egg yolks
12 oz/375 g plain flour
9 oz/285 g butter
olive oil
oregano
basil
seasonings

Rub the butter into the flour and knead lightly to form a ball. Chill.

Cook the broccoli in a little water until *al dente*. Chop the onion finely and crush 2 cloves of the garlic. Sauté in a little olive oil until soft. Wipe and slice the mushrooms and add to the onion pan. Cook until the juices flow.

Slice the tomatoes. Chop 2 more cloves of garlic with a few basil leaves and a sprig of oregano. Combine the herb/garlic mixture with a generous amount of black pepper, a little salt and a pinch of brown sugar.

Place the Torta di Dolcelatte in blender or food processor with the remaining garlic and the egg yolks. Process until smooth.

Divide the dough in half. On a lightly floured board roll out two rounds to fit into an 8 in/20 cm loose-bottomed deep caketin, or a soufflé dish if using hot. Place one round of dough on the base of the dish/tin. Cover with the broccoli, gently levelling. Spoon over half of the Torta di Dolcelatte mixture. Scatter over this the mushrooms and onions. Layer with the tomato slices and then sprinkle over the garlic and herbs. Pat down gently and spoon over the remaining Torta di Dolcelatte, levelling the top. Cut the second round into eighths and crimp the outside curves (making petticoat tails). Carefully place on the top and bake at gas mark 4/350°F/180°C for 45–50 minutes. Allow to stand 10 minutes in a warm place before serving. If using cold, cool, then chill in the tin. Before serving run a knife around the edge and slip off the sides of the tin.

Tarte au Chaume

Chaume is a semi-soft French cheese with a washed, orange rind and, as my partner says, a taste verging on a smell. The tart is recommended for picnics when the light is golden, the air crisp and the poignancy of Autumn touches you. Make the most of these short fleeting days before the murk of winter sets in. Take plenty of rugs and woollies and a good bottle of soft claret. Pick blackberries for pudding, elderberries for a sauce next time you make the tart, and sloes for gin or sherry.

12 oz/400 g plain flour
6 oz/200 g unsalted butter
1½ lb/750 g slender leeks
6 oz/200 g Chaume
2 cloves garlic
a little oil or butter
pepper

Rub the butter into the flour and with a little water bind together. Chill.

Clean the leeks and cut into ½ in/1.5 cm lengths. Peel and crush the garlic. Slowly cook the leeks and garlic in a little butter or oil until meltingly soft. Remove the cheese rind and cut the Chaume into small cubes. Stir through the leeks and season with pepper and sea salt.

Roll out two-thirds of the pastry and line a 9 in/23 cm flan ring or dish. Press well into the sides and neaten the top. Roll out the remaining pastry into an oblong. Cut into narrow strips ½ in/1 cm wide. Turn the leeks into the pastry shell levelling the top. Lay the strips over the leeks to form a lattice.

Put in a hot oven (gas mark 6/400°F/200°C) for 30–35 minutes until golden brown.

To keep warm for a picnic, immediately wrap in a double layer of greaseproof and then in several layers of newspaper.

Serve hot, warm or cold with an Elderberry and Port Sauce (p. 237) or other piquant chutney or relish.

Sage and Cidery Pudding

This recipe and the next are in the spirit of steak and kidney puddings: hearty, robust fare for winter eating. Serve with hot red, white and green (spring) cabbage — cook each separately and minimally to preserve colour, bite and flavour.

12 oz/350 g plain or 85%
  wheatmeal flour
½ tsp dried sage, crumbled
1 tsp baking powder
6 oz/175 g vegetable suet
8 oz/250 g tiny onions
6 cloves garlic
1 medium Bramley apple
1 medium celeriac
8 oz/250 g shiitake mushrooms
8 oz/250 g parsnips
½ pt/300 ml dry cider
olive oil
white pepper, salt

Peel and trim the onions and garlic and put to brown a little in 2 tbs oil. Peel and cut the parsnips and celeriac into ¾ in/2 cm chunks. Add to the onions. Trim the stalk end of the mushrooms then tear them up roughly. Combine with the other vegetables. Fry, stirring, over a moderate heat until the celeriac and parsnip are also beginning to colour. Pour over the cider and season with salt and white pepper. Cover and simmer 10 minutes.

Sift the flour with the sage, baking powder and a pinch of salt. Add the suet, combining it with a fork. Add enough cold water to make a firm dough, drawing it together with your fingertips. Roll out three-quarters of the dough and fit into a lightly oiled pudding basin. Trim the edges, level to the rim of the basin. Core and slice the apple. Using a slotted spoon, pack the bottom of the basin with some of the vegetables, cover with a layer of apple slices and then the rest of the vegetables and more apple. Reduce the cooking liquor to ¼ pt/150 ml and pour over the filling. Roll out the remaining pastry and use to cover the top. Brush the edges with a tiny amount of water and pinch to seal. Cover with lightly oiled paper and foil and tie down. Stand in boiling water and cook for 3 hours. Do not allow the pan to boil dry. (If you have a pressure cooker, you can reduce the boiling time very considerably – to about 1 hour under low pressure, but you will need 20 minutes boiling before putting under pressure. Remember to leave the pressure to decrease slowly rather than placing it under a cold tap.) Serve from the basin, wrapped in a large napkin.

Stout Pudding

No, the name does not refer to one's shape after overindulgence; rather to its prime ingredient – a bottle of stout (Guinness or similar). The dark beer gives a wonderful richness to the gravy of the pudding. Serve with mealy boiled potatoes to mop it up with.

A substantial wine is needed to cope; try a big Syrah from the Rhône or its Australian counterpart from the Hunter Valley.

12 oz/350 g plain flour
6 oz/175 g vegetable suet
1 tsp baking powder
salt
8 oz/250 g shallots
1 lb/500 g leeks
4 cloves garlic
½ medium swede
8 oz/250 g turnips
8 oz/250 g carrots
12 oz/375 g flat field mushrooms
1 small bottle stout
pepper
rosemary, thyme
1 bay leaf
oil

Peel and trim the shallots and garlic and quarter. Wash the leeks and cut into 1 in/2.5 cm slices. Fry the leeks, shallots and garlic in 2 tbs oil until lightly browned. Scrub or peel the swede, turnip and carrots and cut into ¾ in/2 cm chunks. Cut the mushrooms in halves or quarters, depending on size. Add to the pan and continue to fry over a moderate heat, stirring from time to time, until the root vegetables begin to colour. Add the stout, herbs and seasonings. Bring to the boil and simmer for 10 minutes in a covered pan.

Make the pastry, sifting the flour, baking powder and salt and combining with the suet. Mix to a stiff dough with cold water and roll out three quarters of it to line a lightly oiled pudding basin. Fill with the vegetables, packing them down well. Reduce the cooking liquor and then pour it over. Roll out the remaining pastry to cover and seal the edges. Cover with paper and foil and tie down. Boil for 3 hours and serve from the basin or turned out onto a deep plate.

Soured Cream Tart

A.k.a. an 'Auntie Daphne', from whose recipe this is adapted. Other soft fruits can of course be used – blackcurrants or blueberries are particularly delicious. Cook them briefly until they pop and thicken with a couple of teaspoons of arrowroot. Add a dash of Crème de Cassis or Myrtilles.

For a soft, flowery, unusual dry Muscatty wine, try the Argentinian, Etchart Cafayate Torrontes.

4 oz/125 g fine plain flour
2 oz/60 g unsalted butter
1 oz/30 g golden caster sugar
2 oz/60 g soft brown sugar
1½ lb/750 g sweet cherries
¼ pt/150 ml soured cream
2 eggs and 1 yolk
1 tbs rosewater

Rub the butter into the flour and stir in the caster sugar. Mix together the egg yolk and the flower water – if unavailable use plain cold water with a drop of almond essence. Combine with the flour to make a stiff dough. Roll out in a round for an 8 in/20 cm pie dish, covering the base and sides. Neaten the edge. Cover with greaseproof paper and line with beans or rusks. Bake 7 minutes only at gas mark 5/375°F/190°C, then remove filling and paper. This is known as baking blind. Turn oven down to gas mark 2/300°F/150°C.

Stone the cherries. Place them in the pie shell. Beat together the eggs, soured cream and soft brown sugar. Pour gently all over the cherries. Bake slowly until set, about 1½ hours. Allow to cool, then chill until serving.

Oyster Mushroom and Soured Cream Tart

Oyster mushrooms or pleurots are becoming more widely available. If your local greengrocer or supermarket is still only selling fairly anaemic buttons, create a demand, ask repeatedly. Greengrocers are worth cultivating; using one regularly will make them more kindly disposed towards you. Discover where good local restaurants shop. Often the so-called exotica is hidden away in cold rooms in the back for special customers; become one of the élite and the world is your oyster mushroom.

Failing the fraternising, you can grow your own fancy mushrooms. Kits are available for pleurots and stropharia (the brown cap mushroom) and little space or effort is required to harvest a reasonable, continuous supply.

Delightful hot as a main course with a spicy Gewürztraminer. Make them as individual tartlets (doubling the soured cream mixture), as bonne bouches or starters, and hand around with something light and sparkling: an aromatic Moscato Spumante perhaps. Alternatively, serve chilled al fresco with a Portuguese *dry* Moscato, Joào Pires.

8 oz/250 g plain flour
4 oz/125 g butter
1 tbs blue poppy seeds
1 tbs white sesame seeds
12 oz/375 g oyster mushrooms
4 oz/125 g shallots
2 cloves garlic
1–2 tbs sesame oil
5 fl oz/150 ml cultured soured
   cream
½ a lemon
1 tbs fresh chives
black pepper, sea salt
paprika

Rub the fat into the flour until it resembles fine crumbs. Stir in the poppy and sesame seeds. Add enough water to bind, kneading only lightly with the fingertips. Chill, then roll out to line an 8 in/20 cm flan dish or ring. Press well into the sides and flute the top. Prick the base all over with a fork. Bake the pastry case blind for 10 minutes at gas mark 5/375°F/190°C, using ceramic beans or dried crusts to weight the base of the pastry and prevent rising.

Meanwhile peel and finely chop the shallots and garlic. Cook them over a low heat in the sesame oil until soft and golden. Trim the fibrous stalks from the mushrooms and slice into thin strips. Add to the pan and cook a further 5 minutes, stirring from time to time. Cool.

In a small bowl beat the soured cream with the chopped chives, a squeeze of lemon, a good grinding of black pepper and a pinch of sea salt.

Put the shallots and mushrooms into the pastry case, pressing down gently and levelling the top. Spoon over the soured cream mixture, spreading it carefully to the edges. Lightly dust with paprika and bake at gas mark 1/275°F/140°C for 30 minutes or until the top is set but not browned.

Raised Plum Pies

Gooseberries are traditionally the only fruit that has been served in a hot-water crust but I find plums are also very good done this way. The arrowroot, in cooking, combines with the plum juice in a delicate jelly-like way. Greengages are excellent too, when you can find them. If making the pies with gooseberries, pop a tiny spray of elder-flowers under the lid for a lovely Muscat-scented taste.

1½lb/750g plain flour
9oz/270g vegetable margarine
    (the block variety is better, e.g.
    Baking Flora or Tomor)
½pt/300ml water
1–2lb/500g–1kg plums –
    preferably Victorias
1–2tbs arrowroot
dark muscovado sugar
1 egg
(if the plums lack flavour add 1tsp
    pudding spices)

Prepare the plums by halving and stoning them. Place them in a large bowl and sprinkle with the arrowroot, adding sugar and spices if desired. Turn them about until all are coated with the arrowroot. Use the larger amount if the plums are very juicy.

Melt the margarine with the water. Do not boil. Sift the flour into a bowl, make a well in the middle and pour in the hot water and margarine. Work quickly to bring all together, kneading lightly. The dough should be very malleable but not sticky. Divide the dough into six equal balls. Keeping the bowl warm and covered, work on one pie at a time.

Pinch off the top quarter of the ball, return to the bowl. Using the thumb and forefinger begin to hollow out the centre of the dough ball. Work round and around to get an even thickness, pushing the sides out. Don't push your fingers through the base but ensure that it is not too thick (about ¼in/0.5 cm is ideal). Continue moulding until you have a little round 'pot' 2½ × 2½in/ 6 × 6 cm. Pin a double-thickness greaseproof paper band around it and stand on a baking sheet. Pack tightly with the prepared plums, layering one on top of the other with no gaps. Roll or press out the reserved quarter of the pastry ball to fit the top. Brush the edges with a little beaten egg and pinch together to seal. Trim to neaten, decorate by imprinting with fork tines if desired. Repeat with the remaining dough and plums. Brush the tops of the pies with the egg before placing in a hot oven (gas mark 6/400°F/200°C) for 45 minutes. Take out of the oven, remove the paper bands and brush again with egg, this time also covering the sides. Sprinkle very lightly with sugar and return to the oven for 10 more minutes.

Allow to get quite cold before serving with double cream, lightly whipped and folded through with ground almonds and a little icing sugar.

Salsify Pie

Salsify is known as the vegetable oyster. Well, maybe. This recipe is in the tradition of fish pies but does not, I hope, falsify the salsify which is an excellent vegetable in its own right. It is interchangeable with scorzonera. They are long roots dug at any time from mid-October through the whole winter. The home gardener can also force the leaves for chards to eat raw in salads in the spring. Scorzonera has black-skinned roots. Both are similar in appearance to horseradish, which must not be substituted.

A deep oval pie dish with a rim is ideal, but failing that a casserole or soufflé dish could be used. Individual pies could be made in ramekins. If liked, true puff paste could be made rather than the rough puff dough which is explained here.

Mashed potatoes, much sneered at in the past, are making a comeback after the slurs and slurry of the instant mash days. Serve piled in a white volcano erupting a lava of golden butter.

Steamed kale, with its seaweediness, complements the maritime theme as would a Muscadet.

8 oz/250 g plain strong flour
6 oz/180 g butter or hard vegetable margarine (Tomor or Granose)
1/2 a lemon
water
1 1/2 lb/750 g salsify
8 pink peppercorns
4 juniper berries
2 bay leaves
milk
1/2 pt/300 ml single cream or half milk/half cream
4 oz/125 g oyster mushrooms
1 very large sweet onion – about 12 oz/375 g
a little oil or butter
1 egg yolk
2 hardboiled eggs (optional)

Sieve the flour with a good pinch of salt into a large bowl. Cut the butter or margarine into small dice, dropping them into the flour. Using a wide-bladed knife, turn them in the flour until well dusted in it – do not try to combine any more than this. Squeeze a teaspoon of lemon juice into 3 1/2 fl oz/100 ml very cold water. Add most of this to the flour and fat, gently combining with the knife to make a soft dough. Add the rest of the water if needed but take care to avoid overdoing it and ending up with a sticky mess. (If you have been too splash-happy cut up 1/2 oz/15 g butter, toss it with a little under 1 oz/20 g flour and add it to the bowl with the knife.) Keep everything very cold; use the knife as much as possible to form the dough, finishing off with your fingertips if necessary. Wrap and chill for 20 minutes.

Dust the rolling surface and pin with flour and gently roll out to an oblong between 1/4–1/2 in/0.5–1 cm thick. Fold into thirds and seal the edges by pressing together with the rolling pin. Rewrap and chill. Roll and fold three more times, resting and chilling between each stage. Ensure that the sealed edges are towards you when rolling. Flour well when rolling to prevent sticking.

Prepare the filling between the various rolling steps. Peel and chop the onion into good chunks. Sweat in a small amount of oil or butter for 5 minutes. Under water, pare the salsify with a potato peeler. Cut obliquely into 1 in/ 2.5 cm pieces. Add to the pan. Cut the mushrooms into fine strips and stir all together. Place a blade of mace, the crushed juniper berries and a bay leaf on the top of the vegetables. Pour over milk to cover and simmer very gently until everything is only just tender, with a slight firmness in the middle. Drain off the milk, reserving it for soup. Remove the bay leaf. Put into the pie dish with the crushed pink peppercorns, a generous grinding of sea salt, a fresh bay leaf and the chopped hardboiled eggs, if using. Pour over the cream.

Beat the egg yolk with 1 tsp water and a little salt. Brush the rim of the pie dish with this. Roll the pastry out to $\frac{1}{4}$in/0.5 cm thick. Cut a strip of pastry to fit on the lip of the pie dish all the way around. Press the strip onto the egg-washed rim then brush it with the wash. Lay the remaining pastry over the dish, gently sealing the edges. Trim away the excess. Boldly scallop the crust by indenting with the point of the knife every 1½in/3 cm around the edge.

Lie the trimmings one on top of each other to re-roll. Make shapes to decorate the pie. I like to borrow a Norwegian motif of fish chasing each other's tails in a circle (I use a children's biscuit cutter) but moon and stars or hearts and flowers are all other possibilities. Leave it plain if you wish. Make an x-cut in the centre and fold back the points. Brush the top with the wash and bake at the top of a medium-hot oven (gas mark 5/375°F/190°C) for 30 minutes. Cover with greaseproof if the pastry browns too fast.

Sussex Puddle Pudding

Sussex Pond pudding was served up at school, in Sussex, as a dingy brown sponge. Fair comment on Sussex ponds perhaps, but it wasn't until much later that I discovered that the true pond pudding was really a suet crust enclosing a whole lemon. This recipe is a scaled-down version of the original, made in individual pudding basins with kumquats and limequats. Serve with cream, smetana or custard.

A vin de pays Catalan, Clos St Martin, a relatively dry Muscat, is an interesting and not cloying choice.

8 oz/250 g plain flour
½ tsp baking powder
1 tsp mixed pudding spice
*   (optional)*
pinch salt
4 oz/125 g vegetable suet
cold water to bind
4 kumquats
4 limequats
light muscovado sugar
a little butter

Prick the fruit all over with a darning needle or fine skewer. Sift the flour with the baking powder, spice and salt. Stir in the suet, with a fork. Combine well. Add enough water to make a quite firm dough. Roll out to a little under ¼ in/0.5 cm thick. Cut into four. Lightly grease the pudding basins with the butter. Line them with the pastry, leaving the ends of the paste hanging over the sides. Into each basin put ½ tbs sugar, then a limequat and a kumquat and top with a bit more sugar. Fold over the ends of the pastry, pinching to seal. Cover each basin with a double thickness of buttered grease-proof paper and foil and tie down. Stand in a large covered pan of boiling water and boil for 2 hours.

You must serve hot; cold suet crust is unpleasant. Invert the basins onto warm plates. When the crust is opened a pool of hot citrusy syrup will seep out and the fruit will be very tender. Lovely on cold cheerless winter days – comfort food.

Sablé Italienne

A good green salad with a little bite to it is very good with this layered dish. Tender young spinach leaves or some sorrel, peppery argula (rocket), land cress, lamb's lettuce, dandelions or watercress would all contribute good pokey flavours against a buttery foil of a Tom Thumb-type round lettuce.

In the summer drink it with a Frascati but in the winter use a Chianti Classico.

4 oz/125 g butter
1 oz/30 g rolled oats
5 oz/150 g plain flour
4 wholemeal digestive biscuits, crushed
¼ pt/150 ml plain yoghurt (the Greek strained sheep's milk is best)
2 large well-flavoured tomatoes
2 eggs
8 oz/250 g flat, dark mushrooms
3 cloves garlic
8 oz/250 g Mozzarella (the small plastic bags that contain the cheese in water are the next best thing to an Italian deli on the corner. Danish Mozzarella has a wholly different texture)
1 tbs olive oil
¼ pt/150 ml passata (sieved tomatoes)
fresh oregano or basil

Line the sides and bottom of a loose-bottomed 8 in/ 20 cm cake tin with silicone paper or very well greased greaseproof. Rub the butter into the flour and then stir in the oats and biscuit crumbs. Press half this mixture onto the base of the tin. Peel and chop 2 cloves of garlic, wipe and slice the mushrooms. Place these in a frying pan with the oil and cook until the juices run black. Spread over the bottom of the tin.

Unwind the Mozzarella, pulling it into thin strips. You should not be able to grate it – Mozzarella is a wet, fresh cheese. Using half the cheese cover the mushrooms. Spoon over the passata. Peel the remaining clove of garlic and chop it with the basil or oregano. Combine with a pinch of sugar and a pinch of salt. Sprinkle over the passata and then cover with the rest of the Mozzarella. Cut the tomatoes into fine slices and lay over the second Mozzarella layer. Season well with fresh black pepper. Beat together the yoghurt and eggs and pour over the tomatoes. Top with the remainder of the crust crumbs, very gently patting it level.

Bake at gas mark 5/375°F/190°C for 40 minutes until set and nicely brown. Remove from the oven and set in a warm place for 5 minutes before slipping off the sides of the tin.

Set on a plate and serve hot or cold in wedges. A hot garnish of caramelised button onions is attractive and tasty. Cold, it can be decorated with tassels of spring onions and cherry tomatoes.

Raised Chestnut and Mushroom Christmas Pie

Even vegetarians like to be traditional at Christmas. This raised pie looks wonderful as the centrepiece of the Christmas feast: all glazed and golden, decorated with pastry holly and ivy. Surround with tiny rosemary-roasted potatoes, brussels sprouts, carrots baked in honey and orange, and buttered parsnips. Serve with either Cranberry or Elderberry and Port Sauce (page 237). The rich fragrant filling is layered inside an old-fashioned hot water crust. It can be made in an 8 in/20 cm deep springform cake tin, but for real glamour a lovely fluted-edged hinged pir mould should be used.

Push the boat out and serve a really fine Bordeaux – a Château St Christophe would do admirably.

2 lb/1 kg mushrooms – try to obtain a selection of different kinds: flats, button, chestnut or brown cap, pieds de mouton, oyster or shiitake
8 oz/250 g dried chestnuts
1–2 bay leaves
12 oz/375 g stoned prunes
4 cloves garlic
2 sweet red onions
2 strong English onions

Soak the chestnuts overnight. Drain and place in a covered casserole with a little water and half the wine. Add a pinch of sugar, a little salt, a generous grinding of black pepper and the bay leaves. Cover and cook in a slow oven until fairly soft. Then chop coarsely.

Meanwhile, stew the prunes until plump. Drain and then chop.

Wipe and thickly slice the mushrooms. Finely chop 2 cloves of the garlic. Melt 1 oz/30 g butter in a heavy-

bunch of fresh sage
½ btl red wine – a claret or other
    Bordeaux or an East European
    Merlot
1 egg
2 oz/60 g butter
1 lb/500 g plain flour
6 oz/200 g vegetable margarine
    (the block variety is better, e.g.
    Baking Flora or Tomor)
⅓ pt/200 ml water
salt, black pepper

bottomed pan over a low heat. Add the garlic and cook for a couple of minutes. Put the mushrooms in with the garlic, gently combining. Cover and cook slowly for 15 minutes, shaking the pan occasionally to avoid sticking.

Peel the onions and cut in two lengthways. Slice and sweat with the remaining garlic, crushed, in the rest of the butter. When softened add some finely chopped sage and the remaining wine. Simmer for 10 minutes.

Melt margarine with the water. Sift the flour with 1 tsp salt. Make a well in the middle and pour in the hot water and margarine. Work quickly to bring all together, kneading lightly. The dough should be very malleable but not sticky. Use two-thirds to line the tin, pressing well into the sides and bottom. Avoid too much thickness at the corners. Keep the rest of the dough warm and covered.

Place a layer of mushrooms over the base, then a layer of chestnuts, a layer of onions and then one of prunes. Repeat the layers, filling the pie shell and finishing with a mushroom layer. Lightly press down.

Roll out the remaining dough and cover the pie, sealing the edges with the egg beaten with 1 tsp water. Crimp boldly. Use the trimmings to fashion holly leaves and berries and ivy tendrils and leaves. Brush the top of the pie with the egg wash, garland with the holly and ivy, brush again. Cut a 1 in/2.5 cm cross in the centre and fold back the cuts.

Put in a moderately hot oven (gas mark 6/400°F/200°C) for 1 hour. Slip off the sides, brush again with wash and return to the oven for another 15 minutes. Serve on a large platter with all the Christmassy trimmings you like.

This pie can also be served cold. A hot jelly of claret and gelozone should be poured through the centre vent whilst the pie is still warm and then the whole allowed to cool and set.

Port and Stilton Undercurrants

Traditional partners port, Stilton and walnuts are combined in a rich pâté in a pastry shell and then glazed with a port wine and redcurrant reduction. If pressed for time you could cheat by using a quality bottled redcurrant jelly, but be warned, many commercially available varieties are sickly sweet. Equally good hot or cold.

And to drink, a reasonable Bordeaux, perhaps the reliable Mouton Cadet. A cheaper alternative would be an East European Merlot – either would be most acceptable here.

8 oz/250 g Stilton, crumbled
2 oz/50 g walnuts, broken
2 medium onions, roughly
*   chopped*
2 large cloves garlic, crushed
1 oz/30 g butter
4 oz/125 g button mushrooms
2 egg yolks
1 lb/500 g redcurrants
6 oz/180 g sugar
3 fl oz/100 ml port
shortcrust pastry to line an
*   8 in/20 cm flan ring*
or 4 crumpet rings
seasoning

Place the flan ring or crumpet rings on a heavy baking sheet. Roll out the pastry to fit the ring(s). Using your thumbs or knuckles, press the pastry down to the base, taking care not to stretch the dough. Flute the sides of the pastry by vertically pinching the dough between your index fingers. Neaten the top with a sharp knife and crimp. Fill with ceramic beans or crusts and bake blind for 10 minutes at gas mark 6/400°F/200°C.

Melt the butter in a heavy-bottomed pan, sauté the onions and garlic until just beginning to colour. Reserving a couple of perfect specimens, chop the mushrooms and add to the pan. Cook a further 5 minutes then add the walnuts; after another couple of minutes pour on half the port. Allow to bubble up then take off the heat and transfer to a food processor, with the Stilton and egg yolks. Whizz in several bursts of a few seconds each, so that you have a fairly smooth purée but leaving some texture. Season with freshly ground black pepper.

Pile the mixture into the pastry case(s) and level the top(s). Bake at gas mark 6/400°F/200°C for 20–25 minutes.

Meanwhile finely slice the remaining mushrooms, put in a small saucepan with the port and 1 tbs water. Simmer until the mushrooms are cooked. Using a slotted spoon, remove and set on a plate. Place the redcurrants in the pan with the cooking liquor. Cook until they pop. Add the sugar, heat gently, stirring until melted then boil hard until reduced and thick. Do not allow to caramelise or scorch.

When the pâté is firm and pastry golden, arrange the mushrooms over the top and glaze with the hot redcurrants spooned through a sieve.

Elderberries and cranberries can also be used to great effect.

Onion and Apple Tart Renversée

Bramley apples, the best cooking apples, give a tarter flavour and would be better married with a mellow cheese such as Double Gloucester. I prefer Cox's Orange Pippin, a truly great dessert apple which retains its individuality in this dish. The flesh is never white but a rich cream. The texture is meltingly grainy and the perfume aromatic. Do not overseason as you would lose the apple's special charms.

You can make it more like a savoury Tarte Tatin if you omit the bottom layer of pastry (line the bottom of the tin with baking paper) and use puff paste instead.

Rowan Brook Chardonnay from Chile is aged in oak for lovely smokiness but it is still fruity, very good with the apple and onion combination.

12 oz/400 g plain flour
6 oz/200 g butter
2 large strong onions
2 medium apples
8 oz/250 g Cheddar cheese
nutmeg

Rub the butter into the flour until it looks like fine crumbs. Add a little very cold water to make a soft dough. Chill, wrapped in greaseproof paper, whilst you prepare the tin and filling.

Line the sides of an 8 in/20 cm loose-bottomed cake tin, with greased greaseproof or baking parchment.

If you wish, you could use a food processor's slicing blade to thinly and evenly slice the peeled onions and apples and the cheese. Whichever way you choose to slice them, turn them all into a large bowl and toss together with a *little* grating of nutmeg.

Roll out half the chilled dough to fit the base of the cake tin. Gently lift in. Pile all the cheese, apple and onion slices on top and level. Roll out the remaining pastry into another 8 in/20 cm round and place over the filling. Press down very lightly with the flat of the hand.

Bake at gas mark 6/400°F/200°C for 45 minutes.

To serve hot: keep warm for 5 minutes then invert onto a warmed serving plate. Brussels sprouts cooked in olive oil, garlic and plum tomatoes make a good, cheering winter accompaniment. In the warmer months a salad of red, red tomatoes, garden herbs and unguent green olive oil is almost unbeatable whether the tart is hot or cold.

To take on a picnic, leave in the tin, turning it out only when you have reached the grassy spot.

Plum and Almond Tart

Dare I suggest that the perfect drink with this tart is Armagnac? Or perhaps an Orange Pekoe Darjeeling, in the late afternoon with the wasps buzzing around the plums left on the tree and the still warm sun dappling through the leaves.

12 oz/375 g plain flour
8 oz/250 g butter
4 oz/125 g brown sugar
12 oz/375 g small dark plums
2 oz/60 g ground almonds
2 eggs, separated
3 tbs milk

Rub 4 oz/125 g of the butter into 8 oz/250 g of the flour and add enough water to bind. Roll out and line a 10 in/ 25 cm flan tin. Brush lightly with a tiny bit of egg white and pop into the oven at gas mark 7/425°F/220°C for 5 minutes.

Whilst the shell is baking, cream together the sugar and remaining butter until light and fluffy. Beat in the egg yolks. Fold in a little at a time, alternately, the almonds, the rest of the flour and the milk. Whisk the egg whites until stiff and fold through the mixture.

Spoon into the pastry case, smoothing the top gently. Halve the plums and remove the stones. Place, in concentric circles, cut-side down on the almond mixture. Bake at gas mark 4/350°F/180°C for ¾ hour.

Serve warm with pouring cream or cold with whipped cream.

Quinces, or the fruit from the garden japonica, are also very good in this tart. If you prefer, you can use a richer pastry for the base, adding an egg yolk and icing sugar.

Jalousie of Kohlrabi

Kohlrabi's distinctive, rather delicate flavour is enhanced but not swamped by clotted cream and a dusting of nutmeg. The crisp, flaky golden crust makes a good counterpoint. If required for a picnic make sausage-roll-sized puffs.

If you want to use a vegetable margarine instead of butter, take care, the soft ones do not make good flaky pastry – look for the block ones. The kosher Tomor or the red-labelled Granose both work well.

Eat hot or cold with a spicily soft Austrian white, a Grüner Veltliner, and a salad of mixed leaves and herbs.

12 oz/375 g plain, strong flour
8 oz/250 g butter
1/2 tsp lemon juice
ice cold water
2 medium kohlrabi, red or white
6 oz/180 g clotted cream
nutmeg
1 egg yolk

Rub a quarter of the fat into the flour and make a soft dough with the lemon juice and water. The amount of water will vary according to the flour used but start with about 1/4 pt/150 ml. Add it fairly cautiously; too much will make the dough sticky, too little will mean the pastry won't rise. It is the steam from the proportionately large amount of water trapped between the impermeable layers of fat sandwiched by thin layers of dough that gives flaky pastry its lightness. On a floured surface, lightly roll the dough out to an oblong 1/4 in/0.5 cm thick. Over two-thirds of the paste, smear little dabs of a quarter of the remaining butter. Fold the dough into three, ensuring alternate pastry and fat layers. Seal the edges by pressing firmly together with a rolling pin. Wrap in greaseproof paper or a floured teatowel and leave in the fridge for 1/2–1 hour.

With a sealed end rather than the folded edge towards you, roll out the dough again to the oblong and repeat the fatting/folding process, chilling between each rolling, three more times, using the same amount of fat each time.

Meanwhile, wash the kohlrabi and pare away any knobbly bits. Put into a large saucepan of boiling water for 20 minutes. Drain. Peel and cut into ¼in/0.5 cm slices when cool.

Roll out the pastry in a large rectangle (14 × 12 in/35 × 30 cm approx) to about ¼in/0.5 cm thick. Place on a heavy baking sheet. In the centre third of the pastry (14 × 4 in/35 × 10 cm) lay overlapping slices of kohlrabi. Dust well with nutmeg and dot all over with the clotted cream.

Cut the two outside thirds in slanting strips, 1 in/2 cm wide, leaving a gap before the filling. The lefthand fringe should be a mirror-image of the right. Fold the first strip from the lefthand side over the filling, then the first from the righthand, the second from the left and the second from the right and so on down until all have been plaited in. Pinch the top and bottom cut ends together then brush all over with the egg yolk beaten with 1 tsp water and a pinch of salt. Place in a hot oven (gas mark 6/400°F/200°C) for 25–30 minutes. Cover with a greaseproof paper if the pastry seems to be browning too quickly.

The Jalousie will be richly brown, light and crisp when done. Transfer to a large platter and serve at once, or cool on a rack.

Tropical Strudel

The filling in this strudel can be varied – spiced apples are traditional, dried cherries are a variation on a classic and prunes and pecans would be rich and delicious.

Have the strudel warm with smetana and the Romanian sweet white, Tamaioasa, beautifully fragranced and slightly syrupy.

1 lb/500 g strong plain flour
about 5 oz/150 g vegetable
    shortening – soft white fat, e.g.
    Trex
5 fl oz/175 ml water
1 tsp white vinegar
good pinch of salt
1 mango
2 bananas
8 oz/250 g dried pineapple chunks
½ a fresh coconut
2 oz/60 g wholemeal breadcrumbs
2 oz/60 g brown sugar
2 tsp ground cinnamon
1 tsp finely grated lemon rind
2 oranges

Sift the flour and the salt together. Warm the water with 1 oz/30 g of the vegetable shortening and add the vinegar. Cool to lukewarm. Melt the rest of the vegetable shortening. Make a well in the centre of the flour and pour in most of the water, enough to make a soft, almost batter-like dough. Knead it for quarter of an hour. It will start to get less sticky, then it becomes smooth and leaves the bowl cleanly. Form it into a ball and brush it with some melted shortening. Cover the dough with a teatowel and leave for an hour.

On a large work surface – preferably a table that you can walk around, so you can stretch the dough from all angles – lay a clean tablecloth. Work some flour into it all over. Place the dough on the cloth. Brush it with more fat. Dust your hands with flour and, using your knuckles, begin to spread out the dough. Once it has been spread a little, pick up an edge of the dough and get your hands underneath it. Gradually stretch it across the backs of your hands. Work from the middle to the sides, backwards and forwards, easing the dough, pulling it thinner and thinner until you can see the pattern of the tablecloth through it. Carefully patch any holes and cut off the thicker edges. Leave 15 minutes then brush with melted shortening again.

While the dough is resting prepare all the fillings. Mix together the sugar, breadcrumbs and cinnamon. Grate the orange rind and squeeze the juice. Grate the coconut, coarsely. Peel the bananas and mango and slice thinly.

Scatter the fillings evenly all over the dough, sprinkling them with the orange juice. Roll the strudel up, using the tablecloth to help. Cut into lengths and place on a greased baking sheet. Brush again with melted fat and place in a moderate oven, gas mark 5/375°F/190°C, for 30 minutes. Dust thickly with icing sugar and serve warm.

Croquembouche

Croquembouche means literally to 'crunch in the mouth' and is normally a name given to dessert creations covered in a crisp glaze that crackles when eaten. Carême designed elaborate pyramids to be coated in caramel, confections of sugar and paste that were architecturally stunning. In the same style as chocolate profiteroles, these choux pastry puff balls, filled with Brie and cranberry, are stacked in a pile, and fine caramelised onion strips are spooned over the mound immediately before serving. Alternatively, individual pyramids of four puffs, three on the base and the fourth atop, drizzled with the rich glazed onions, would look delightful surrounded by fresh salading.

A light wine, maybe a German Niersteiner or a crisper Sèvre et Maine would be a very good choice when using these puffs as a main course. As an appetiser, try them hot with a Muscat de Frontignan well-chilled in straight glasses with frosted rims. I was first offered Muscat as an aperitif like this at Mortagne au Perche and it was lovely.

6 oz/200 g plain flour
4 oz/125 g butter
4 eggs, well beaten
½ pt/300 ml water
1 lb/500 g ripe Brie
8 oz/250 g cranberries
3 cloves garlic
1 large or 2 small English onions
  (the strong ones)
2 oz/60 g brown sugar
1 tbs sesame oil

Melt the butter with the water, do not boil. Add the mustard and stir. Tip in the flour all at once and stir, beating well as it thickens. Continue to cook over a low heat until the flour paste leaves the sides of the pan cleanly and is one ball. Take off the heat and gradually incorporate the beaten egg. Add a couple of tablespoonfuls at a time and beat very well after each addition.

Using a forcing bag and a plain ½ in/1.5 cm nozzle, pipe walnut-sized balls onto a greased baking sheet. Alternatively, use two teaspoons to shape even-sized balls. With a wetted finger gently smooth the top of each ball. Bake in a hot oven (gas mark 7/425°F/220°C) for about 10–15 minutes, until they are well risen, light and brown. Either split and fill immediately or remove and place on a wire rack to cool. Using a sharp knife slit one side to allow the steam to escape.

To make the filling, place the cranberries over a low heat until they pop and have thickened. Either put the Brie and the peeled garlic in a food processor or finely chop the garlic and mash into the Brie. In each puff put a heaped teaspoon of the cheese mixture and a scant teaspoon of the cranberries. Build up a pyramid (using a mathematical formula if it helps: 16, 9, 4, 1 for a four-sided version or 15, 9, 6, 3, 1 for a three-sided affair) on a heatproof plate. Heat through in a moderate oven.

Meanwhile very finely slice the onion(s). Brown in the sesame oil, stir in the sugar off the heat. When the sugar has melted shake the pan over a high heat until the sugar darkens and bubbles. Spoon over the pile of puffs and serve.

In the summer, try chopped fresh peaches or apricots and the much maligned cottage cheese. Cottage or curd cheese, especially from the smaller dairies, can be very good and served hot, as here, becomes interesting in a way longtime dieters may never have imagined. St Agur, the rich and creamy blue cheese, is fabulous with apricots or pears.

Christmas Crackers

These crisp, golden Christmas Crackers are delicious and whimsical. They can be made half-size using small leeks for Christmas party hors d'oeuvres.

Instead of white wine use a red and swap the Caerphilly for Stilton.

Drink a flowery sweetish German with the Caerphilly version, one of the Rhine Ausleses for preference, but a Lohengrin St Johanner (Qa.) is a bargain. The Stilton requires a hefty red – the evocatively named Lightning Ridge from Australia (where else) is a blend of Cabernet Sauvignon and Shiraz and has body enough.

12 oz/375 g Caerphilly, grated
4 good sized leeks, at least
    1 in/2.5 cm in diameter
1/4 pt/150 ml sweet white wine
4 or 5 cloves garlic, peeled
a little rosemary and sage,
    preferably fresh
black pepper
filo pastry sheets (available at
    most large supermarkets)
4 oz/125 g melted butter
1 tbs olive oil

Clean, trim and cut the leeks into 3 in lengths. Place them in a heavy-based pan with a tight-fitting lid with the olive oil. Sauté the leeks gently for 5 minutes then add the whole garlic cloves, the herbs roughly chopped and the wine. Grind a little pepper over the top and cover tightly. Allow to simmer on a very low heat until the leeks are very tender. Take off the heat. Set oven to gas mark 5/375°F/190°C. Using a slotted spoon take out the leeks and allow to cool on a plate. Add the Caerphilly to the pan, mashing the garlic and herbs into it with the pan juices. A sort of paste will be formed.

Brush two baking sheets with butter. Place one sheet of filo on your work surface, with the shorter edge towards you. Brush with melted butter then lay the next sheet on top. Brush this with butter too, then spread a 3×2 in/8 $\times 5$ cm line of the cheese paste in the middle of the bottom edge. Place a leek on top of the cheese then roll up the pastry around the leek and cheese to form a Christmas cracker shape. It is easier if you gently pinch the pastry together at the ends of the leek as you roll. The cracker ends hold up better if you use foil-covered cardboard tubes, the sort from the middle of the wrapping paper roll. Cut the tubes into $1\frac{1}{2}$ in/4 cm lengths and place either side of the leek, before rolling up.

A ribbon of leek, chive or welsh onion can be tied at each end.

Place the cracker on the greased baking sheet and brush with a little more butter. Repeat the process using all the leeks to form individual crackers. Space well apart on the baking sheets and bake for 25 minutes until golden brown and crisp.

Serve hot.

Spiced Apple Meringue

Bramley or Grenadier cookers can be used for a tarter flavour, but the faintly aromatic Cox's Orange or the Laxton's dessert apples are my preference here. Many of the lesser known varieties are being rescued by the super supermarkets in their drive to beat their competitors in the diversity stakes. This has to be a good thing. The Victorians grew hundreds of different sorts, showing them at the Royal Horticultural Society. But English apples and pears became the poor cousins, unappreciated in restaurants as pineapples, kiwis and mangoes arrived. The problem is not new. In Owen Thomas's 1904 edition of *The Fruit Garden*, he is already bemoaning the lack of attention paid to apple- and pear-growing in England. He notes the exceptions of Kent, Herefordshire and Worcestershire and applauds the French growers.

The circle is turning slowly and maybe now many orchards previously grubbed up will be replanted, not with green tasteless fruit but with Oranges, Russets, Reds and Reinettes.

Once again the nice 'raisiny' (and very cheap) Moscatel di Valencia would be a most appropriate pudding wine.

The pastry base can be omitted or the meringue can be folded through the apple mixture for equally good variations.

8 oz/250 g plain flour
4 oz/125 g unsalted butter
1 lb/500 g dessert apples
2 oz/60 g brown breadcrumbs
2 oz/60 g Lexia raisins
2 oz/60 g walnuts
2 heaped tsp pudding spices –
   cinnamon, ginger, nutmeg,
   allspice
3 eggs
6 oz/180 g golden caster sugar

Rub the butter into the flour and add enough water to bind. Roll out to line a 10 in/25 cm pie dish. Grate the apple, chop the walnuts roughly and place in a large bowl. Sprinkle all over with the breadcrumbs, spice and raisins. Using your fingers combine all these ingredients until well mixed. Separate the eggs and add the yolks to the apple mixture, using your fingers again to ensure they are well incorporated. Whisk the whites until stiff; whisk in half the sugar a little at a time until stiff and glossy, then fold in the remaining sugar. Pack the apple mixture into the pastry case, levelling the top. Spoon the meringue over ensuring that it is taken right up to the pastry edges. For an extra-special touch, pipe the meringue in big extravagant swirls after having used a little of it to smooth over the top of the apple first.

Bake for 20 minutes at gas mark 5/375°F/190°C, then reduce heat to gas mark 2/300°F/150°C for another 20 minutes. Serve hot, cold or just warm.

Beetroot
and
Cranberry
Consommé

Carrot, Orange and Ginger Soup with Fennel and Ricotta Ravioli

Strawberry and Avocado Salad

Glazed Pear with
Elderberry and Port

Raised Chestnut and Mushroom Christmas Pie

Croquembouche

Choux Swans with Walnut Pâté and Blackcurrant Reduction

Apricot and Banana Crumble

Crumbles are underrated. Perhaps it is because they do not have a fancy name, or because they are so simple to produce. The crumble mixture is infinitely variable and the fruits below can be familiar or exotically different. Try using unusual combinations; be adventurous with flavouring, spices and additions of dried fruits or nuts.

Those old favourites, apple or rhubarb crumble, can be reinvented with the judicious use of cinnamon or raisins or oranges or fresh ginger.

Use either fresh or reconstituted dried apricots depending on availability. Soak dried in a sweet white wine or fruit juice and liqueur. Serve with a crème anglaise or cream.

Drink a Chateau des Hautes Combes, a sweet, fruity white from Bordeaux.

6 oz/200 g plain flour
3 oz/100 g butter
2 oz/60 g soft brown sugar
1 oz/30 g sesame seeds
½ oz/15 g white poppy seeds
12 oz/375 g apricots
3 medium ripe bananas
1 orange

Rub the butter into the flour. Grate the orange rind finely and stir into the flour with the sugar and the seeds. Halve and stone the apricots. Peel and cut the bananas into 1 in/2.5 cm chunks. Mix the fruit together. Lay in an ovenproof dish, squeeze the orange all over, and level. Individual ramekins can be used and look more 'dressed up'. Pat the crumble mixture on top of the fruit. Bake for 30 minutes at gas mark 5/375°F/190°C.

Redcurrant and Raspberry Crumble

Humble fare but fruity and with a bit of bite. The jewel-like colour of the sharpish fruit makes a wonderful contrast with the sweet, coarse topping. Lovely served hot with a good dollop of clotted cream.

A cheap sweet white to drink with it is the Moscatel di Valencia.

5oz/150g wholemeal flour
3oz/90g butter
1oz/30g porridge oats
3oz/90g demerara sugar
2oz/60g toasted hazlenuts, finely chopped
8oz/500g redcurrants, topped and tailed
8oz/500g raspberries
4oz/125g strawberries

Rub the butter into the flour; using a fork, stir in the other dry ingredients, combining well.

In an ovenproof dish mix together the redcurrants and raspberries. Add the quartered strawberries. Level and top with crumble mixture. Bake in a hot oven, gas mark 6/400°F/200°C, for 30 minutes.

Carib Prune Pie

My grandmother was born in Trinidad. Ingredients specified by Mrs Beeton were not always to hand there in the Twenties and Thirties, and her elder sister, Myra, devised a pie out of Beeton's bakewell tart recipe. It became something of a family legend. 'Granny' Myra's prune pie was served on high days and holidays, weddings and christenings. Although she purported to give away the recipe as wedding presents and to her sister, nobody could make it like Myra. Little wonder, she never quite parted with the whole recipe! The joke is on Myra though; her deception of my grandma gave birth to this transcendent version, which bears little resemblance to its progenitors.

In true Grandma fashion, it is made with butter and served with cream and liberally flavoured with best West Indian rum. Devour it hot (Myra's descendants would say with custard) or warm or cold. Any way it is toothsome, like eating black velvet.

Eat it with a small glass of well-chilled Pineau de Charente.

12 oz/375 g stoned prunes – the best are from Agen but failing those make sure they are large and juicy, without chemical additives to plump them up
2 large eggs and 1 yolk
8 oz/250 g unsalted butter
8 oz/250 g and 1 tbs plain flour
4 oz/125 g golden caster sugar
1 oz/30 g icing sugar
1 double measure dark rum

Sieve the icing sugar together with 8 oz/250 g flour and rub in 4 oz/125 g of butter until it looks like fine crumbs. Make a well in the centre and drop in the egg yolk and 2 tsp cold water. Gradually work the fat/flour into the middle, forming a soft dough (if your flour is particularly absorbent a little more water can be added, but be cautious). Wrap in greaseproof paper and chill.

Stew the prunes in a little water until very soft. Mash or purée in a food processor with the rum.

Roll the pastry out between two sheets of greaseproof paper lightly dusted with icing sugar. Peel off the top sheet and flip the dough over on to a deep 8 in/20 cm pie dish. Fit the pastry into the dish before removing the second sheet. Neaten the edges. Spread the prunes evenly in the lined pie dish.

Beat the remaining butter with the caster sugar until very light. Beat in the eggs, one at a time. Fold through one tablespoon of plain flour and very gently spoon over the prunes, levelling the top.

Place in the oven at gas mark 3/325°F/170°C and turn down to gas mark 1/275°F/140°C after 10 minutes. Cook for another hour until the top is set.

Choux Swans with Walnut Pâté

A pâtisserie display prompted this recipe. The 'swans' should sail proudly across a puddle of shimmering Blackcurrent Reduction (p. 244). Whilst undeniably visually appealing, the blackcurrants' sharpness cuts the richness of the nutmeats and the pastry and provides a delicious contrast. How whimsical you wish to be is up to you. The edges of the puddle could be decorated with new potato 'boulders', broccoli 'bushes' and fine bean 'reeds' – but that's pushing even the limits of kitsch.

A jammy Gamay wine, a Beaujolais Supérieur (not a Nouveau) with a medium body perhaps, could cope with the fruit and the nuts.

6 oz/200 g plain flour
4 oz/125 g butter
4 eggs, well beaten
1/2 pt/300 ml water
6 oz/180 g shelled walnuts
8 oz/250 g shallots
2 gloves garlic
2 small sticks celery
1 large parsnip
2 egg yolks
2 oz/60 g fresh wholemeal
*   breadcrumbs*
red wine
winter savory
nutmeg
olive oil
white pepper, salt
a truffle or two (optional extra)

Grate the parsnip. Finely chop the shallots, garlic and celery. Soften and then brown the parsnip, shallots, celery and garlic in a little oil. Add a good splash of red wine and reduce away. Remove from the heat. Chop the savory – if you have no savory, use a *little* rosemary with a bit of sage. Either coarsely grate or finely chop the nuts. Add the herbs, nuts, breadcrumbs and chopped truffles, if using, to the pan. Combine well. Beat the egg yolks and use to bind the mixture. If it is very dry, add a tablespoon of red wine. Season well with nutmeg, white pepper and salt. Pile into a greased heatproof dish, cover and steam for 45 minutes, either on top of the stove or in a moderate oven.

Melt the butter with the water (do not boil). Add the flour all at once. Beat well and cook over a low heat until the flour paste leaves the sides of the pan cleanly and is one ball. Take off the heat and gradually incorporate the beaten egg. Add a couple of tablespoonfuls at a time and beat very well after each addition, until the mixture no longer looks very glossy.

Using a forcing bag and a plain ½ in/1.5 cm nozzle, pipe six 'S' shapes, about 3 in/7.5 cm long overall, onto a greased baking sheet. At the top (smaller) end of each S, pull the nozzle and twist to break off the paste to form the 'beak'.

Divide the remaining mixture into six pear-shaped mounds, smoothing the surface with a wetted knife or finger. The rounded bottom of the 'pear' is the swan's breast.

Bake in a hot oven (gas mark 7/425°F/220°C) for about 10 minutes. Remove the S shapes ('necks') and allow a further 15–20 minutes for the 'bodies' until they are well risen, light and brown.

Using a sharp knife, slit from the 'breast' to the 'tail' to allow the steam to escape. Fill the cavity with the hot nut pâté. Push the bottom of the S into the breast slit so the swan's neck stands upright. Serve immediately.

Allow everything to cool before assembling if you wish to serve cold.

Coulibiac

Originally a Russian fish pie, much taken up by the French; the pastry is a brioche dough and the filling is in layers. Buckwheat kashka is authentic but if you are unable to find it, use rice instead. I have used aubergines but other vegetables could be substituted. A Gewürtztraminer from Alsace will go with this hearty dish very well.

Dough

1 lb/500 g strong plain flour
6 oz/200 g butter
1/4 oz/7 g dried yeast
4 eggs
1 tsp salt
pinch sugar
4 fl oz/120 ml warm water

Filling

2 large aubergines
8 oz/250 g mushrooms
8 oz/250 g shallots
2 cloves garlic
bunch of parsley
6 chives
1/2 tsp allspice
good pinch ground cloves
1/2 tsp cinnamon
black pepper, salt
butter
madeira
vegetable stock
thyme
oil
5 eggs
6 oz/200 g kashka – buckwheat
   grains
1 tbs potato flour

Prepare the dough by first sieving the flour, salt, sugar and yeast. Beat the eggs with the water and soften the butter. Pour half the egg mixture onto the flour, drawing it in to make a dough. Work in the softened butter, squidging it between your fingers. When the butter is all incorporated, knead in the rest of the egg, a little at a time. If the dough is very sticky, add a small amount of flour, but be cautious. Knead well and leave to rise in a warm place for 3 hours. Push down sharply on the dough in the bowl, knocking it back and knead, flouring lightly if necessary. Keep wrapped in the fridge until ready to use.

Boil 4 eggs in their shells for 10 minutes, plunge into cold water.

Slice the aubergines lengthwise into fairly thick slices. Salt and leave to stand. This draws the bitterness out of the aubergine. Recent correspondence in foodie magazines seems to suggest that most aubergines grown today are not bitter anyway. I still salt – up to you!

Peel and chop the shallots and garlic. Soften with 2 oz/60 g butter. When just beginning to colour, add the chopped mushrooms with the finely chopped herbs (not the thyme) and all the spices. Cook, stirring, for a couple of minutes then pour in a glass of Madeira and 1/4 pt/150 ml stock. Season with salt and pepper. Simmer for

10 minutes. Slake the potato flour with a couple of teaspoons of stock and stir into the mushrooms. Stir continuously as the sauce thickens. Cook for a couple of minutes then remove from heat.

Place the kashka in a pan with 1 oz/30 g butter and a pinch of salt. Pour on 6 fl oz/200 ml boiling water. Stir around and bring to the boil. Cover tightly and reduce heat to a simmer. The grains should be soft and the water absorbed after 15 minutes. Fluff up with a fork.

Scrape the salt off the aubergine. Lay out on a grill pan and brush with oil. Sprinkle with a little thyme and place under a hot grill. When nicely browned, turn and do the same to the other sides.

Peel and chop the hardboiled eggs

Divide the paste into two. Roll out one half to an oblong 10 × 5 in/25 × 12.5 cm and the other to 14 × 9 in/35 × 22.5 cm. Place the smaller but thicker piece on a baking sheet lined with silicone paper. Beat the remaining egg with a teaspoon of water. Brush all over the dough base. Begin to layer up the four fillings in the following order: kashka, mushrooms, eggs and finally aubergine. Repeat the layers at least once. Cover with the second sheet of dough, pinching the edges together to seal. Trim to neaten and then crimp. Use the trimmings to decorate and brush all over with the remaining beaten egg.

Bake in a moderate oven (gas mark 4/350°F/180°C) for 1¼ hours. Cover with greaseproof during cooking if getting too brown.

Serve with stir-fried cabbage and Beetroot Julienne (p. 166).

Curried Peach Tartlets

Curry powder is added to the flour in the rich flan pastry to give subtle flavour and colour. To show the crust off, make the tartlets using crumpet rings instead of flan dishes.

Serve with a simple salad of Little Gem-type cos lettuce, dressed merely in freshly squeezed lime juice, and have a nicely chilled bottle of Premiers Côtes de Bordeaux, a relatively inexpensive, delicious sweet white wine.

In the winter when fresh peaches are unavailable use ½in/1.5cm slices of a small pineapple rather than tinned peaches.

12oz/375g flour
7oz/210g butter
2 egg yolks
1 tsp good curry powder
2 tbs water with a few drops of lime or lemon juice
12oz/375g soft, loose goat's cheese
8oz/250g shallots
2 cloves garlic
3 large freestone peaches
¼tsp ground turmeric
pinch chilli powder
½in/1.5cm fresh ginger, finely grated
¼tsp ground cumin
½tsp garam masala
½tsp black mustard seeds
a little ghee or sunflower oil

Sift together the flour and curry powder. Rub in the butter. Beat the egg yolks, water and lemon or lime juice together, just enough to mix well. Combine with the flour to make a stiff but soft dough. To avoid adding too much liquid, do not tip it all in at once, rather add three-quarters and then the rest if needed. If the flour you are using is very absorbent it may be necessary to add a very little more water.

Scarcely knead at all to draw it all together, then rest in a cool place, wrapped in greaseproof paper.

Peel and finely chop the shallots and garlic. Heat a tablespoon of ghee or oil in a large flat pan. Add the mustard seeds and heat until they pop, add the rest of the spices (except the garam masala) and the ginger and fry over a low heat for a minute. Stir in the garlic and shallots. Cook, covered (a baking sheet will improvise as a lid if necessary), for 10 minutes until soft. Pour boiling water over the peaches, peel, halve and stone them. Pour ¼pt/150ml of the water into the pan, add the garam masala and stir well. Add the peaches, cut-side down. Simmer, spooning the curry mixture over the peaches, for about 7 or 8 minutes. Using a slotted spoon, remove the peaches and set on a plate. If the peaches are very juicy you will need to reduce the curry sauce by turning up the heat and stirring constantly until thick.

Stand the crumpet rings on a baking sheet. Roll out the pastry. It may be rather delicate so it is easier to divide it into 6 balls and roll each between two sheets of grease-proof paper. Peel the top layer of the paper off and invert the pastry on its backing paper over the crumpet ring. Ease the paste into the ring form, pressing well into the base before removing the second paper layer. Trim the top edges. An attractive rope-edge can be made on the crust by impressing a knife blade on a diagonal slant every 1/4 in/0.5 cm. Prick bases all over with a fork and bake blind, using rusks or beans (dried or ceramic) to prevent rising, at gas mark 5/375°F/190°C for 15 minutes.

Place a good 1/2 in/1.5 cm layer of goat's cheese in the base of the tartlets, top with a peach half, cut-side down, and spoon over the curry sauce. Return to the oven to warm through for 8–10 minutes. Remove the crumpet rings carefully and serve.

Gougère with Ratatouille

The rich crispness of the Gougère is the perfect foil for the soft Mediterranean earthiness of a classic Ratatouille. Frozen and canned travesties of this Provençal vegetable stew exist: the former are tasteless, the latter taste tinny.

The colours remind me of those glorious medieval tapestries, red, purple, gold and green. The smell is of Summer and sheer pleasure.

Ratatouille is heaven on its own, chilled and eaten with the sun on your face – but, please, only good olive oil will do!

A Côtes du Luberon or Ventoux would be an appropriate choice or any good VDQS from the region.

6 oz/150 g plain flour
2 oz/60 g butter
3–4 eggs lightly beaten
1/2 pt/250 ml water
4 oz/120 g Franche Comte or Gruyère cheese
5 cloves garlic, if available green garlic for preference
1 lb/500 g shallots or sweet yellow onions
3 large peppers, red, green and yellow
2 medium aubergines
1 lb/500 g courgettes – I prefer the finger-thin ones; if fresh the skins will pierce very easily
1–1 1/2 lb/500–750 g well-flavoured tomatoes
dark, thick green olive oil
fresh herbs – thyme, marjoram, rosemary, sage

Slice the aubergines, sprinkle with salt, cover with a plate and leave for half an hour.

Melt the butter in the water. Tip in the flour and beat hard over a low heat until the mixture forms a ball and leaves the sides cleanly. Take off the heat and add the egg a little at a time, beating very well after each addition. It will look rather slippery as you first add the egg, but as you beat and incorporate it the texture will change. The mixture should be quite stiff but soft. Finely dice the cheese and combine with the paste. Season with a little salt and pepper. When cold, spoon into a 12 in/ 30 cm round on a greased baking sheet.

If you have time, it is worth charring the pepper skins under a hot grill or directly in the gas flame and then removing the blackened skin under cold water. The flavour of the peppers is improved, making them sweeter.

Peel and chop the onions or shallots and the garlic. Cover the bottom of a large pan with oil and start to soften the onion and garlic. Rinse and squeeze dry the aubergine and add to the pan. Aubergine acts rather like a blotter, soaking up the oil. Add a little more oil as necessary, not allowing the pan to get too dry. Cook over a low heat, covered, whilst you slice the courgettes. Add to the pan, combining well. Cut the peppers into strips, discarding the seeds. Add to the pan with the roughly chopped tomatoes and the finely chopped herbs. Stir well and cook on a low heat for 45 minutes. Season generously with freshly ground black pepper and a little sea salt.

Heat the oven to gas mark 7/425°F/220°C, then bake the Gougère for 30–40 minutes until well-risen and golden brown.

To serve, slide the ring onto a large flat dish and fill the centre with the ratatouille.

Brandied Peach Ring

Slightly warm peaches, sweet thick crème pâtissière and crisp glazed choux pastry combine to make an impressive dessert that warrants something rather grand to have with it. Champagne is rather overpriced now but a sparkling Saumur is worth trying instead.

For the paste

6 oz/200 g plain flour
4 oz/125 g butter
3–4 eggs lightly beaten
½ pt/300 ml water

For the cream

2 oz/60 g plain flour
5 oz/150 g caster sugar
1 tbs unsalted sweet butter
4 large eggs
1 vanilla pod
1 pt/600 ml full cream milk

6 large ripe peaches
¼ pt/150 ml brandy
icing sugar

Pour boiling water over the peaches. Peel and stone. Cut into eighths. Lay in a small saucepan with the brandy and warm gently. When hot, turn off the heat and allow to stand.

Mix together the 2 oz/60 g flour, caster sugar, 1 tbs butter and 4 eggs in a bowl. Beat well. Using a sharp knife, insert the point between the flat sides of the vanilla pod. Slide it up and down, scraping out the tiny seeds. Put these in a pan with the pods and the milk. Slowly heat until boiling. Pour onto the egg mixture, stirring hard all the while. Strain back into the pan and cook over a low heat for 3 or 4 minutes. Ensure that you never stop stirring. If you do this following a figure-eight pattern, you will ensure that it does not catch (burn or stick) anywhere on the bottom. The cream should now coat the back of a spoon well. Pour into a dish to cool. Continue to stir from time to time as it cools.

Melt the butter in the water. Tip in the flour and beat hard over a low heat until the mixture forms a ball and leaves the sides cleanly. Take off the heat and add the egg a little at a time, beating very well after each addition. It will look rather slippery as you first add the egg, but as you beat and incorporate it the texture will change. The mixture should be quite stiff but soft. When cold, spoon into a 12 in/30 cm round on a greased baking sheet. If you have time, pipe the paste in interlocking

S-shaped swirls to form the round. Bake in a hot oven (gas mark 6/400°F/200°C) for 30 minutes until well risen and richly brown.

Turn up to gas mark 9/475°F/240°C. Run a knife all the way around the outside of the ring and fill with the peaches and crème pâtissière. Dust thickly with sifted icing sugar and return to the oven briefly to glaze. Serve immediately.

Asparagus Éclairs

The size of these light, elegant pastries can be altered to suit the occasion. Tiny gherkin-sized ones are lovely, hot or cold, as nibbles. The larger 8–9 in/20–22 cm sort would make a stunning late Spring lunch, made with fresh English spears and served with tiny new potatoes and the first sweet crop of local vegetables. To complete the spurge splurge, fresh strawberries and champagne. A French sparkling Chardonnay is a good, reasonably priced alternative – try a Baron de Beaumont.

Out of the short asparagus season they are still worth making with tinned or the now available (and superior) frozen asparagus.

The choux paste cases can be made in advance.

6 oz/200 g plain flour
4 oz/125 g butter
4 eggs, well beaten
1/2 pt/300 ml water
1/2 tsp wholegrain Dijon mustard
1 1/2 lb/750 g asparagus, steamed
  and cooled, or tinned
2 small yellow onions
1 large clove garlic
8 oz/250 g fromage frais
1 oz/30 g unsalted butter
1 oz/30 g plain flour
Raclette cheese to top (optional)

Melt the butter with the water; do not boil as this would result in the reduction of the liquid and consequently cause a problem with the proportions of dry ingredients to wet. Add the mustard and stir. Tip in the 6 oz/180 g of plain flour all at once and stir, beating well as it thickens. Continue to cook over a low heat until the flour paste leaves the sides of the pan cleanly and is one ball. Take off the heat and gradually incorporate the beaten egg. Add a couple of tablespoonfuls at a time and beat very well after each addition, until the mixture no longer looks very glossy. If you are tired and this is not what your right arm's for, you can cheat. Warm the bowl of your mixer. Tip in the cooked flour ball, and beat in the eggs on a fairly slow speed with a paddle or K-type beater.

Using a forcing bag and a plain ½in/1.5 cm nozzle, pipe the required length éclairs onto a greased baking sheet. At the end of each piped length, lift the nozzle up and back over the éclair. This avoids a pointy nib which would brown too quickly, and gives a nice rounded end instead.

Bake in a hot oven (gas mark 7/425°F/220°C) for about 10 minutes for the cocktail size. The bigger ones will need a further 25 minutes or so at gas mark 4/350°F/180°C until they are well risen, light and brown. Remove and place on a wire rack to cool. Using a sharp knife, slit one side to allow the steam to escape.

Chop the onion and garlic very finely and fry until delicately browned in the butter. Sprinkle over the flour and cook for 2 minutes over a low heat, stirring constantly. Stir in the fromage frais and season well. If making small éclairs: chop the asparagus and fold through the mixture; spoon into the pastry cases and heat through before serving immediately. With the larger éclairs you may wish to keep the spears whole, laying them inside the pastry on top of a layer of the fromage frais mixture. Cover the asparagus with some more of the creamy mixture. Heat through in a moderate oven.

A delicious addition, particularly when fresh asparagus is not available, is a thin slice of Raclette cheese melted over the top of the hot éclair just before serving.

6
Pasta and Pizza

asta and pizza merit their own chapter in this book in recognition of the way these two Italian staples have caught the imagination of the world.

Marinetti wanted to outlaw pasta, but its spread across the globe has been unstoppable. Spag Bol is cooked up in countless halls of residence. West Indians have created a spicy Bajan 'national dish' of macaroni pie. Macaroni cheese (a.k.a. macker-cheese, sorry) has been a long-time favourite with all three of my children. Mauritians have a sweet-and-sour-style spaghetti. The Turks make a kind of ravioli. And I remember a nasty sort of stew in hospital in Nigeria which contained grub-like pasta.

Who invented pasta is a moot point; theories abound, but it is likely that it was the Chinese, whose rich culinary heritage brought us that other Italianised marvel – ice cream.

As these chapters are loose gatherings rather than straitjackets, I have included under this heading a couple of noodle dishes with different ethnic backgrounds. Strictly speaking, one could have argued for pizza to come under pastries or breads, but it doesn't.

Whether you feel the effort involved in making fresh pasta is worthwhile – I do, but certain luminaries do not – you should try it at least once. Of course there is no other way to make filled pastas such as ravioli, tortellini and the like, and who could miss them out? Dried pastas vary enormously; some have a much higher egg content than others – check the packet.

Pizza bases are not difficult to make, so pass by the ready-mades and the instant mixes and you will be glad you did.

The classic pizza requires a good Mozzarella. Look for those marked *pasta filata*; this will indicate that the cheese has been made in the correct, spun, way. You cannot buy real Mozzarella off a block – that which is sold in supermarkets is as much Mozzarella as squash is orange juice – and you cannot grate it. Pull or chop it into bits and scatter it over. Mozzarella was originally made with buffalo milk, but now is made mostly from cow's milk. It is possible to find the Mozzarella di Bufala, but it is very expensive and probably should be reserved for salad use, with basil, olives, garlic and tomatoes. Some cheeses are blends of buffalo and cow's milk and they are a good compromise. Avoid poking and prodding the cheese, and consume quickly – it does not keep. When Elizabeth David wrote *Italian Food* in 1954, many of the fresh cheeses, including Mozzarella, Mascarpone and Ricotta, were very difficult to find. We are fortunate now to have several large importers and producers supplying good quality authentic cheeses. One enterprising expat Italian has begun to make a grana (Parmesan-type) cheese in Sussex.

Some pasta sauces are well-known classics, others are traditional but not so well-known. It is enough sometimes to dress the pasta in butter or olive oil and black pepper. The next refinement could be grated hard cheese, of which Parmesan is probably the best known. Then there are the blue cheeses; Gorgonzola is excellent, crumbled and stirred through hot pasta. Do not ignore the best of the British blues either – Blue Cheshire works brilliantly. The cream cheeses, especially Mascarpone which is a particular favourite of mine in both sweet and savoury dishes, make rich sauces with no effort. Any of the creams, single, soured, double or clotted, is good with pasta.

If you need to watch the cholesterol level, you will not be missing out as the olive oil-based sauces, pesto being the most common, are arguably the best accompaniments to pasta. You can make pesto in a mortar and pestle or in a food processor. For speed, and it is best freshly made, I use a hand-held wand-type blender. While basil is the most common herb used for pesto, you can use other herbs for different flavours – try a mint pesto or a marjoram pesto. The method is the same: leaves, garlic, pine kernels (or pecans or hazel-nuts or even, on one memorable occasion, almonds) and finely grated dry cheese (Pecorino or Parmesan, but also other grana and the Spanish cheeses, Mahon and Manchego) are pounded or puréed together to a paste and then oil is added, as in the mayonnaise (see p. 49), until a soft creamy buttery consistency is reached. Try a similar method with garlic (the Provençal aïoli), puréed black olives (tapenade), grilled sweet red peppers or sundried tomatoes. All these fragrant pastas can be used in salad dressings, on hot vegetables and to season soups, stews and other dishes.

The ultimate topping for pasta is reputed to be white truffles. Although I have eaten the black truffles of the Perigord I have yet to try the fabled Italian white truffles. It was with a certain amount of envy that I watched Valentina Harris, on her televised travels, sit down to a plate piled high with the most exquisite pasta over which was shaved the Piedmontese truffles. The wafer-thin slices fluttered down onto the delicate tanglefood. It is probably fortunate we do not yet have smell-e-vision; I was in torment just watching and drooling.

Pasta does not have to be a savoury food; I include a few sweet pastas too. The winning recipe of a Christmas pie competition I judged last year contained fresh tagliolini, used like Greek Konafa – baked, not boiled, in a sweet pastry shell with nuts, peel and sugar. Dried pastas – macaroni, stelle, fafallette, penne – can all be made into baked milk puddings in the same way as rice pudding.

You need not restrict yourself to savoury pizza either; in the Italian Tyrol they make red fruit tarts on a sweet bread dough base.

Pasta and pizza are the best of fast foods and are even better when time and trouble are taken over them.

Tagliatelle with Avocado

This recipe is written for those truly in a rush. It is possible to make this dish, from getting in the door to getting it on the table, in 15 minutes – I know, I have done it!

Assuming you will have a little time to savour it, open an oak-aged Chardonnay, either an Australian or a New Zealander, a nice buttery one.

1 lb/500 g fresh tagliatelle or wide-ribbon noodles
½ pt/300 ml soured cream
2 cloves garlic, peeled
8 oz/250 g shallots or spring onions
8 oz/250 g oyster mushrooms
2 soft but not overripe avocados
1 oz/30 g butter or margarine
1 wineglass white wine
1 oz/30 g flaked almonds

Put a large pan of water on to boil. If the kettle boils faster, use that and pour it into the pan when boiling.

Push the garlic through a press into a lidded skillet. Add butter, put on low heat and cover. If using spring onions you can snip with scissors over the pan for speed, otherwise peel and chop shallots. Add to pan, shaking. Slice mushrooms, stir into shallots. Turn up heat. In small separate pan toast almonds briefly. Throw pasta into pan in which water is boiling. Add wine to mushrooms and reduce. Peel avocado, cut into small cubes. Stir into mushrooms and shallots with the soured cream, warm through but *do not boil*. Drain tagliatelle, combine with sauce, gently tossing until mixed. Serve with toasted flaked almonds on top of mound of pasta.

Serving note: the top narrow part of the avocado could be reserved, brushed with lime juice and cut into a fan to decorate the plates.

Sesame, Ginger and Soy Vermicelli

The hair-fine strands of rice vermicelli are 'cooked' in the liquor from the vegetables which is poured over the noodles in individual bowls and left to stand briefly, before serving.

4 oz/125 g shiitake mushrooms
2 tbs dried black fungus – available from Chinese grocers; dark, thin and almost translucent, it looks much like a contraceptive cap!
8 oz/250 g welsh or spring onions or shallots
4 sticks green celery
3 medium carrots
3 cloves green garlic
1 in/2.5 cm root ginger
2 tbs white sesame seeds
3 tbs shoyu soy sauce
1 tbs clear honey
2 tsp lemon juice
2 tbs toasted sesame oil
6 oz/180 g rice vermicelli – exceptionally fine noodles, much finer than egg-thread noodles

Pour ½ pt/300 ml boiling water over the black fungus and leave to stand. Peel and thinly slice the garlic and ginger. Chop the onions into 2 in/5 cm lengths. Slice in half lengthwise and flatten each piece. Cut into fine strips. Wash the celery and slice obliquely into thin crescents. Scrape the carrots and trim the ends. Before cutting into thin rounds, you may like to cut four or five grooves, equally spaced around the sides, running from top to bottom. This will give a simple flower shape. Cut the fresh and dried mushrooms into thin strips. Reserve the soaking water.

Heat the oil in a saucepan and pop the sesame seeds in it. Add the garlic and ginger and cook over a medium heat for a few minutes. Add, in this order, allowing a minute or so between each addition: carrots, mushrooms, onions, celery. Stir while frying. Pour over the soy, lemon juice, honey and soaking water and cook until the vegetables are just tender. Divide the dry vermicelli between four small deep bowls. Ladle over the liquid. Allow to stand in a warm place for 3 minutes – keep the vegetables hot. Add the vegetables to the vermicelli and serve.

Lasagne

Lasagne in vegetarian restaurants has become something of a cliché. An inedible one, too, more often than not. Because there is an insistence on using pulses, regardless of whether they are appropriate, the lasagne is mushy and stodgy or, after three hours under the inevitable hot lights, dry and hard. If you feel you must use lentils, use the grey Continental ones not the red which will turn to so much infantile pabulum. Cook, with bay leaf, pepper and onion, until just softening, before putting in a rich but quite liquid tomato-based sauce.

I prefer to stick to the vegetables listed, occasionally adding aubergine or courgette in season.

Drink a good Chianti or, perhaps more interestingly, an Amarone – a very big wine, also known as Recioto della Valpolicella.

1 red pepper
1 green pepper
1 lb/500 g yellow onions
4 cloves garlic
1 lb/500 g mushrooms – flats
preferably
2 tbs dried porcini (ceps)
1¹/₂ lbs/750 g good plum tomatoes
– tinned if necessary
basil, fresh or preserved in oil
2 bay leaves
2 ribs of celery, with leaves
1 tsp fresh chopped oregano
pinch of thyme
salt, pepper
sugar
olive oil
1 pt/600 ml milk
1 oz/30 g butter
1 oz/30 g plain flour
nutmeg
Parmesan cheese
pasta sheets

Warm the milk and leave to infuse with some black pepper, a generous grating of nutmeg and a bay leaf.

Pour a little boiling water over the porcini and allow to stand.

Peel and chop the onion and garlic. Pour a little oil into a large heavy-bottomed pan and, over a low heat, fry the onion and garlic in it. Cut the peppers into ¹/₂ in/1 cm dice and the celery into ¹/₂ in/1 cm slices. Finely chop the celery leaves. Add to the pan and turn up the heat slightly. Allow everything to brown slightly, stirring from time to time to prevent sticking or burning. Roughly chop the mushrooms and add to the pan. Cook a further 5 minutes. Skin the tomatoes and chop or break up with your fingers or a fork. Add to the pan, stir until up to the boil. Pour in the porcini and their soaking liquor, a bay leaf, oregano, thyme, a pinch of sugar, a little salt and some black pepper. Cover, reduce the heat and simmer for at least 45 minutes but preferably an hour.

Combine the flour and butter, with a wooden spoon, in a pan over a low heat. When the mixture forms a ball that leaves the sides of the pan cleanly, remove from the heat and stir in the strained milk, a little at a time, to begin with. Stir well after each addition of milk to avoid lumps. Return to the heat and stir constantly until the sauce coats the back of the spoon well. Take off the heat. Grate some Parmesan; how much is up to you – I would suggest 3oz/90g. When I worked for a motor factors, Dee the number plate fabricator explained Parmesan to one of the van drivers – 'It smells like sick but it tastes great.' Stir it into the sauce and adjust the seasonings.

Prepare the lasagne sheets as necessary. Fresh lasagne needs only a few minutes in boiling water, some dried needs 15 minutes and some requires no precooking at all – check the packet.

Stir the chopped basil into the tomato sauce. Spoon half of the tomato mixture into the base of a large flat baking dish. Smooth down and cover with a layer of pasta. Pour over half the cheese sauce, scattering with some more cheese if desired. Add another layer of lasagne sheets and cover that with the rest of the tomato. More pasta, then a final coating of cheese sauce, dusted with a grating of cheese. Cover for the first 25 minutes of cooking in a moderate oven gas mark 5/375°F/190°C. Uncover and continue cooking for another 20–25 minutes, by which time the top should be nicely browned. If it is looking a bit pallid, pop under a hot grill before serving.

Lasagne Verdi

Please, fresh not frozen spinach. The texture has gone from the pulverised mush that is left after defrosting. Perpetual spinach, although not as fine-leaved as ordinary spinach, can be cropped for months and need not take up much space in the garden. Use it to edge paths, or tuck a few plants into the border. Tiny new leaves are delicious, raw, in salads. Never, never cook spinach in boiling water – the small amount of water left clinging to the leaves after washing is all that is necessary. A good knob of butter or some olive oil, easily absorbed by the leaves, adds richness and flavour.

Spinach and wine are not easy bedfellows but try an Italian (of course) red such as Conero, made with the Montepulciano grape. Mellowed out after ageing it is very capable of coping with the spinach and the Gorgonzola.

dried or fresh lasagne sheets –
*   either plain or verde pasta*
2 lbs/1 kg spinach
4 cloves garlic
8 oz/250 g Gorgonzola
1 pt/600 ml milk
2 oz/60 g butter
1 oz/30 g plain flour
12 oz/375 g yellow or Spanish
*   onions*
2 egg yolks
2 tbs fresh breadcrumbs
1 tbs freshly grated Parmesan
1 bay leaf
salt, peppercorns
nutmeg

Warm the milk with the bay leaf and a couple of crushed black peppercorns. Leave to infuse.

Wash and strip the spinach of any large stalks. Shake dry and tear into small pieces. Crush 2 cloves of garlic and place in a pan with 1 oz/30 g butter, over a low heat. When the butter has melted, add the spinach, turning it about like a salad so the leaves all get some butter on them. Cook tightly covered for 8–10 minutes. If the spinach has produced a large amount of liquid, turn up the heat and boil it off. Take care not to scorch it, though. Season with salt, pepper and freshly grated nutmeg.

Prepare the lasagne sheets by simmering in a large pan. Some brands do not require this precooking and others need only a minimal dip in the boiling water.

Peel and chop the onions and the remaining 2 garlic cloves. Put to soften, over a low heat, in 1 oz/30 g of the butter. When soft and lightly golden, stir in the flour.

Cook, while stirring, for a couple of minutes. Take off the heat and gradually stir in the strained milk. Return to the heat and cook, stirring continuously until the sauce coats the back of the spoon. Remove from the heat. Cut the Gorgonzola into small chunks and stir into the onion sauce. Beat in the egg yolks.

Place half the spinach in the base of a greased flat baking dish. Cover with a layer of lasagne, topped with a layer of onion and Gorgonzola. Add another layer of pasta and repeat the spinach, lasagne and Gorgonzola layers. Combine the Parmesan with the breadcrumbs and scatter over the top. Place in a moderate oven (gas mark 4–5/ 350°–375°F/180°–190°C) for 40–50 minutes. Allow to stand for 5 minutes in a warm place before serving.

Lasagne Michael Gray

When we first moved to our cottage Michael used to cook on Tuesdays. This has gone by the board now, but here is his culinary triumph, slightly adapted by me.

Serve with a rich German Auslese or a red that is mellow but light such as the Vin de Pays des Bouches du Rhône.

2 large bulbs Florence fennel
3 large tomatoes – I like using golden ones here if possible
1 lb/500 g plum tomatoes or 14 oz/400 g tinned tomatoes
4 sweet onions
2 oz/60 g butter
2 tbs chervil
1 lb/500 g Ricotta
8 oz/250 g Fontina – if unavailable, Raclette or similar melting cheese
2 oz/60 g chopped walnuts
salt, pepper
nutmeg
lasagne sheets, fresh or dried – the number will depend on the dimensions of the dish and the pasta!

Peel and slice the onions and garlic and fry in 1 oz/30 g butter. Scald the plum tomatoes and chop. Chop any tinned tomatoes. Add to the onions when turning colour. Cover and simmer for 5–15 minutes, the longer time if using fresh tomatoes.

Roughly chop the fennel and braise in a pan with a little over ½ oz/15 g butter. Cook until softening.

Using the remaining butter, grease the inside of a large flat ovenproof dish. If using lasagne sheets that need precooking (some dried ones do not) cook them until just *al dente*. I often do this in a roasting tin of barely simmering water. Fresh pasta takes scarcely a couple of minutes.

Cover the base of the dish with the fennel; grind a generous amount of black pepper over it. Chop the chervil finely and scatter over the fennel. Lay on some lasagne sheets, patchwork-quilt fashion, to cover, then top with the Ricotta, seasoned with a little salt. Cover the Ricotta with more lasagne. Spoon over the onions and tomato mixture and dust with nutmeg and a little salt. Slice the Fontina thinly and place in two wide borders down either side of the dish. Fill the centre strip with the walnuts, cover, and bake at gas mark 4/350°F/180°C for 35–40 minutes. Five minutes before the end of cooking, scald and peel the fresh tomatoes. Slice them transversely as thinly as possible. Remove the cover and lay the tomatoes down in the centre of the dish in an overlapping band. Return to the oven to finish cooking. Stand 5 minutes, then serve.

Pizza Bianca

This pizza is white. Have a white wine too – a Tuscan Avignonesi made from the Chardonnay grape, or an Umbrian Orvieto.

But have a dark salad for a good contrast. Use black olives or grapes or the very dark feuilles de chênes.

12 oz/375 g strong plain flour
¼ oz/7 g dried yeast
½ tsp salt
warm water
4 tbs olive oil
1 lb/500 g tiny stewed artichokes
or 14 oz/420 g bottled or tinned
    artichoke hearts
4 oz/125 g button mushrooms
2 small white aubergines –
    flavourwise, the more ordinary
    purple can also be used
8 oz/250 g white onions
4 cloves garlic
parsley, marjoram
1–2 tbs white wine vinegar – to
    taste, depending on how
    piquant you like it
8 oz/250 g Mozzarella

Sift the flour, yeast and salt. Make a well in the centre and pour in 2 tbs oil and 7 fl oz/200 ml warm water. Work to a soft dough, adding more water if necessary. Knead well until smooth and allow to rise in a warm place for about 1 hour.

Peel and thinly slice the onions and garlic. Soften in a covered pan over a low heat in the remaining oil – do not brown. Cut the aubergines lengthwise, into thin slices. Add to the pan and continue to cook slowly. Slice the mushrooms and chop the herbs, including some stalks from the parsley. You should have about a tablespoon of chopped herbs. Add the vinegar to the pan with the mushrooms and herbs. Season with salt and white pepper. Keep covered and stew until all is tender, then reduce any liquid by turning up the heat.

When the dough has doubled, knock it back by pushing it down sharply in the bowl and knead briefly. Press or roll out to a 14 in/35 cm round. Lay on a heavy baking sheet. Rest for 10 minutes. Put into a hot oven (gas mark 7/425°F/220°C) for 10 minutes. Quarter the artichokes and slice or pull the Mozzarella into small pieces. Take the base out of the oven, reduce heat to gas mark 5/375°F/190°C. Prick and gently press down the dough if it has puffed up too much. Cover with the onions, aubergine and mushroom mixture. Scatter the Mozzarella over that and then top with the artichokes. Return to the oven for a further 10 minutes, until the base is cooked through. Serve.

Calzone

A calzone is a sort of pizza pasty, a pizza folded over on itself. Because the filling is so enclosed I like them, made small, for picnics. A good green salad, a robust Italian Merlot and a checked tablecloth and you're away.

1 lb/500 g strong flour
1/4 oz/7 g instant dried yeast
warm water
olive oil
salt, black pepper
4 large red onions
4 cloves garlic
8 oz/250 g mushrooms
1 lb/500 g plum tomatoes
fresh herbs – either basil, marjoram
    or oregano, and a little parsley,
    including the stalks
sugar
8 oz/250 g Mozzarella cheese or
    freshly grated Parmesan

Sift the flour with the yeast and 1 tsp salt. Make a well in the centre, pour in 2 tbs olive oil and 8 fl oz/240 ml warm water. Work together to make a stiff dough, adding a little more water if necessary. Knead well until pliable and smooth. Leave in a warm place to rise.

Whilst it is proving, make the rich tomato sauce. Peel and chop the onions and garlic and fry until soft in some olive oil. Chop the mushrooms and add to the onions. Scald the tomatoes and peel and chop. Add to the pan with the chopped or torn herbs. Season with a pinch of sugar, salt and black pepper. Cook the mixture down slowly to a good, thick, aromatic mass.

Divide the dough into eight balls. Roll each out to teaplate size. On half of the disc place a good couple of tablespoons of sauce, cover with some Mozzarella or Parmesan, moisten the edges then fold over and seal. Put on a baking sheet and cook in a hot oven (gas mark 7/425°F/220°C) for about 20–25 minutes until puffed and brown.

You could add a few chopped black olives to the sauce.

Florentine Calzone

This time the turnover is made large with a layered filling of garlic and mushrooms, spinach and Ricotta. Serve with a Tomato and Red Pepper Coulis (p. 233) and freshly grated Parmesan.

A big Syrah from the top of the Rhône is recommended to deal with the spinach – a St Joseph maybe.

1 lb/500 g strong flour
¼ oz/7 g instant dried yeast
warm water
olive oil
salt
4 cloves garlic
8 oz/250 g porcini (ceps) – if
    unavailable use ordinary fresh
    mushrooms, with a few dried
    ones for flavour
4 oz/125 g shallots
1½ lb/750 g spinach
5 oz/150 g Ricotta
nutmeg, white pepper
freshly grated Parmesan

Sift the flour with the yeast and 1 tsp salt. Make a well in the centre, pour in 2 tbs olive oil and 8 or 9 fl oz/about 225 ml warm water. Work together to make a stiff dough, adding a little more water if necessary. Knead well until pliable and smooth. Leave in a warm place to rise.

Peel and chop the garlic and fry it with the porcini, roughly cut up, in a little olive oil. Peel and finely slice the shallots. Place in a heavy-bottomed saucepan, cover and soften over a low heat. Wash the spinach and shake off any excess water. Strip away the stalks and tear the leaves into pieces. Combine with the sautéing shallots. Cover and continue to cook for 10 minutes. The leaves should now have reduced to a pulpy mass. Uncover and turn up the heat to dry out the spinach. Stir to prevent sticking and to break down into a purée. Remove from heat. Season with white pepper and freshly grated nutmeg.

Knock back the dough by pushing it down sharply in the bowl. Dust your work surface with flour and have ready a large oiled baking sheet. Flour your hands, pick up the dough and drop it onto the surface. Roll it around under your hands, flattening as you go. Then pat it and press it out into a large round, 20 in/50 cm in diameter. On one half of the dough, place the porcini, leaving a clear border all around the edge. Cover with the spinach and top with the Ricotta. Damp the edge with water and fold the dough over, pinching the edges together well. Transfer carefully onto the baking sheet. Allow to stand 10 minutes before placing in a hot oven (gas mark 7/425°F/220°C) for 20–25 minutes. Drizzle with a little rosemary- or basil-flavoured olive oil before rushing to the table.

Fruit Pizza

I have tried two methods for making this sweet pizza. The first used a thick cooked purée of fruits – apple and blackberry and gooseberry were most successful – topped with Mozzarella in the usual way. The second way, described below, uses fresh fruits: peaches, plums, apricots, bananas and strawberries are all very good. Barely cooked chunks of pink rhubarb in the Spring work amazingly well.

The yeasted pastry base (p. 118) could be substituted, adding a little icing sugar to the flour.

Serve warm with a Monbazillac or a Loupiac.

7 fl oz/200 ml milk
1 oz/30 g butter
2 oz/60 g sugar
12 oz/375 g strong plain flour
¼ oz/7 g dried yeast
¼ tsp salt
1 egg white
mint (optional)
12 oz/375 g Ricotta or for a richer pizza, half and half with Mascarpone
honey
1 lb/500 g nectarines or greengages

Scald the milk. Stir in the butter and 2 tbs sugar and allow to cool to blood heat. Sift the flour with the yeast and salt. (You could add a hint of ground spice – cloves, ginger or cinnamon perhaps, especially if the fruit is a little bland.) Pour on the milk and work to a soft dough. Add more liquid, either milk or water if the dough is too dry. Knead well until smooth, then allow to rise.

When the dough has doubled, push it down sharply in the bowl to knock it back. Knead briefly, then roll or press out to a circle 14 in/35 cm in diameter. Place on a greased baking sheet and allow to rise for 10 minutes.

Lightly whip the egg white and brush the dough. Sprinkle with a little sugar and bake for 15–20 minutes at gas mark 7/425°F/220°C.

Chop the mint, if using, and beat into the Ricotta with the honey. Scald and skin the fruit. Cut nectarines into eighths and greengages into quarters. Heat a grill.

Take out dough. Gently press any overpuffed areas down and quickly spoon on the Ricotta in a nice even layer, allowing a clear 1in/2.5cm border around the edge. Cover with the fruit. Work fast but try and arrange them in a pattern, not just higgledy piggledy. Brush the fruit and the exposed edge of the base with the remaining egg white and dredge with sugar. Place under a hot grill to caramelise the sugar, and serve.

Dolcelatte and Pear Pizzette

In Elizabeth David's wonderful book *Italian Food* she mentions a yeast pastry as the upmarket base for pizza. I have adapted her guidelines to use the fermipan dried yeast. This yeast does not require a soaking period and can be rubbed into the flour with the fat. These small pizze use this melting dough as a foil for rich creamy blue cheese over Conference pears. Cut the dough into 3 in/7.5 cm rounds for an entrée or main course and 1½ in/3–4 cm rounds for hors d'oeuvres. A salad of green and black grapes and chicory complements the dish well, as does the warm Brussels Sprout salad (p. 180).

An Italian white, possibly a frizzante Frascati, seems a good match.

12 oz/375 g plain flour
5 oz/150 g butter
¼ oz/7 g dried yeast
2 egg yolks
1 whole egg
12 oz/375 g Dolcelatte
1 tbs double cream
2 cloves garlic
1 lb/500 g Conference pears

Sieve together the flour and the yeast. Rub in the butter until the mixture looks like crumbs. Rub in one of the egg yolks. Beat the second with a couple of tablespoons of water. Make a well in the flour and tip in the yolk and water. Draw in the four, quickly and lightly, to make a soft dough. Do not knead heavily; unlike other yeasted doughs the gluten does not require stretching and developing. If necessary add a little more water, but beware, just enough is important, too much is a disaster. Cover with a teatowel and leave in a warm place for 2 hours. The dough will not rise as much as bread dough; it *is* a pastry.

Roll out the dough to about ¼in/0.5 cm thickness, cut into rounds as described above. Place on a baking sheet and prick all over. Bake at gas mark 6/400°F/200°C for 7–10 minutes depending on the size. Do not allow to brown. Remove from the oven.

Place the Dolcelatte, cream, egg, and garlic in a blender or processor and whizz until smooth, just a few good bursts. Alternatively, press the garlic; mash the cheese and cream together; beat in the egg and garlic.

Fennel and Ricotta Ravioli

Ravioli are small packets of pasta dough enclosing tasty fillings – leftovers were originally used. Well-seasoned, aromatic or rich fillings work best to give maximum impact. The Turks claim to have invented the ravioli but I don't think you would find many Italians who would agree with that. Other cuisines have similar dishes – Russian piroshki, Indian samosas and Chinese won ton, to name just three.

1 small head fennel
2 oz/60 g ricotta
1 clove garlic
a little olive oil
8 oz/250 g strong plain flour
2 eggs
salt, black pepper

Chop the garlic and fennel and sweat in the oil, in a covered pan over a low heat, until meltingly soft. Stir in the Ricotta. Season with plenty of black pepper.

Make the pasta dough by working the eggs into the flour with ½ tsp salt. Combine with a little water (approx 1–2 tbs) and knead well. Work until smooth and elastic. Put through pasta rollers until very thin and silky or roll out with a rolling pin. This dough is more than sufficient for the ravioli; use the extra for lasagne sheets. Making a smaller quantity is not practical. Using a 2 in/5 cm cutter, stamp out rounds. Place a teaspoon of filling on each, wet edges and seal. Leave on wire rack.

To serve: either boil in simmering water and serve with butter and a little fresh grated Parmesan, or *in brodo*: poach the ravioli for 3–5 minutes in a clear soup. The Carrot, Orange and Ginger (p. 20) is particularly recommended for this ravioli filling. Serve in flat soup plates with a garnish of orange zest and some feathery fennel leaves.

Peel and quarter the pears. Remove the cores and cut into thin strips. Arrange them, fan-like, on the pastries. Spoon a good tablespoon of the cheese mixture over the pears and return to the oven allowing 3–5 minutes for them to warm right through. Serve immediately.

Chocolate and Hazelnut Tortellini alla Panna

Aimed at true chocoholics, this pudding is very rich. For contrast, if desired, only half the dough need have cocoa in it. Tortellini look like navels and are slightly more fiddly than ravioli which can be made instead. If you cut the paste into squares instead of rounds before folding and twisting them, they would be cappelletti (little hats).

In the spirit of real gluttony that this recipe inspires, drink Marsala, heavy and heady, or cut through the richness with a spumante from Piedmonte, an Italian region noted for the richness of its food.

Any leftover dough can be rolled very thin, cut into wide ribbons, boiled, and served with toasted pine kernels and puréed avocado.

7 oz/225 g strong plain flour
1 oz/25 g good cocoa powder – not drinking chocolate
4 egg yolks
1 egg white
1 tsp hazelnut oil – if unavailable, use a tasteless vegetable oil
3¹/₂ oz/100 g dark chocolate – at least 52% cocoa solids
3¹/₂ oz/100 g toasted hazelnuts
¹/₂ pt/300 ml double cream
1–2 tbs Kahlua or, at a pinch, Tia Maria

Grate and combine the chocolate and the hazelnuts. If the chocolate is very bitter stir in a little icing sugar. Add a dash of Kahlua if desired. Stand in a warm but not hot place.

Sift the flour with the cocoa. Make the pasta dough by working the egg yolks into the flour. Combine with the oil and knead well. Work until smooth and elastic. Put through pasta rollers until very thin and silky, or roll out with a rolling pin.

Using a 2 in/5 cm cutter, stamp out rounds. Place a dab of chocolate filling on each. Lightly whip the egg white until it just breaks up. Brush it around the edges of the dough and fold over to make semi-circles. Press the cut edges together to seal. Turn the parcel around the tip of your floured finger as if making a ring, bring the points together and pinch hard. Set on a rack or floured towel whilst making the rest.

Cook in simmering water with a knob of unsalted butter for about 5 minutes. If you do not have a very large pan cook in batches, keeping hot. Drain and place in a large flat ovenproof dish, sprinkle on the liqueur and pour over the cream. Place in a hot oven (gas mark 6/400°F/200°C) for 5 minutes until warmed through. Serve immediately.

The tortellini could also be cooked, drained and dressed with warmed liqueur and served with a dollop of Mascarpone.

Cannoli

Well, really an adaptation of cannoli. Cannoli are a sweet Sicilian pastry, and tubular – hence the name. I have taken great liberties with them. Here they are savoury and … conical. I changed the shape for convenience; I do not possess a dozen lengths of 1 in dowelling but I do have cream horn moulds. If you happen to be the proud owner of so many broomhandle cutoffs, the accepted way is to cut the dough into 4 in/10 cm circles, then roll them around the greased wooden lengths. I use my wok for the deep frying; it uses less oil due to the dished shape.

Traditionally they are Ricotta-filled, but with the addition of nuts, chocolate and crystallised fruit.

A crisp green salad and a crisp 'green' wine are called for – Portuguese vinho verde would fit the bill.

6 oz/175 g plain flour
good pinch ground allspice
½ oz/15 g butter
1 tbs Marsala
1 tbs brandy
1 egg white
sunflower oil
8 oz/250 g Ricotta
small bunch chives
2 cloves garlic
1 tsp grated zest of a lemon
1 oz/30 g salted roasted pistachios
a few basil leaves
1 small red pepper
a few stoned black olives
salt, black pepper

Sift together the allspice and flour. Rub the butter into the flour and make a stiff dough with the brandy and marsala. Cover and leave in a cool place for 3 hours.

In a gas flame, or under a hot grill, roast the red pepper. Turn it as the skin blisters and blackens. Scrape away all the papery charred bits, cut open and remove the pitch and seeds. Chop into small pieces. Place in a bowl with the crushed garlic, the lemon rind, chopped olives and the shredded basil. Snip the chives into the bowl. Season with a little salt and some black pepper. Leave to stand.

Divide the dough into thirds. Roll out thinly into three rounds 12 in/30 cm across. Cut each circle into quarters. Wrap each quarter around a cream horn mould and seal the join with a dab of lightly beaten egg white. Deep fry in hot fat, three or four at a time, until crisp and golden. Cool on a rack lined with kitchen paper, removing the moulds when able to handle.

Just before serving add the pistachios and Ricotta to the red pepper and herbs and combine with a fork. Check seasoning. Fill the pastries with a teaspoon and arrange on a bed of lettuce.

Apricot and Amaretti Ravioli

Using pasta for puddings is not unheard of: Mrs Beeton gave a recipe for a macaroni pudding as a nursery sweet. Valentina Harris recalled Italian children crunching on deep-fried, sugar-dusted ravioli as breakfast on the way to school. The pasta dough must be rich and eggy. The filling needs to be generous. Other fillings that could be tried are prunes and walnuts or spiced grated apple.

Amaretti are tiny button macaroons with the scented bitter flavour of apricot kernels.

An Orange Muscat and Flora from Australia is less rich than the French Muscats of Frontignan and Beaumes de Venise, but that is an asset here, especially if you decide to serve the ravioli with a crème anglaise. The citrusy hints and lovely caramelly flavours more than make up for any lack of body.

This amount of dough is twice as much as you need for the filling, but it is easier to handle in this quantity. The leftovers can be rolled extremely thin and cut into wide (³/₄in/ 2 cm) ribbon noodles. Dried over backs of chairs on teatowels, they can be stored loosely wrapped in the fridge until the next day. Cook in boiling water and serve dressed with toasted flaked almonds, the zest of a sweet orange, a little ground cinnamon and unsalted butter. Alternatively cut the rolled pasta in sheets for lasagne made with Ricotta, orange and fennel.

8 oz/250 g strong plain flour
2 eggs + 2 extra yolks
1 egg white
1 tsp orangeflower water
1 small orange
4 oz/125 g dried apricots
2 oz/60 g amaretti
2 oz/60 g sugar
1 stick cinnamon bark

Pare the zest of the orange, ensuring no white pith is removed, and cut into very fine strips. Reserve. Soak the apricots and half the amaretti in the juice of the orange for at least an hour. Mince or chop finely together or process in bursts on a machine. Do not turn into purée. Crush the remaining amaretti and combine with the apricots.

Make the pasta dough by working the eggs and yolks into the flour with the merest pinch of salt. Combine with the orangeflower water or, if unavailable, a little orange juice, and knead well. Work until smooth and elastic. Put through pasta rollers until very thin and silky, or roll out with a rolling pin.

Place a teaspoon of filling at regular 2 in/5 cm intervals down a strip of dough. Whip the egg white until just broken up and slightly bubbly. Brush the egg white around the little mounds of filling. Lay a second pasta sheet over the first and firmly press together between the mounds. Cut into squares with a very sharp knife or a fluted pasta wheel. The wheel has the advantage of further helping to seal the parcels whilst providing an attractive edging. If you do not possess one you can use the floured tines of a fork to imprint a pattern on the borders of the squares. Place the filled ravioli on a rack or floured teatowel in a cool, dry place while using up the rest of the dough and filling.

Dissolve the sugar in a large pan of water, add the orange peel and the cinnamon stick. Bring to the boil and poach the ravioli, six at a time, for 3 or 4 minutes or until they rise to the surface and the pasta is soft but still retains a bite (*al dente*). Keep the cooked ravioli hot in a covered dish over boiling water. Dress them with a small amount of unsalted butter to prevent sticking.

Serve on warmed plates with either an Apricot Coulis (p. 234), spiked with Amaretto, a light orange syrup or a delicately almond-flavoured Crème Anglaise (p. 231). In a hurry, a good homemade apricot jam, sieved and warmed with Amaretto, could stand in as the sauce.

Dry any leftovers on teatowels and the next day deep-fry in oil and dust with a mixture of ground cinnamon and icing sugar.

Won Tons

Won tons are Chinese 'ravioli' but the shapes, unlike Italian pasta, are looser, not so well defined. The won tons can be rolled or folded and rolled, but here I have chosen to make large saucer-shaped parcels, allowing just one per person in a soup plate of clear broth.

Two fillings are given. If you can find callaloo use it instead of spinach for the second.

A small proportion of buckwheat flour can be used in the dough for colour and flavour.

Dough

7 oz/200 g strong flour
2 eggs
2 tbs water
2 tsp sesame oil
1 tsp salt

Filling I

3 oz/90 g mung beansprouts
2 oz/60 g shiitake mushrooms
1 large yellow onion
½ a mooli
2 cloves garlic
1–2 carrots
1–2 tbs shoyu soy sauce
1 tsp arrowroot
good pinch five-spice powder
sesame oil

Sift the flour and make a well in the centre. Lightly beat together the eggs, water, oil and salt. Pour into the flour and work into a soft dough. Knead well for about ten minutes, until quite silky. Cover and leave for an hour.

Make the filling.

I: Cut the onion, mooli, garlic and carrots into fine strips. Heat a little oil in a wok and stir-fry the vegetables until the onion is lightly browned. Add the rinsed and drained beansprouts. Cook for a minute. Combine the shoyu with the arrowroot and pour over the beansprouts. Cook and stir for another minute or so. Season with the five-spice powder. Cool.

II: Finely chop the garlic and ginger and fry for a minute in a little oil with the aniseed and the mustard seeds. Add the chopped spinach, spring onions and oyster mushrooms if using. Cook stirring over a moderate heat. Add a little soy when the vegetables are tender.

Roll out the dough very thinly until it is almost transparent. Cut into eight rounds about 5 in/12.5 cm across – use a sharp knife around a saucer. On four, place a

Filling II

12 oz/375 g spinach or chard
1/2 in/1 cm fresh ginger root
2 cloves garlic
5 spring onions
4 oz/125 g oyster mushrooms
   (optional)
1/2 tsp aniseed or 2 star anise
1/2 tsp white mustard seeds
splash of soy
peanut oil

mound of the filling. Wet the edges and cover with a second round of dough. Pinch the edges together, fluting between two fingers. Knead together any scraps of dough and re-roll. Allow to dry slightly before cutting into fine strips for noodles.

Stand the won tons on a wire rack until needed. Poach in just-boiling water for about 8 minutes, drain and place in a large soup plate. Drizzle on a few drops of soy sauce. Alternatively, top with a few chopped black beans – these are fermented soy beans available in packets or tins and are quite piquant and pungent; do not overdo them. Ladle over a strong clear (miso-based) broth. Decorate with carved vegetable slices or spring onion flowers.

The won tons can also be cooked in the simmering broth.

7
Eggs

lthough I devote a chapter to them, I no longer eat eggs just as eggs very often. If you abhor the battery house you must accept that eggs are not always plentiful. I buy eggs from small producers who are on intimate terms with their hens. In severe weather there simply are no eggs, and the cook must plan menus accordingly. Measures introduced ostensibly to protect the consumer from salmonella are actually squeezing the healthiest (small) flocks out of business, thereby preserving the interests of the large battery barons. The Danish have got rid of battey cages – why can't we? The British have an obsession with the notion of cheap food. Price and profit are all, quality and compassion come very much lower down the scale.

Do not be misled by terms such as fresh farm eggs or country eggs, they don't mean anything. Take the time to find a good source for your eggs – cooking would be impoverished without their versatility. Elsewhere in these pages, eggs enrich sauces, gild pastries and bind farces. In this chapter they take centre stage with fluffy soufflés, light batters and delicate baked custards.

Quails' Eggs in a Nest

All the pleasure of egg and chips, daintily. Pullets' eggs could be used instead but allow only 1 or 2 per person. Accompany with fried whole button mushrooms and cherry tomatoes.

The addition of parsnips to the potato nests is a good variation – omit the thyme and dust with nutmeg.

With this simple repast have a reasonable Merlot – velvety, fruity and rich, possibly one of the upcoming Chileans that are difficult enough to pronounce *before* drinking them. Try saying '*Errazuriz Panquehue*' after a couple or three glasses! My mother read Spanish (and French) at Cambridge and then met my father in South America – they do say 'Spanish is the loving tongue'. Unfortunately, due to intransigent school timetabling, I had to give up *my* Spanish 'O' level for a German 'A' in order to study Food and Nutrition. I threw the whole lot up by the end of the first year for an ill-fated teenage marriage – Spanish would have been better perhaps.

1 dozen quails' eggs
4 large Desirée potatoes
2 parsnips (optional)
thyme
olive oil or sunflower oil
4 medium red onions
1–2 tbs balsamic vinegar
4 cloves of garlic

Peel the potatoes and coarsely grate them. Rinse in a colander under the cold tap. Turn into a clean teatowel and blot dry. Crumble dried thyme over the potato, season with salt and pepper and combine with a fork. Heat oil in a roasting tin, about ¼ in/0.5 cm deep. When hot, arrange the potato into four 'nests'; do not pat down – keep it looking 'twiggy'. Spoon over the hot oil and place in a hot oven (gas mark 6/400°F/200°C), basting occasionally, until golden brown. This takes about 20 minutes.

Peel and halve the onions. Slice them and place in a frying pan with the finely chopped garlic and a little oil. Fry until soft. Stirring, add the vinegar and allow to boil off.

Plunge the quails' eggs into boiling water for 2 minutes, then place them directly into cold water. Peel and keep warm.

Dish the nests onto plates, fill with the onions and top with the eggs.

Batter Pudding and Ravigote-Sauced Vegetables

Yorkshire pudding with a difference. It never looked so dressed up before. In our local pubs, frozen 'yorkies' (*sic*) are sold swimming in a harsh onion and MSG gravy – this is somewhat a similar idea but rather more 'taste full'. The vegetables can be varied according to season. A parisian baller for root vegetables will improve the look of the finished dish, otherwise cut into neat chunks.

Ravigote sauce caught my attention some years ago because two very different sauces seemed to be called the same thing. *Larousse Gastronomique* confirms this and I acknowledge assistance from that quarter whilst developing this version of a classic French sauce.

A Mâcon blanc can be used for the sauce and to drink with the meal.

4 eggs
4 oz/125 g plain flour
1/4 pt/150 ml milk
2 leeks
8 oz/250 g mushrooms – button
    will do, but ceps or shiitake are
    better
2 large carrots
1 celeriac
2 cloves garlic
2 tbs white wine
2 tbs green peppercorn vinegar
1 oz/30 g flour
3 oz/90 g butter
oil
1/2 pt/300 ml vegetable stock
1 tbs dried mushrooms
3 tbs double cream
8 oz/250 g small shallots
parsley
thyme
1 bay leaf
salt, pepper, white peppercorns

Make a roux: melt 1 oz/30 g butter and stir in 1 oz/30 g flour. Cook, stirring over a medium heat, until the mixture leaves the sides of the pan cleanly. Off the heat, beat in the vegetable stock little by little. Season with salt and pepper. Return to the heat and bring up to the boil, stirring constantly. Simmer over a gentle heat for an hour.

Make a batter with the 4 oz/25 g flour, eggs and milk, beating well. Allow to stand. Pour 1/2 pt/300 ml boiling water over the dried mushrooms and simmer, covered, for 30 minutes. Reduce the liquid by half, by boiling rapidly.

Prepare the vegetables, peeling, chopping and trimming. Save one shallot and chop it finely. Braise the rest of the vegetables in a little oil until just tender. Add the dried mushrooms, reserving the cooking liquor.

Place the finely chopped shallot in a pan with 4 crushed white peppercorns, chopped parsley (including the stalks), a twiggy bit of thyme and the wine and vinegar.

bring to the boil and boil hard to reduce by half. Stir in the roux-based sauce and the mushroom cooking water. Boil again and reduce by half again. Strain through a sieve into a clean pan.

Pour a little oil in the bottom of 4 straight-sided 6 in/ 15 cm cake tins and heat in a hot oven (gas mark 6/400°F/200°C) until smoking. Immediately pour the batter equally between the tins and bake for 20–25 minutes until risen and golden.

Cut the remaining butter into small pieces. Reheat the sauce and, when not quite simmering, whisk in the butter, one piece at a time. Keep whisking and add the cream in a thin stream – do not stop whisking whilst on the heat and do not boil. Check seasoning. Keep warm by putting the saucepan over another pan of scarcely simmering water. Ensure the vegetables are hot.

When the batter saucers are cooked, slide onto serving plates, fill with the vegetables and ladle over the sauce. Serve immediately.

Aubergine Sandwiches

The horseradish in the filling is quite pungent. If you do not care for it use one of the milder mustards, herbs (e.g. mint) or more garlic. Hummus or tahini make excellent alternative fillings.

Serve with a crisp Entre-Deux-Mers or a Californian Chenin Blanc and a watercress salad or green vegetables.

2 large aubergines
1 tsp freshly grated horseradish or creamed horseradish
1½–2 tbs soured cream
1 tsp potato flour
2 shallots
1 lime
2 cloves garlic
1 small Cox's Orange Pippin
4 oz/125 g plain flour
1 tbs sesame seeds
7 fl oz/200 ml lager or cider
4 eggs
salt, pepper
oil

Prepare the batter 6–12 hours before needed. Sift the flour with ½ tsp salt. Stir in the sesame seeds. Make a well in the centre and add the egg yolks and 3 tbs of the beer. Beat the egg yolks, drawing in the flour gradually to make a smooth paste. Add the rest of the beer, little by little to avoid lumps. Cover with a plate and stand in a cool place. Put the egg whites in a separate covered dish.

Cut the aubergines lengthwise into ¼ in/0.5 cm thick slices. Heat a little oil in a frying pan and cook one side of each slice until golden. Remove from the pan and place cooked-side up on a plate.

Either grate or finely chop the shallots and garlic and fry in no more than 1 tsp oil. As they begin to colour sprinkle on the potato flour, stir around and remove from the heat. Grate the apple and add to the pan with the horse-radish, combining well. Add the soured cream. Season with salt and pepper. Use the mixture to sandwich pairs of aubergine slices. You can, if you prefer, roll single slices up around the filing and secure with a toothpick. The uncooked sides of the aubergine slices should be on the outside of the 'sandwich'. Heat the oil to 350°F/180°C and finish the batter by folding through the whisked egg whites. Dip each sandwich in the batter and deep fry at 370°C/190°C for 5–8 minutes. Fry 2 or 3 at a time, depending on size. Drain on crumpled paper and serve at once with thin slices of lime.

Brie Fingers

I tried deep-frying Brie after being given, as a cocktail nibble, a rather rubbery cube of deep-fried Cheddar. Camembert fritters often turn up on restaurant menus, but I prefer the fingers of Brie, cooled enough to pick up and dip into the spicy fruit sauce but still hot enough to be runny inside the crisp exterior. The fruit sauce is variable; try also apricots, peaches, gooseberries or elderberries.

Serve with a Gewürztraminer and a cos-based salad.

1 lb/500 g slightly under-ripe Brie
6 oz/180 g breadcrumbs – white or
    wholemeal
1/2 tsp celery seed
coarsely ground black pepper
1–2 eggs
8 oz/250 g red plums or pink
    rhubarb, depending on season
3 shallots
2 dates
1/4 tsp ground or grated ginger
3 tbs vinegar
light muscovado sugar to taste
3 cloves garlic
1/2 tsp ground allspice
salt
sunflower oil

Very finely chop the shallots, garlic and dates. Stone the plums or chop the rhubarb. Combine the fruit, shallots, garlic, dates, allspice and ginger. Add a good pinch of salt and 2 tbs sugar. Put all to simmer, covered, with the vinegar, adding a *little* water if necessary to prevent sticking. Cook slowly until soft and pulpy. Sieve. Check seasonings adding more sugar, salt or vinegar as necessary. Reheat when required.

Cut the Brie with a sharp knife into batons, 3×3/4 in/ 8×2 cm. The best way to do this is herring-bone fashion across the wedge of cheese. Whether you cut the rind off or not is up to you. I like it so I leave it. Beat one of the eggs on a plate. Combine the breadcrumbs with a generous amount of coarsely ground pepper and the celery seed. Spread a thick layer of crumbs on a plate. Coat the batons with egg and then crumbs. Beat the other egg when necessary. Replenish the crumbs on the plate as they get used up. Chill the batons for half an hour and then dip in egg and breadcrumbs again. This may sound rather tedious but a double layer of egg and breadcrumbs does stop any leaks and gives an extra crunch. Chill until required.

Heat the oil to 365°F/185°C and fry until crisp and golden. Do not fry too many at once. Drain and serve with a puddle of sauce.

Mushroom Fritters

Serve with a sauce of some piquancy – perhaps a Tomato Coulis (p. 233) with chopped capers or gherkins, or a fiery chilli-based sauce. Alternatively, accompany with the cold Red Cabbage in Cider (p. 177) or any of the other Blini side dishes (p. 166).

The choice of wine will vary according to the sauce chosen, but a light red such as the Domaine les Colombies, a Corbières, is good with the mushrooms and cheese.

1 lb/500 g small mushrooms,
*   without their stalks*
2 eggs, separated
4 cloves garlic, crushed
8 oz/250 g Double or Single
*   Gloucester cheese, grated*
4 oz/125 g plain flour
seasonings
oil for deep frying
bamboo skewers

Make a paste with the cheese, egg yolks and garlic. Season to taste with salt and pepper. With a small spoon, fill the mushroom caps with the cheese mixture. Pair up the mushrooms, cheese sides together, and impale each pair on a skewer. Beat enough cold water into the flour so that it resembles single cream. Whisk the egg whites until softly mounding, then fold through the batter.

Heat the oil to 350°F/180°C, then dip the skewered mushrooms into the batter, coating well, and pop into the hot oil. Fry until crisp and golden. Drain and serve immediately.

Timbale with Truffled Eggs

*L*arousse states that a 'timbale' is a crust containing something. The encyclopaedic *Joy of Cooking* says, contradictorily, that it is a crustless quiche, a less exuberant soufflé. I will stick with *Larousse* and call the latter a savoury custard.

This recipe is an amalgam of two Brillat-Savarin recipes, with twists of my own. The filling for a *Flan* Brillat-Savarin is put into a glazed crust made from a brioche. This should be one of the tall brioches, the same shape as the Italian panettone. Alternatively, you can use the small brioches, one per person. This dish could be made with a cottage loaf and flat mushrooms, if you are not in an extravagant mood.

If you are eating it as an extra-special breakfast, drink Buck's Fizz, but for a lunch or supper use a soft fruity red. A Château de la Jaubertie is rather claret-like and lovely.

---

1 brioche mousseline
2 black truffles
2 tbs Armagnac
5 oz/150 g butter
8 eggs
2 tbs cream
2 tbs freshly grated Parmesan
  (optional)
salt, black pepper

Cut the top off the brioche and hollow it out, leaving a reasonable crust. Melt 2 oz/60 g butter, season it well with black pepper and combine it with the Armagnac. Brush this all over the brioche, inside and out. Place in a hot oven (gas mark 6/400°F/200°C) for 7 or 8 minutes.

While it is in the oven, make the scrambled eggs. Melt another 2 oz/60 g butter in the top of a double boiler. Lightly beat the eggs with a pinch of salt and pour into the butter. Stir until the eggs are just cooked, then stir in the cream. Melt the rest of the butter and gently heat the thinly sliced truffles in it.

Stir half the truffles into the eggs and then pile the mixture into the brioche case. Spoon the rest of the truffles and the butter over the eggs and sprinkle with the Parmesan. Replace the brioche lid and return to the oven for 3 minutes. Serve.

Ricotta Pancakes

An Italian relation to blinis perhaps? The raised cakes are delicate, with a little graininess. Sweetened and flavoured with orange or lemon rind, and proffered with a drizzle of honey and juice and a dusting of cinnamon, they make a good tea-time snack or a rustic pudding. They will be more elegantly formed if you use crumpet rings. Fry in butter for the sweet version and olive oil for the savoury. The latter can be served with a topping of char-grilled vegetables – peppers, aubergine, courgettes and tomatoes, scattered with herbs. Also very good with a fragrant, rich Neapolitan-style tomato ragoût.

The sweet version could be served with a Muscat and Orange Flora from Australia and the savoury will be happy in the company of a Sangiovese alla Romagna.

8 oz/250 g Ricotta – if, like me, you have a sporadic supply, cottage cheese can be used after giving it a few bursts in the food processor to break down the lumpy curds a bit
2 oz/60 g plain flour
1 oz/30 g fine yellow polenta (cornmeal)
¼ pt/150 ml milk
¼ oz/7.5 g dried yeast (the fermipan sort)
salt or sugar
olive oil or butter
black pepper or lemon or orange rind, finely grated

Everything should be at room temperature. Sieve together the flour, polenta, yeast and sugar or salt. Stir the Ricotta, work in the flour and beat in the milk. Season with pepper or zest as required. Allow to stand for 40 minutes.

Heat a griddle or a cast-iron frying pan. Grease with oil or butter. Drop tablespoons of mixture onto the hot surface. They will start to look set but the smell will tell you when the base is golden. Flip over with a palette knife – they are delicate; do it quickly. Fry until golden on both sides. Regrease the pan before adding more batter. Keep the cooked ones hot, wrapped in a napkin on a plate over hot water. Serve immediately. In all probability you will have to return to the kitchen and begin again – the pancakes are just too moreish.

Banana Soufflé

This is an impressive-looking pudding, ready in double-quick time. It can bake whilst you are eating the previous course. To speed up even more, bake in individual ramekins for 7–10 minutes. Unexpected guests will be impressed! The flavours are very fresh and fruity, the texture almost celestially light.

It is a myth that soufflés are impossibly difficult; in this recipe machines lighten one's load further.

Try a honeyed pudding wine such as a Muscat: Beaume de Venise is probably the best known but the Rivesaltes or the Frontignan are very acceptable too.

4 large bananas
1 orange
1 passion fruit
4 eggs, separated
8 oz/250 g golden granulated sugar
1 tbs dark rum (optional)
icing sugar to dust
butter or margarine to grease
1 large fragrant ripe mango

Peel the bananas and break into pieces. Place in a blender or food processor with the egg yolks, rum and the juice of the orange. Halve the passion fruit and scoop the pulp and seeds into a sieve. Press as much of the flesh and juice as you can through into the processor's bowl. Discard the seeds. Liquidise the banana mixture until smooth.

Whisk the egg whites until peaky, then whisk in the sugar, a couple of tablespoons at a time, until very stiff and glossy. Gently fold the banana mixture into the egg whites, carefully combining the two.

Spoon into a lightly-greased deep straight-sided dish and bake for 15–20 minutes at gas mark 6/400°F/20°C until well risen and just set. Dust the top with icing sugar before rushing it to the table.

Serve with a puddle of mango sauce, made by simply sieving the mango pulp whilst the soufflé is in the oven.

Scandinavian Omelette

An Omelette à la Norvégienne is a Baked Alaska (see Chapter 11); this is not the same thing at all! It is a more substantial northern cousin of the students' favourite, Spanish omelette. It is cut in wedges and serves four people. Piquant toppings, based on vinegar, can be added if desired.

It would make a good lunch with rye bread and lager or dry cider.

1 medium apple – the Revd Wilks is the best variety to use; it holds its shape, and is neither sweet nor tart
5 eggs
3 oz/90 g Jarlsberg cheese
1/2 oz/15 g butter
1 shallot
2 oz/60 g plain four
3/4 pt/450 ml milk
pinch of allspice, salt

Sift together the flour, allspice and a pinch of salt. Beat the eggs, flour and milk together well. Quarter and core the apple and thinly slice. Add to the eggs. Peel and quarter the shallot and slice it finely too. Combine with the egg and apple. Slice the cheese wafer-thin, using a mandolin-type grater. Stir into the mixture. Melt the butter in a large frying pan. Pour in the eggs when the butter smells mouthwatering – the 'point of fragrance'. Preheat the grill. Cook the omelette over a moderate heat. Lift the edges, tilting the pan to allow the still runny egg mixture to cook also. Ensure an even distribution of apple, onion and cheese. When almost set, place under the grill to brown the top. Rush to the table.

The omelette is nice cold with salad and chutney too – almost a quiche without a crust!

Baked Savoury Custard

The custard can be turned out onto a plate or served from the dish. It can be eaten hot or cold. It looks very pretty when cooked in ramekins, inverted onto a plate and garnished with a fine lattice of lightly cooked vegetables (courgette, pepper and carrot for example). Pour a lovely fresh-tasting coulis around the base of a cold custard; the colour contrast is almost as important as the flavour. For a hot custard, serve with a dark mushroom sauce or a light, minted pea and soured cream one. A more substantial dish can be made of the custard if you include 4 oz/125 g of cooked rice.

Some people complain that red wine tastes metallic with eggs. It will be noted from previous selections in this chapter that I do not experience this unpleasant reaction. However, with this dish I would advise against a red and plump instead for a Sauvignon Blanc, one of the 'gooseberry' ones, either a Californian Mondavi Woodbridge or a Menetou-Salon from the Loire.

6 eggs
12 fl oz/350 ml milk or milk and
    cream
3 tbs finely chopped parsley
1 tbs chopped chives
1–2 oz/30–60 g finely grated fresh
    Parmesan
butter
salt, pepper

Butter a soufflé dish or 4 medium or 6 small ramekins. Cover the base and sides with chopped parsley. Heat the chives in a little butter, cooking them very briefly. Place them in a bowl and season with salt and pepper. Add the Parmesan and eggs and beat well. Bring the milk almost to the boil and pour onto the egg mixture in a thin steady stream while stirring rapidly. Pour the resulting custard into the prepared dish(es) and stand in a roasting tin of hot water. Bake at gas mark 4/350°F/180°C for 35–40 minutes until set. Allow to stand for 5 minutes before turning out. Run a round-bladed knife round the edge before inverting onto a plate.

If having cold, chill and unmould just before serving.

The custard can be altered by adding various purées – try cooked lettuce, watercress, sorrel or spinach. Mushrooms or leeks can be used sliced, finely chopped or puréed. Root vegetable purées become very delicate and refined – salsify, carrots and jerusalem artichokes are all very good. Bottled or tinned globe artichoke hearts, puréed with garlic, make, I think, the best custard of all.

The recipe is also an excellent way of using small amounts of precious things: chanterelles, truffles or asparagus.

Greengage Clafoutis

A clafoutis is a batter pudding from the Limousin in central France, originally made with cherries: a sweet toad-in-the-hole. I like greengages, or ReineClaudes, as they are known in France. While I normally applaud scale reductions made in the name of daintiness, I find the 'new' clafoutis, made in a pastry tartlet shell, too far removed from the essence of the dish. They are just a pleasant fruit tart. In Provence a similar pudding is made with cherries, but they are set in custard. This makes for a richer dish and is worth trying.

If greengages are unavailable, use damsons, plums, nectarines, quartered quinces or halved crab apples. In the spring new rhubarb is delicious – serve with single cream spiked with ginger wine.

The Limousin offers no local wine but a wealth of intoxicating countryside. In the Creuse, where we stayed, the rolling meadows are unsprayed and full of wild flowers. The tiny roads wind their way through farmyards seemingly unchanged since before Zola's *Earth*, stretching back in their continuum to the Middle Ages. We saw a peasant sowing seed from a pouch slung around his neck, a horsedrawn harrow, and many farms where the only concession to technology was a beat-up 2CV van, in some cases literally held together with string.

Many picnics were had by streams, rivers and lakes; just simple food – baguettes, fresh cheeses, salads, glorious sweet butter and all manner of local jams. The owners of our gîte, M. and Mme Durand, made us welcome on arrival with wine, orange juice for the children and a Gâteau Creusois – a fragrant, slightly grainy cake studded with almonds. The perfect start to an idyllic stay. Tourists have yet to catch on. Postcards home were difficult – there were none except in Aubusson. Unlike in the Dordogne, slightly further south, we saw no other GB stickers for a fortnight. The only other foreign car we met while pootling along the byways belonged to a German who bemusedly asked us if we were lost.

However, if clear water and fresh air are not enough, open a bottle of Côtes de Montravel or one of the Muscats. We tried many that holiday, chilling the bottles in the waters of the *étangs*. One particularly glorious day we had a Muscat de Lunel; it seemed a little lighter than those of Rivesaltes and Frontignan and made very pleasant drinking in the hot spring sunshine.

1 lb/500 g ripe greengages
4 oz/125 g plain flour
6 oz/180 g caster sugar
4 eggs
½ pt/300 ml full cream milk
½ oz/15 g butter
1 vanilla pod (optional)
icing sugar

Sift the flour with the sugar and make a well in the centre. Beat the eggs, then beat in the milk. Slit the vanilla pod and scrape the tiny beans into the milk. Pour a little milk mixture into the flour and beat until smooth. Gradually add the rest of the milk and eggs. Leave the batter to stand until required.

Butter a shallow baking dish. Put in the greengages. I like to leave them whole but if you prefer you can halve and stone them. Pour over the batter and bake at the top of a gas mark 4/350°F/180°C oven for 35–40 minutes. When risen and nicely browned, dredge lightly with icing sugar and serve immediately.

Mrs Hartley (*Food in England*) and Mrs Beeton both give recipes for batter puddings with fruit but they seem, on the whole, to have been boiled ones – the Tunbridge Fried Cherry Batter being an exception. I would much rather the browned crust of the clafoutis.

Spiced Crème Caramel

Crème caramel is very popular in Spain and Mexico where it is known as 'flan'. Hoardings show wide-mouthed children spooning in packet-mix instant 'flan'. This seems a shame when it is so easy to make. Making your own, you are in control of the flavourings and the degree of sweetening – important points. Vanilla is the classic flavour but cinnamon with cardamom is delectable. An elusive almond perfume is added by steeping some nuts in the warm milk. Use coffee beans in the same way for a delicate coffee flavour. Make the custards in darioles or ramekins.

Serve with small glasses of chilled Oloroso or Amontillado – sherry is not just an aperitif.

1 pt/600 ml milk
6 oz/180 g golden caster sugar
2 sticks cinnamon
4 cardamom pods
1 oz/30 g almonds
2 in/5 cm piece of sweet orange rind
 – ensure there is no pith
2 eggs + 2 extra yolks
4 tbs water

Crush the almonds between two sheets of paper with a rolling pin. Place in a saucepan with the milk, 2 oz/60 g sugar, cinnamon sticks and orange peel. Crush the cardamoms and add to the pan. Warm gently, stirring occasionally until the sugar melts. Bring slowly to the boil then remove from the heat and leave in a warm place to cool down slowly.

Lightly grease the darioles and stand in a roasting tin of hot water. Melt the rest of the sugar in the water. When it is dissolved, boil hard until it becomes a deep rich amber – not a black coffee colour, as that will have a burnt taste with a bitter edge. Pour some caramel into each of the moulds, running it around the base and halfway up the sides.

Beat the eggs and the extra yolks together. Strain the milk and beat gradually into the eggs. Strain the custard into a jug and pour gently into the moulds.

Place in a moderate oven (gas mark 4/350°F/180°C) for 35–45 minutes or until a blade slipped into the centre comes out clean. Cool and then chill. To serve, loosen the edges and invert on a plate – if you have children they may insist on doing this. Accompany with fresh sliced peaches scattered with toasted flaked almonds.

Double-Ovened Chestnut Soufflés

When I determined to write this book, in order for prospective publishers to take notice, I entered a number of cookery competitions. The spin-offs, apart from the contract, were delightful. Foreign holidays and kitchen appliances aside, there were marvellous opportunities to meet other cooks and exchange ideas. The very first gathering for me was at the 1988 Cheese Challenge. I was very pregnant and rather wide-eyed at the proceedings in the basement of a Mayfair hotel. For my trouble I got a microwave which was sold before unpacked when I returned home. Chris Bussey, a chef from Kentallen, got a car for his wonderful garlic and stilton soufflés – and I lifted from him the notion of re-baking a soufflé. I have since seen similar processes but to him must go my acknowledgements and grateful thanks. Is he still roaming the Highlands in his Maestro?

Penfolds are Australia's largest wine producers. Quantity in this case does not mean a lack of quality. I have several favourites from their cellars. Their Bin 2, the Shiraz/Mataro, is robust and tasty – very good with the chestnuts and not so expensive that you could not sacrifice some to the cooking pot.

4oz/125g dried chestnuts
4 cloves garlic
2 shallots
6 eggs
1/2pt/300ml double cream
nutmeg
sage
rosemary
black pepper, salt
red wine
olive oil

Soak the chestnuts overnight.

Peel and chop the garlic and the shallots. Fry in a little olive oil – a flameproof casserole dish is easiest. Pour in 4tbs wine and reduce. Add the chestnuts and their soaking liquor. Add several sprigs of sage and rosemary and season liberally with black pepper and a little salt. Bring to the boil, cover and cook slowly, either on the top of the stove or in the oven.

When the chestnuts are soft, remove the herbs. Reduce any remaining liquid and purée them with 5 egg yolks.

Whisk 6 egg whites with a pinch of salt until stiff. Fold through the chestnut mixture. Check seasoning, adding a little finely chopped sage if desired. Spoon into large well-buttered ramekins and stand in a roasting tin of boiling water. Cover with foil.

Bake at gas mark 4/350°F/180°C for 40 minutes, until set. Remove and cool slightly. Turn up the heat to gas mark 7/425°F/220°C. Beat the remaining yolk with the cream. Turn each soufflé out onto a small ovenproof gratin dish. Spoon the cream generously over the soufflés and dust with freshly grated nutmeg. Return to the oven for 15 minutes and serve.

Spoonbread

Cornbread at its lightest and most delicate, spoonbread is similar to a soufflé but is slightly gritty in texture. Other flavouring can be added – grated Parmesan, minced olives, finely chopped chives or spring onions for example. If you prefer, make it for breakfast in ramekins, placing a spoon of marmalade in the base of the greased dish.

As a supper dish serve it with a Provençal country red and a dark green salad.

2 oz/60 g cornmeal
3 eggs
1/2 tsp salt
1 oz/30 g butter
3/4 pt/450 ml milk

Butter a soufflé dish using half the butter. Heat the milk until it begins to bubble around the edges. Pour onto the cornmeal, stirring well. Stir in the butter and season with the salt. Return to the heat and cook over a low heat, while stirring, until the mixture is thick. Take off the heat. Separate the eggs. Whisk the egg whites until stiff. Beat the yolks into the warm cornmeal/milk mixture. Fold through the egg whites and spoon into the buttered dish.

Bake in a hot oven (gas mark 6/400°F/200°C) for 35–40 minutes.

Soufflé aux Marrons

Chestnuts are very adaptable. In this recipe they are sweet and delicate, and in the next savoury and more substantial. Although fresh chestnuts can be used, I choose, against my norms, to make this with canned, unsweetened chestnut purée. This is because my supplies of English sweet chestnuts are a bit iffy – many, when peeled, are bad. It also means that this *is* a larder standby for one of those mysterious unexpected guests we are all supposed to have regularly turning up on our doorsteps, if cookery features are to be believed.

Drink something heavy and sweet with this – you could also make a sauce based on Malmsey or Marsala.

If you are in a hurry, cook in individual ramekins.

12 oz/360 g natural chestnut purée
2 oz/60 g stoned prunes
6 eggs
3 tbs brandy
1 vanilla pod
8 oz/250 g caster sugar
butter
icing sugar

Cook the prunes in a little water until soft. Drain the purée with the brandy. Beat in the chestnuts. Slit open the vanilla pod and scrape the tiny seeds into the chestnut mixture. Whisk the egg whites until stiff, then whip in the caster sugar.

Butter a soufflé dish. Warm the chestnut mixture, beating, over a low flame. Beat in the egg yolks then fold in the meringue. Turn into the dish and bake at gas mark 6/400°F/200°C for 30 minutes until puffed and set. You *must* force your guests, expected or not, to eat it without delay.

8
World Food

As the world shrinks with faster, more accessible travel so we are exposed to a far greater diversity of food. Unfortunately at the same time the imperialism of the North American food chains, working on the aspirations of the poorer countries, is leading to a standardisation (Westernisation) of restaurant food. It has happened with hotels already. It has become difficult, once inside your hotel, to tell where in the world you are. The national character has been all but erased. So it will be with food if we do not champion the authentic cooking of other nations. If you do not believe this, look no further than France where Parisian café owners are already under threat from junk-food outlets. The Champs Elysées has, in the eyes of many, already succumbed.

In the scope of this book it is impossible to do more than note a few dishes – each cuisine, whether Arab, Russian, Chinese or any of the others, demands a book to itself. In all of these cultures there are vegetarian dishes, and ideas that will transfer readily to a dish without meat that preserves the identity of the original concept.

Throughout the book there are influences from all over the world; this chapter seeks to re-establish certain dishes previously debased by vegetarians and to bring others to wider notice.

Samosas

All of the Indian dishes in this chapter could be made at once and served in individual dishes as a thali (or tali). Accompany the thalis with rice, nan, raita and pickles.

Samosas are a convenient way of using up any curry leftovers, just like ravioli, piroshki and pasties. The filling specified is aloo mutter – pea and potato curry – which can be made on its own.

I used to make samosas with a pancake batter, cooking each pancake on one side only, enclosing the filling (uncooked side out) and then deep frying. That method works and is quite nice but this dough is better.

If you have only had supermarket samosas, do make your own and eat them straight away – they are best hot.

8 oz/250 g plain flour or half and
half plain and wholemeal
3 tbs melted ghee or oil
3–4 fl oz/90–120 ml very warm
water
1 tsp salt
oil – soya or peanut
1/2 tsp cumin seeds
1 small fresh green chilli
1 tsp coriander seeds
pinch turmeric
12 oz/375 g waxy potatoes
12 oz/375 g shelled peas
2 medium onions

Dry roast the cumin and coriander seeds in a small pan over a medium heat. Shake the pan continuously so they do not burn. Allow them to darken slightly and notice the change in the aroma. Tip onto a clean sheet of paper and allow to cool. Grind as finely as possible.

Scrub the potatoes and cut into 1/2 in/1 cm chunks. Peel and finely chop the onion. Mince the chilli. Fry the chilli and onions in 2–3 tbs oil until nicely browned. Add the potatoes and spices and cook, stirring, over a medium heat for 7 minutes. Add the peas, a good pinch of salt and a splash of water. Stir around, cover and simmer until the potatoes are tender. Allow to cool.

Sift the flour(s) with 1 tsp salt. Using your fingertips rub in the ghee or oil. Add enough of the warm water to make a firm dough. Knead it for 10 minutes until smooth. Pinch off a large walnut-sized piece, keeping the rest of the dough covered, and roll out to a 5–6 in/13–15 cm diameter circle. Cut the round in half. Use each half to form a cornet, sealing the overlapping edge with water. Fill with a very generous teaspoon of aloo mutter and seal the top edge, pinching the sides together. Repeat with the rest of the dough.

Deep-fry in hot oil until deep golden. I use a wok for this but other large pans will do. Serve immediately, after draining on crumpled greaseproof or kitchen paper.

Sag Bhagee

The spinach or other greens cooked in good Indian restaurants are always my favourite dishes in the selection provided for a thali. Balti dishes are like Indian woks. I use my Cantonese one with no difficulty. Don't, as one rather disreputable curry house did, use tinned spinach. If you have no time to make panir, cross cultures and use cubes of smoked tofu (soy bean curd).

Curry spices and spinach – I would forget about a suitable wine. 'Tuskers' all round?

2 lbs/1 kg fresh chard or spinach – the former is preferred for its delicious stems
2–3 tomatoes
1 large mild onion
1/2 tsp mustard seeds
1/2 tsp fenugreek
1 stick cinnamon
3 cloves garlic
1/2 in/1.25 cm root ginger
1/2 tsp coriander seeds
1/2 tsp ground turmeric
pinch of chilli powder
1/2 tsp cumin seeds
salt
ghee or soya oil

For the panir

2 pt/1 1/4 l milk
2 tbs white malt vinegar mixed with 4 tbs warm water

The panir has to be made the day before it is needed to give it time to drain. Bring the milk up to the boil over a high heat. You will need to stir it to avoid it catching on the base of the pan. If it does stick and burn, the cheese will be tainted by that nasty scorched-milk flavour: you have been warned. Once boiling, immediately remove from the heat and slowly stir in the vinegar and water. Stop adding the vinegar as soon as the milk curdles. Pour the curdled milk through muslin, squeezing out as much liquid as possible. Hang the solids up to drain thoroughly in the muslin, then press into a flat cake between two plates.

The next day cut the panir into cubes of about 3/4 in/2 cm. Peel and chop the onion and garlic. Wash the chard or spinach and roughly chop. Grate the ginger. Crush the coriander and fenugreek. Heat a wok, balti dish or large pan. Add a little ghee or oil and allow that to get hot. Fry the cubes of cheese until browned. Remove with a slotted spoon. Add the seeds, spices, including the ginger, onion and garlic and fry, stirring, for a couple of minutes. Stir in the chard or spinach with a good pinch of salt. Keep stir-frying for a couple of minutes then cover with a baking sheet or lid and turn down the heat. Cook for 8 minutes, then add the quartered tomatoes and the panir cubes. Cook, stirring constantly but carefully, so as not to break up the panir, for a further 5 minutes. Serve.

Garlic Risotto

Y ou cannot make risotto with anything other than Italian rice – pudding rice, although more like it in shape than long grain, is just not the same and must not be substituted. Look for Arborio. The second prerequisite is a good stock. For this recipe, I use the clear broth from the French Garlic Soup (p. 29). Other stocks can also be tried.

Forget about those mixed veg'n'rice creations fraudulently posing as risottos in women's magazines and chill cabinets – a good risotto should be simple. The impostors have onions, sweetcorn, peas, peppers, peanuts, mushrooms, raisins, egg and goodness knows what else all jostling for position in amongst the separate grains of rice. A risotto is a creamy, almost soupy dish of great integrity. Its accompaniments are best kept to cheese and butter with only one or two others.

Drink a Soave Classico; you can put some in the risotto too, instead of the Marsala, if you prefer.

1 lb/500 g Arborio rice –
sometimes sold as risotto rice;
check the small print. It should
say 'Product of Italy'. This is a
generous amount for 4 people.
3 oz/90 g butter
4 oz/125 g Parmesan cheese

Divide the garlic into cloves and peel. Place in a saucepan with the sage, cloves, crushed peppercorns, salt and water. Bring to the boil. Cover and simmer for 1 hour. Strain the soup, squeezing the pulp but not pressing it through the sieve. Reheat the broth and keep it on a low flame.

3 tbs Marsala
2 shallots
4 bulbs garlic
2¹/₂ pt / 1.5 l water
small bunch of sage
2 cloves
7 white peppercorns
1 tsp salt

Melt half the butter in the bottom of a large pan. Gently fry the very finely chopped shallots in it. When softened and slightly coloured, add the rice and stir it around in the butter until it has all been covered in it. Do not fry the rice. Add the Marsala and let it reduce away. Add a ladleful of stock. Stir it through. Watch the rice as it absorbs the broth; add more but do not add too much at once. Do not let it boil dry. The rice, as it absorbs the liquid, will become creamier and the risotto will need continuous stirring. The total cooking period will vary according to the rice but will be approximately 25 minutes. You may not need to add all the broth. When it is done the risotto will be creamy but not runny. The rice will be tender with a slight resistance in the centre and it will not be sticky.

Stir in the rest of the butter and half the cheese, grated. Serve with the rest of the cheese handed separately.

If you want to make a mushroom risotto, grind 1 tbs dried mushrooms to a fine powder and add this to the broth. Cook 8 oz / 250 g sliced fresh porcini (use brown caps if unavailable) in butter, with herbs to taste, and stir into the risotto with the cheese. Artichoke hearts, preserved in olive oil, make an excellent alternative to the mushrooms.

I look forward to a risotto with white truffles.

Piroshki

More small parcels, this time Russian. Made large they are called piroghi. The piroshi differ from region to region. The word means 'little pie'. The dough varies, along with the cooking methods. Plain bread dough, rich brioche, shortcrust, puff paste, choux paste, cream cheese or cottage cheese pastry and even blinis are all used. The parcels are baked, boiled or fried. Fillings range from the exotic – truffles, to the more mundane – cabbage. It is possible to by a hinged mould that shapes, cuts and seals the dough into small semi-circular pasties but I sometimes like to cut mine into equilateral triangles, folding the points up and sealing them over the filling to make pyramids.

I am giving a cheese pastry, but do use the other doughs for this filling and experiment with other fillings too.

10 oz/300 g plain flour
¼ tsp salt
8 oz/250 g cream cheese
9 oz/275 g butter
1 small white cabbage
1 tbs dried mushrooms
a few spring onions
1 tsp dill seeds
3 eggs
1–2 tsp poppy seeds
white pepper

You do need to make the pastry the day before and leave well wrapped in the fridge to chill. It is delicate and rather difficult to handle if you do not. Sift the salt into the flour. Cut 8 oz/250 g of the butter, and the cream cheese, into the flour with two knives or a pastry blender – the sort with U-shaped wires attached to a wooden handle. Process in a machine with caution; do it in bursts only. Form into a soft dough and chill well.

Hardboil 2 of the eggs.

Pour 2 tbs boiling water onto the dried mushrooms and leave to stand. Finely chop the onions and the cabbage and fry gently in the remaining butter with the dill seeds. Add the mushroom water and the finely chopped mushrooms and simmer until tender. Chop the hardboiled eggs and add to the cabbage. Season generously with the white pepper.

Roll the dough out to ⅛ in/0.25 cm thick, on a lightly floured surface. You may find it easier to do this on silicon paper. Dust the paper with flour. Cut the dough as you wish: circles, squares or triangles. Put a teaspoon of filling on each and seal by brushing the edges with the remaining egg, lightly beaten, and pinching or crimping.

Carefully transfer to a greased baking sheet. Brush the piroshkis with egg and scatter with poppy seeds. Bake at gas mark 5/375°F/190°C until nicely browned; depending on size this will take between 10–20 minutes.

Moussaka

Arto der Haroutunian traces the origins of moussaka from the medieval dish of *muh-klabah* as made in Baghdad. In his book, *Middle Eastern Cookery*, he gives three recipes for Arab, Armenian and Greek moussaka. My recipe borrows from all three traditions and, although it contains no meat, is very much in the spirit of the original dish.

Drink the fine Lebanese wine, Château Musar. It is extraordinary that anything as everyday as winemaking can continue in the Bekaa Valley and yet here is a great wine, with nothing everyday about it. Alternatively, find another Cabernet Sauvignon/Syrah blend, the Australian Bin 389 from Penfolds.

2 large aubergines
olive oil
salt
8 oz/250 g shallots or red onions
3 cloves garlic
2 sticks of celery, with leaves
4 oz/125 g long grain rice
2 oz/60 g lentils
½ a lemon
½ tbs fresh chopped coriander
  leaves
2 tbs fresh chopped chervil or flat
  parsley
12 oz/375 g flat mushrooms

Slice the aubergines, crossways, into ¼ in/0.5 cm slices. Sprinkle with salt and allow to stand.

Mince or very finely chop the shallots, garlic, celery and mushrooms. You can do this in a food processor in short bursts, but do not purée it. Heat 2 tbs oil in a large pan. Add the crushed allspice, the cinnamon, cloves and a generous grinding of black pepper. Fry for a minute then add the minced vegetables. Fry, stirring, until beginning to brown. Add the lentils and rice and continue to stir over a medium heat for another couple of minutes. Pour on the stock and add the juice and ½ tsp of the finely grated zest of the lemon. Add the herbs. Cover and cook

2 tbs chopped walnuts or pistachios
½ pt/300 ml vegetable stock – can include a slosh of your chosen wine
1 cinnamon stick
5 allspice berries
2 cloves
black pepper
nutmeg
2 egg yolks
4 oz/125 g Kefalotiri or Hahloumi cheese
½ pt/300 ml smetana

slowly until the rice and lentils are done and the stock is almost absorbed; about 20 minutes. Stir in the chopped nuts.

Scrape or rinse the salt off the aubergines. Pat dry. Fry in hot olive oil until lightly browned either side. The aubergine will absorb quite a lot of oil, especially if the oil is not hot enough. Expect to add more oil between batches but allow it to heat before adding more aubergine slices.

In an ovenproof dish, layer up the aubergine slices and the rice/vegetable mixture, like a lasagne, beginning and ending with aubergines. How many layers you can make will depend on the dimensions of the dish.

Mash the cheese and egg yolks and work in the smetana. You can whizz this briefly in a liquidiser if you prefer. Season with a little salt and a generous grating of nutmeg before carefully spreading it all over the top of the aubergines. Bake in a moderate oven (gas mark 4/350°F/ 180°C) for 30–40 minutes. The top should be set and nicely browned. Serve.

Goulash

Paprika, the Hungarian pepper, in *A Modern Herbal* (1931) by Mrs M. Grieve, F.R.H.S. (but presumably not C.O.O.K.), is referred to as 'a tasteless cayenne'. It may not be fiery, as cayenne, but it most certainly has taste. Goulash, or Guylas, depends on it. Add it towards the end of cooking, like garam masala in Indian foods. If the ground paprika you have is not a vivid red, discard it – it is either stale or of inferior quality.

Goulash should be quite liquid – lots of spicy rich gravy, almost soup-like. Mop up the sauce with plain boiled potatoes, poppy-seeded bread or wide-ribbon noodles dressed in butter and caraway seeds.

Hungary produces some very good wine. Traditionally the red came from the Kadarka grape but now much is Pinot Noir, Cabernet Sauvignon and Merlot. Drink a Merlot from Eger, also known here as Medoc Noir; it will be quite gutsy enough to partner the goulash. Eger in the North East is home too for Bikavér – the famed Bull's Blood. Far from being sanguinary, it is actually a blend of Kadarka, Pinot Noir and Merlot grapes. As with Chianti, look for a bit of age if you want refinement.

2 very large, thick mushrooms –
   tea-plate sized
2 large, well-coloured carrots
2 cloves garlic
12 oz/375 g red onions
8 oz/250 g fresh plum tomatoes –
   tinned ones will make it too
   tomatoey!
3 large peppers – 1 deep red, squat
   and knobbly; 1 ordinary red
   capsicum and 1 long white one
1 small dried chilli pepper
1–2 tbs ground paprika
1 tsp caraway seeds
a piece of lemon peel
some Hamburg parsley*, including
   the root
1/2 tsp marjoram
salt, white pepper
1 pt/600 ml strong stock
1/4/150 ml red wine
2 oz/60 g butter
soured cream to serve (optional)

Peel and finely slice the onions and garlic. Cut the carrots and mushrooms into 1 in/2 cm chunks. Chop the tomatoes. Cut the peppers into strips, 1/2 in/1 cm wide. Crush the caraway seeds. Melt the butter in a large pan. Add the seeds and fry for a minute. Stir in the mushrooms, carrots, onions, garlic, tomatoes and peppers – including the chilli. Stir occasionally, while cooking over a moderately high heat for 5 minutes. Pour on the stock and wine and add the chopped parsley (*if unavailable use flat parsley and a small piece of celeriac), lemon peel, marjoram and salt and pepper. Allow to cook slowly, in the oven, on the hob or, as traditional, over an open fire, for 90 minutes. Stir in the paprika and cook a further 10 minutes. Serve in soup plates with a flourish of soured cream.

Banana Korma

Hats off to my daughter, Jessamyn; hers was the finishing touch in this recipe. Mild and delicate, not for old colonels who need their heads blowing off. Serve with saffron rice and fresh peas with ginger.

If you can, buy whole spices and grind them yourself in your *hummumdusta* – this wonderful word, according to Harvey Day in his 1955 book, *Curries of India*, means mortar and pestle. I love this little book, passed on from my father. Its small quirky cartoons are endearing, the recipes enticing and the commentary interesting and informative.

12 oz/375 g button onions
12 oz/375 g shiitake mushrooms
1 lb/500 g broad beans
8 oz/250 g small carrots
8 oz/250 g tiny new potatoes
1/2 pt/300 ml good vegetable stock
4 small bananas
1/2 pt/300 ml plain yoghurt
1 1/2 oz/45 g creamed coconut
1/2 tsp cumin seeds
5 cardamoms
1/2 tsp coriander seeds
4 cloves
2 sticks cinnamon bark
4 cloves garlic
1/2 tsp fresh grated ginger
1/2 tsp ground turmeric
1/2 tsp black peppercorns
1 tsp garam masala
salt
1 bay leaf
ghee or peanut oil

Prepare all the vegetables first. Peel the onions, trimming the top and bottom, but only quartering if on the large size. Trim the mushrooms. Scrub the carrots and potatoes. Cut the carrots into quarters, lengthwise. Shell the broad beans. Peel and finely slice the garlic.

Crush the seeds, cloves and peppercorns in the *hummumdusta*. If you have not got one, try putting the spices between two sheets of clean writing paper and rolling backwards and forwards with a hefty pin. Or use a mallet!

Melt a tablespoon of ghee in a large pan over a fairly low heat. Add all the spices and garlic and fry, stirring, for a couple of minutes. Throw in the onions, carrots and potatoes. Stir around so that they get coated in the spices. Cover and cook for 5 minutes, shaking from time to time. Add the beans, stock, a little salt and the bay leaf. Bring up to the boil then turn down and simmer until all the vegetables are tender.

Cut the bananas into 1/2 in/1.25 cm pieces. Combine with the yoghurt and garam masala. Turn up the heat to reduce the curry liquid. Stir to avoid sticking. Remove from the heat and add the crumbled creamed coconut. Allow this to melt into the curry then add the yoghurt and banana. Reheat gently, mixing well, until steaming but on no account allow it to boil. Serve dusted with a little paprika and a sprig or two of coriander leaves.

Almond Curry

A friend, long ago, gave me a recipe for an almond curry from her days in the Far East. I carelessly misplaced it and have had to invent my own. Use either as a side dish or as a sauce on steamed long green beans or braised chard or spinach. If you cannot get long beans – Chinese grocers are the best source – use French beans instead. You can use ready-ground almonds but the flavour is better if you grind them fresh.

Despite the recent protestations of some wine writers, I still find it difficult to appreciate wine with curries. I would far rather have fruit juice, mango or pineapple, with soda, or serve lager. However, if you must, use a Riesling – a sweetish Spätlese.

1 red onion
4 cloves garlic
1 dried red chilli
1/2 in/1.25 cm fresh root ginger
1/2 tsp ground coriander
1/2 tsp turmeric
1/4 tsp cayenne
pinch of ground cumin
pinch salt
very generous grinding of black
  pepper
12 oz/375 g freshly ground
  almonds
1 tbs peanut oil
3 oz/90 g creamed coconut – this is
  sold in a block
1/2 pt/300 ml boiling water

Peel the onion, garlic and ginger. Roughly chop them and put into a food processor (unless you happen to have a large grinding stone in your kitchen). Process in bursts until almost smooth. Heat the oil and fry the chilli, coriander, turmeric, cayenne, cumin, salt and black pepper for a couple of minutes, stirring continuously. Add the onion paste and continue cooking over a low heat for 10 minutes. Add the almonds and cook for a further 5 minutes. Pour the boiling water onto the coconut and stir until it is dissolved. Add to the curry and simmer a further 10 minutes. Do not cover. Stir occasionally. Remove the chilli before serving.

This sauce can also be used for dipping, satay style or over deep-fried eggs. The eggs are boiled, in their shells, for 4–6 minutes depending on size. Then they are plunged into cold water and peeled, before being fried in hot oil until golden. The eggs could also be accompanied by a more Chinese plum sauce.

Channna Dhall

Although I have eaten dhall curries made from all manner of pulses including chick peas, mung beans and red lentils, I favour the small golden-yellow split peas. There must also be a garnish of crisp garlic. Almost but not quite bitter and slightly nutty, it is the essential counterpoint to the dhall. I prefer by dhall with a nan or puri rather than rice. I remember with affection the Pakistani chefs, flown in for Expo '67 in Montreal, who made the most extravagant puris. They rose like cumulus in the kitchen, were whisked on silent feet to the restaurant and sank gently back on a large white damask napkin by your plate. The waiters took us into the kitchens to watch these miracles. They made delicate milky puddings and decorated them with the finest sheets of silver and gold. Every meal there, and there were quite a few in the too-short year, was wondrous and my eight-year-old delight in food from the subcontinent has never diminished.

Curries were often served at home. My grandmother, now ninety-six, still makes her special chicken curries for guests. Hers is a hybrid, though, with influences from old colonials and the West Indies. A hybrid and not a bastardised version – curry has meant mince fried with a packet of dried 'minestrone soup', some water and a teaspoon or so of curry powder elsewhere.

8 oz/250 g small yellow split peas – if you buy these from an Indian grocer they will be marked 'channa dhall' (or dal); they are smaller than European yellow split peas which are known as 'matar dhall'. Husked mung beans can be substituted.
pinch of turmeric
3 large cloves garlic
1 shallot (optional)
2 tsp ground cumin
1 tsp ground coriander
1 bay leaf
1 dried chilli
2 tomatoes
black pepper, salt
ghee or oil
2 pt/1.25 l water

Pick over the split peas, rinse and then dry them in a tea-towel. Dry-fry them, stirring or shaking the pan, until they begin to colour. Add the water, turmeric, cumin, chilli, coriander, bay leaf and quartered tomatoes. Season with a little salt and pepper. Bring to the boil and cook slowly for 75–90 minutes, until the dhall is soft. Peel and thinly slice the garlic and shallot if using. Fry quickly until crisp in a little hot oil or ghee. Spoon on to the top of the dhall immediately before serving.

Cheese Churros

Driving the mountain road through the tiny tax-haven state of Andorra high in the Pyrenees there are billboards everywhere the eye can see for hyped supermarkets, restaurants, snackbars and 'Xurros'. Churros, as the rest of Spain knows them, are choux fritters. Gleaming steel machines extrude long sausages of paste, a twirling blade lops off 3-inch lengths which plop into the boiling oil below. Magically they rise to the surface and, crisp and golden, are automatically lifted out and dumped in a tray of sugar. Then, and only then, does the human hand intervene with a pair of tongs. After being turned in the sugar, they are bagged and handed to wild jugglers who try vainly to avoid burning their fingers.

This recipe is for savoury churros, flavoured and dusted with cayenne and Mahon. Mahon is a hard, granular cheese, quite similar to the Italian Parmesan. It has a distinctive bright orange rind. The churros can be used for *amuse geules*, to dip in Guacamole (p. 175) or as an accompaniment for a soup, ragoût or salad. They are best eaten hot.

Try a Spanish red – a Gran Sangredetoro Reserva from Catalonia is full, hefty and spicy.

If you have not got a forcing bag or can't be bothered to make one from greaseproof, just drop heaped teaspoonfuls into the hot oil.

18 fl oz/500 ml milk
14 oz/400 g plain flour
2 eggs
2 tsp salt
½ tsp cayenne pepper
4 oz/125 g Mahon
half and half olive and sunflower
oil for deep frying

Sift together the flour and cayenne. Grate the cheese on a fine rasp. Lightly beat the eggs in a small bowl or tea cup. Heat the milk and salt. When the milk comes to the boil tip in the flour and beat hard. Continue cooking and stirring hard until the mixture forms a ball and leaves the sides of the pan cleanly.

Remove from the heat. Add the eggs a little at a time, beating well after each addition. When all the egg is incorporated, beat in half the cheese. Scrape the mixture into a forcing bag with a ½in/1.5 cm star nozzle. Heat the oil so that a 1in/2.5 cm cube of bread browns in barely 60 seconds; or check on a fat thermometer – 370°F , or a little under 190°C. Squeeze out 2½in/6.5 cm lengths and drop into the fat. Fry until nicely brown, scoop out and drain on crumpled paper.

Dust with the remaining cheese and a little cayenne to taste before serving immediately.

Satay

There are few cases for the use of beancurd but satay is one. It actually works quite well, picking up the flavours of the marinade. Do not buy the tofu in the juice-box cartons, it is too sloppy. You need to find the blocks that look like packaged cheese. The smoked variety gives an interesting flavour variation. Serve as an appetiser or as a small part in a many-dished Far Eastern meal. Serve with the typical peanut sauce and/or a tomato chilli one.

8 oz/25 g beancurd – in a block
2 tbs shoyu soy sauce
2 cloves garlic
1/2 tsp grated ginger
2 oz/60 g red-skinned peanuts
1 tbs chopped red onion or shallot
1 small green chilli
1 lime
salt
1 oz/30 g creamed coconut
3 tbs boiling water
1 tbs acacia honey
peanut or soya oil

Mince one clove of garlic and combine with the ginger and 1 tbs of the soy sauce. Cut the beancurd into 1/2–3/4 in/1–2 cm cubes. Place in a dish and dribble over the soy, garlic and ginger. Leave to stand.

Break the creamed coconut into small pieces and pour on the boiling water. Stir until dissolved.

Roast the peanuts in a heavy pan until nicely browned. Rub the nuts in a teatowel to remove the skins. Grind with the onion, chilli, lime juice and salt. If you do not have a large pestle and mortar use a food processor or blender. When fairly smooth, scrape into a pan. Cook over a low heat with a couple of tablespoons of water for 15 minutes. Keep warm.

Drop the beancurd cubes into hot oil. Fry until golden then remove with a slotted spoon. Thread the cubes onto bamboo skewers. Combine the remaining soy sauce with the honey and brush all over the beancurd. Place under a hot grill. Turn and brush with more soy and honey before grilling the other side. Stir the coconut into the peanut sauce and reheat, stirring until hot. Serve at once.

A fleshy white mushroom can be used instead of, or as well as, the beancurd if liked.

Spanakopitas

A Greek treat, available cut from a large pie on roadside stalls. Made in individual pasties, it also makes good food-to-go. If you are not planning a picnic, make it up in a large pie. Layer five sheets of filo, brushing each with melted butter, one on top of the other on a baking sheet. Cover with the spinach to within 1½in/4cm of the edge all the way around. Fold in the edges and cover with four more filo sheets and butter, tucking the overlap under the pie. Bake (at the temperature given below) for about 20–25 minutes.

Feta gives a more authentic salty tang but cottage cheese is surprisingly good for a change.

Try the Australian blend of Shiraz and Mataro – a.k.a. Syrah and Mourvedre; Penfolds call theirs, rather prosaically, Bin 2.

1½lb/750g spinach
1 small onion, finely chopped
2 cloves garlic, crushed
8oz/250g feta or cottage cheese
2 eggs
approx 6oz/200g melted butter
box filo pastry sheets
poppy seeds
1 tbs chopped mint
salt, pepper
freshly grated nutmeg

Wash the spinach, shake off excess water and pull off stalks. Rip into small pieces. In a little of the butter, soften the onion and garlic over a low heat. Add the spinach and cover tightly. Shake the pan occasionally to avoid sticking. When the spinach is a soft, thick mass remove from heat. Beat in the eggs and the crumbled feta or cottage cheese. Stir in the finely chopped mint. Season well with salt and black pepper and, essentially, a good pinch of freshly grated nutmeg.

Spread out a sheet of filo. Brush with melted butter and fold in half. Place a tablespoon of the spinach mixture on the bottom edge. Brush all over with butter again. Fold the two sides into the middle, brush again and then roll up. Place on greased baking sheet. Repeat the process until all the filling is used up. Brush the tops of the parcels with more melted butter and sprinkle with poppyseeds. Bake at gas mark 6/400°F/200°C for 15–20 minutes until crisp and golden.

Couscous and Tajine

Couscous is used like rice in many Arab countries. It is made from crushed wheat semolina, but millet (birdseed) can also be used. The moistened grains are cooked in the steam of the simmering spicy stew below, then the two are eaten together. The stew is known as the tajine. Special two-tiered cooking pots are used but an ordinary kitchen steamer or colander is perfectly adequate.

Couscous, well made, is deliciously light and fluffy. The French around Marseilles and Toulon often eat it now with Ratatouille (p. 98) or other vegetable stews.

A dry red would be my choice for the wine, a Vins de Pays d'Oc, either a Domaine de Rivoyre or a Domaine de Parazols Magee, haute plaine.

1 lb/500 g couscous
8 oz/250 g butter
*4 'Slim Jim' aubergines – these are
    the small striped ones*
2 butternut or pattypan squashes
*8 oz/250 g okra – the short fat pods
    are best*
4 oz/125 g dried marrowfat peas
8 oz/250 g dried chick peas
2 cloves garlic
1½ lb/750 g mild onions
3 oz/90 g sultanas
3 oz/90 g currants
½ in/1 cm root ginger
½ tsp ground cumin
½ tsp turmeric
*1 tsp freshly ground black pepper,
    salt*
½ ground coriander
6 crushed allspice berries
pinch of ground bay leaf
1 stick cinnamon
1 tsp ground cinnamon
1 lemon
*fresh coriander leaves or mint
    leaves*

Soak the peas and chick peas overnight. Place the couscous in a large flat dish. Pour on enough water to cover then pour it off again. Allow the couscous to stand 15 minutes while it swells.

Discard the water in which the chick peas and peas have been soaking and bring them to the boil in fresh water. Simmer until just tender. Put the swollen couscous in a strainer or colander over the pan with the chick peas. After it has steamed for 30 minutes, turn it back into the dish and pour ¼ pt/150 ml warm water with 1 tsp salt dissolved in it over the couscous. Break up any lumps with a fork. Leave for 15 minutes.

Quarter the aubergines, lengthwise. Cut the squashes into large chunks. Trim the okra. Peel and chop the onions and garlic.

Melt half the butter in a large pan. Fry the onions and garlic in it with the cumin, pepper, allspice, coriander and grated ginger. When beginning to brown, add the aubergines, okra and squashes. Fry for a further 10 minutes then add the chick peas and peas with their cooking liquor. Add extra water to cover if necessary.

Add a little lemon peel and the ground bay leaf. Season with a little salt. Simmer.

Return the couscous to the steamer and cook a further 30 minutes over the stew. Add the cinnamon stick to the stew.

Melt the rest of the butter with a few drops of lemon juice. Tip the couscous back into the dish and pour over the butter. Sprinkle with the cinnamon and work lightly with two forks to get rid of any lumps, to distribute the butter and to fluff it up. Push into a border around the edge of the dish and put the tajine in the centre. Top with the coriander or mint leaves.

Tempura

These are Japanese filigree batter-coated deep-fried vegetables. The secret of good tempura is to have the batter ice-cold and the oil deep enough and hot enough. Like a soufflé, make the guests wait for tempura, not the other way around.

Serve with rice balls – Japanese rice is stickier than Indian – or on its own as a light meal or hors d'oeuvres.

Serve a dry Alsatian Muscat or some chilled Fino or green tea, hot and clear in small white bowls.

a selection of fresh vegetables in any combination (about 1 lb/500 g total weight, using 2–3 oz/50–75 g of each vegetable chosen):
> *aubergine*
> *beans, French or Kenyan*
> *broccoli*
> *carrot*
> *cauliflower*
> *courgette*
> *cucumber*
> *green pepper*
> *kohlrabi*
> *mangetout*
> *mushrooms – shiitake or oyster*
> *spring onion*
if you can include lotus root, sweet potato, jicama, or bok choi so much the better

Prepare all the vegetables first. Part of the charm of the dish is the beauty of the vegetable pieces. They should be neat and even and no more than bite-size.

Make the sauce by combining the stock, Sercial – if you can get *mirin* that is more authentic – and the soy. Bring to the boil then turn down to a bare simmer.

Heat the oil to 350°F/180°C. There must be a depth of at least 2 in/5 cm. Keep the oil at this temperature.

Batter

1 egg
2½oz/75g plain flour
2½oz/75g rice flour
7 fl oz/200 ml ice-cold water

Sauce

7 fl oz/200 ml stock
2 tbs Sercial – the driest Madeira
4 tbs kikkoman soy sauce – this is
    Japanese soy
2 tsp grated ginger
1 tbs grated white radish
peanut or soya oil for deep frying,
    flavoured with a little sesame
    oil

Beat the egg then beat in the water. Sift the flours over the egg water and lightly mix together. Dip the vegetables into the batter and drop into the hot oil. Only cook a few at a time. They will cook very quickly. Drain and arrange attractively on individual plates. Give each person a bowl of the hot sauce, scattering in each a little ginger and white radish. Diners dip the vegetables in the sauce before eating.

Use a tea strainer to remove odd pieces of batter to stop them burning while you are frying the tempura.

Tourtière

As a child, I spent six and a half years in Montreal. This was in a period of turmoil for the province, the time following de Gaulle's 'Vive le Quebec libre' speech. The Quebequois are different from the rest of Canada and nowhere is that more apparent than at the table. A Saturday lunch after the exertions of swimming or figure skating would often be a tourtière. Look the word up in *Larousse* and you will be told it means simply a pie dish. In Quebec, it is a two-crust pie, aromatically flavoured with bay, cloves, parsley and white pepper. Traditionally it contains minced pork but I use lentilles de Puy. I believe this preserves the integrity of the dish, unlike most similar substitutions.

The pastry is made with white vegetable fat. Butter is not appropriate. I use a rough puff paste but you could use shortcrust if you prefer.

Drink with a red Bordeaux; nothing too grand, but one with a good proportion of Merlot.

*12 oz/375 g lentilles de Puy – the
    large grey lentils*
2 waxy yellow potatoes
2 large mild onions
4 cloves garlic
8 white peppercorns
3 juniper berries
3 cloves
*1 tsp freshly chopped parsley –
    including the stalk*
2 bay leaves
salt
8 oz/250 g plain flour
8 oz/250 g strong flour
12 oz/375 g white vegetable fat
1 egg yolk
1 tsp lemon juice
oil
water

Peel and chop the onions and garlic. Fry in a little oil until lightly browned. Scrub the potatoes and cut into ½ in/1 cm dice. Wash the lentils by pouring boiling water over them and draining. Place in an earthenware pot with the onions, garlic and potato. Crush the peppercorns and juniper berries. Add to the pot with the parsley, cloves and bay. Stir in a little salt also. Pour on water to cover and cook slowly in the oven until the lentils are just soft. This can be done on the top of the stove, if preferred. It will take about 1½–2 hours.

Meanwhile prepare the pastry. Sift the flours with a pinch of salt. Cut the fat into small dice and toss into the flour. Turn carefully about so all the fat pieces are covered in flour but not rubbed into the flour at all. Bring together into a soft dough, using the lemon juice in about 6–7 fl oz/220 ml cold water. Do not add all of the water at once; you can add more if the flour is very absorbent.

Gently roll out, on a well-floured surface, to an oblong ⅝in/1.5 cm thick. Fold up one third to the middle and the other third over it. Seal the unfolded edges by pressing with the rolling pin. Wrap in greaseproof and rest in the fridge for 30 minutes. Turn the paste so that the folded edge is at right angles to you and roll out to the oblong again. Fold, seal and chill again. Repeat the rolling and folding once more before allowing the paste to rest until needed.

When the lentils are just soft, drain them. Reduce the cooking liquor to 3 tablespoons.

Roll out half the paste to line a large, flattish pie dish to ⅛in/30 mm thick. Beat the yolk with a little salt and 1 tsp of water. Brush all over the base. Spoon on the lentils and pour over the reduced cooking liquor. Roll out the remaining pastry and cover the pie, sealing the edges. Trim and crimp. Brush with the egg and bake at gas mark 5/375°F/190°C for 25 minutes or until golden.

Blinis and Pieces

I like informal 'bitty' meals with good friends. Little dishes of this and that, and people helping themselves whilst relaxing and talking. The Greeks have meze, the Spanish have tapas, the Indians have thalis and the Russians give us blinis: buckwheat pancakes eaten with side dishes.

Assuming you aren't going to wash it all down with vodka, although that might indeed loosen a few tongues, try a dry Tokay Szamorodni made only forty miles from the Russian border. It is produced in the years when the noble rot barely affects the grapes; otherwise Tokay Aszu, sweet like a Sauternes, is made.

You can choose to serve all or only some of the side dishes but I would particularly recommend the beets, recalling as they do that other renowned Russian dish, borsch.

Batter

4oz/125g buckwheat flour
4oz/125g plain flour
2 eggs
1/2pt/300ml scalded milk
1 1/2oz/45g melted utter
1/4oz/7g fermipan dried yeast
pinch salt

Beetroot Julienne

2 large raw beetroots
1/2tsp black mustard seeds
1 tsp citronade vinegar
1/2 an orange – rind and juice
1 tsp honey
1 tbs sunflower oil

Sift the flours, yeast and salt into a big bowl. Make a well in the centre and pour in the scalded milk which must have been cooled to bloodheat. This is *very* important – too hot and it will kill the yeast. Using your hand like a claw, or a slotted spoon, draw the flour in to the liquid gradually. Beat well to make a smooth batter. Cover the bowl with a clean teatowel and leave in a warm place for 30 minutes until doubled in bulk and bubbly.

Lightly beat together the egg yolks and melted butter. Knock back the batter with the spoon and then whisk in the egg/butter mixture. Whip the egg whites until stiffly peaking and fold through the batter.

Heat a large heavy-based frying pan or griddle, grease with a little melted butter. If you have crumpet rings they can be used to give the blinis a good shape, otherwise just spoon 2tbs of the mixture at a time onto the hot pan. When little bubbles break the surface and the batter does not run, flip the pancake over and cook the other side until golden. Keep warm in a teatowel in the oven or on a covered plate over a simmering pan whilst you cook the rest of the blinis.

Mushrooms in Soured Cream

8 oz/250 g firm white mushrooms
bunch of spring or welsh onions
  (scallions)
knob of butter
2 tsp plain flour
¼ pt/150 ml cultured soured cream

Egg and Chives

4 large eggs
handful of chives
1 lemon

Dill Slaw

½ a small white or green cabbage
2 tsp dill seeds
1 tbs blue poppy seeds
1 tbs butter

NB The Red Cabbage in Cider recipe
  (p. 177) is also appropriate.

The accompaniments can be made when the batter is left to prove. Scrub the beet and cut into matchstick pieces. Pop the mustard seeds in the oil then add the beet, vinegar, rind and juice. Combine with a fork, cover tightly and cook, shaking the pan to prevent sticking, for 10 minutes. Drizzle the honey into the pan and toss with the fork.

Boil the eggs for 8 minutes. Chop the chives into a bowl. Add a teaspoon of lemon rind and 2 tsp lemon juice. Peel the eggs as soon as you can bear to handle them, and roughly chop. Toss together with the lemon, chives and some freshly ground salt and pepper.

Shred the cabbage. In a large pan fry the dill and poppy seeds in the butter for a couple of minutes (the fragrance is lovely). Take care not to burn the butter. Add the cabbage, cover tightly and shake over a medium heat for 7–8 minutes.

Thinly slice the mushrooms and chop the spring onions, green tops included. Fry until soft in the butter. Sprinkle over the flour and mix well. Cook for a couple of minutes, then, off the heat, stir in the soured cream. Heat through but do not boil.

Serve the hot blinis on a large platter wrapped in a white napkin to keep warm. People pile whichever combination of the side dishes takes their fancy onto a blini and then top off their creation with another – a Russian sandwich?

9
Vegetables

The British have never been renowned for vegetable cookery. Anne Scott-James, in *The Cottage Garden*, maintains this is because 'the English are a nation of carnivores and have never eaten vegetables if they could get meat'. A frightening proportion of Scotsmen never do eat fresh vegetables. Little wonder they have one of the highest rates of heart disease in the world. It is time vegetables were accorded more respect in this country, from carnivore and vegetarian alike. Alexis Soyer, Reform Club chef, author and contemporary of Eliza Acton, complained of low standards of vegetable cookery in the 1850s. Even today a number of restaurants that make it into *The Good Food Guide* are criticised on this point.

Overcooking has long been a problem but it is not the only one. It would seem often that the vegetables are merely a hasty afterthought, a careless adjunct to the meal. Due to the limitations of space this chapter cannot hope to be encyclopaedic but offers some new *and* traditional ways of serving accompanying vegetables. Some dishes may be used as simple meals in their own right. I include a few rice dishes, though other grains can also be eaten: kasha (buckwheat), millet, bulgar and couscous.

There is never a need to buy prepackaged frozen vegetables. The first peas are more special when you have not tasted any since the previous summer and the memory of their flavour is untainted by the sweet insipidity of frozen peas. We are fortunate that even in the middle of winter there are plenty of fresh vegetables about. Exploit the potential of each season's harvest and enjoy everything in its season.

Cucumbers

My son will eat cucumbers like apples. The best use for Marmite is to team it, in sandwiches, with thinly slices cucumber. One bite and I'm transProusted to another time and place. Not as romantic as madeleines and lime tea perhaps, but still affective. Tiny cucumbers seem impossible to find – I think they are the best for cooking – but the ordinary large ones still make unusual and delicate vegetable side dishes.

Stir-Fried Cucumber

2 large cucumbers
1 oz/30 g butter or sesame oil
1 lime
black pepper, salt

Trim the ends from the cucumbers. Cut into pieces 3 in/ 7.5 cm long. Split each lengthways into eighths. Sprinkle with salt and black pepper. Melt the butter in a wok or large pan. When it reaches the point of fragrance, toss in the cucumbers. Keep them moving around the pan, by stirring or shaking. When just wilted and barely browned, squeeze over the juice of the lime, boil off and serve immediately.

Buttered Cucumber and Dill

Although I have specified dill, carraway or fennel could also be used to great advantage. The dish has echoes of Scandinavia, Poland or Germany. It is good served on its own with black bread, hardboiled eggs and olives.

1 lb/500 g tiny cucumbers
or 2 or 3 ordinary ones
2 oz/60 g unsalted butter
1–2 tsp dill seed
fresh dill weed
3–4 coriander seeds
4 or more white peppercorns
sea salt
1–2 tsp lemon juice or vinegar
  (optional)

Thickly butter a lidded casserole dish. Trim the small cucumbers or quarter the large ones lengthwise. Cut each quarter into 2 in/5 cm pieces. Pack them into the baking dish. Crush the seeds and peppercorns and scatter over the cucumber. Chop the dill weed and sprinkle on top. Add a little freshly ground sea salt. Dot with the remaining butter. Cover tightly and bake for about 40 minutes at gas mark 4–5/350°–375°F/180°–190°C.

Pour over the lemon juice or vinegar just before serving. Alternatively, heat some soured cream in the top of a double boiler and pour onto the cooked cucumbers instead.

Mushrooms

You will not have come this far without noticing a certain predilection for fungi. To me they are 'magic mushrooms'; pyschotropics are not necessary. I do not hallucinate about the extraordinary range of flavours and textures – they are really real. As a nation we chomp our way through an enormous tonnage of mushrooms every year. Sadly, only one per cent are anything but buttons. Things are changing. We have yet to catch up with the French, who now have mushroom boutiques for fungal exotica, and a mushroom museum, but a recent television series was devoted entirely to all aspects of mushrooms, and supermarkets are stocking at least brown cap, oyster and shiitake mushrooms – rather sporadically, it has to be said, up here in the North, where they believe none of us are interested in that sort of fancy thing. After a recent enquiry for porcini at a brand new hypermarket in York the customer was eventually told only *one* of the major chain's stores sold them in the North.

The only place I have been able to find pieds de mouton was Harrods; there ought to be some growing in the local forests but I have yet to discover any. They are also known as hedgehog mushrooms, as their gills look a bit like prickles.

Recently truffles were discovered near Bath; perhaps once again the English too will have truffle hounds sniffing out the knobbly treasures as in France and Italy.

If you want to gather mushrooms – and you do not have to be in the depths of the country to do so, urban parks, playing fields and wastegrounds are likely to be colonised by some species or other – try to get on a 'fungus foray', a guided walk by a mycologist. These are often held in the early autumn; you will find out details from local libraries. Failing this, get a well illustrated book, preferably with colour photographs, and discard any mushrooms you are not sure about. In some areas in France and Italy you are able to take your freshly gathered harvest for checking at the local pharmacy.

You will be able to identify the giant puffball, if you can find one. Nothing else looks quite like it. Only pick white (fresh) ones; if they have gone yellowy leave them alone. The giant puffball can, as its name suggests, grow quite large – about the size of a football. Sliced, egged and breadcrumbed and fried in butter, it is a treat. There are other small puffballs which can be fried whole or put into casseroles.

Morels, which look like an inside-out mushroom, have a wonderful aromatic flavour. They appear in the Spring and may be gathered by hedgerows and in dampish meadows. If you are not entirely certain of your identification it may be safer to avoid morel look-alikes in pinewoods as they may actually be *gyromitra* which is quite poisonous. Only a few morels, fresh or dried, are needed to flavour a whole dish of mushrooms. This is just as well, as I have been unable to find anyone who sells fresh morels, and even the dried are not easily found.

Chanterelles or girolles are trumpet-shaped, apricot-coloured mushrooms. They are lovely raw in salads, giving a slight tang. Alternatively, stir-fry them in butter or oil. They are not improved by long cooking but are good dried. Dried mushrooms of any sort can be finely ground to a powder to scent and season all manner of sauces.

Ceps or bolets, known as porcini in Italy, look like a nice brown bun. The cap is rounded with a rather leathery-looking skin; they do not have gills but tubes whose ends resemble a spongy mass. The flesh is firm and white-to-pinkish and very, very good. Ceps in butter with herbs and garlic are the best filling any omelette has ever been wrapped around.

There are many other mushrooms but space is limited; mention is made elsewhere in the book of oyster, brown cap and shiitake mushrooms. Recipes are liberally sprinkled throughout the book but a couple more follow for good measure.

Stuffed Mushrooms

Shirley Conran's epitaph will doubtless be, 'Life was too short to stuff a mushroom'; but Superwoman has missed out. The very large, tea-plate-sized flat mushrooms that you often find in the supermarkets after Bank holidays (no one has been picking for a few days) take virtually no time and very little effort to stuff. Cooked slowly in a covered dish in red wine they are unbelievably tasty. The cooking juices make the basis for excellent sauces or stock and any leftover mushrooms with their fillings can be processed with butter to make an extremely good potted spread. Fillings can be altered depending on the state of the larder. Simple breadcrumb and herb stuffings are good but try the option below. Try blue cheese, try goat's cheese. Add nuts, add seeds. Alter flavourings, use spice or other herbs. Cook in brandy or stout, cider or white wine. In short, make your own additions and subtractions; experiment.

1–2 large mushrooms per person –
about 5–6 in/12.5–15 cm
across
olive oil
red wine

Wipe the mushrooms and break off the stalks. Chop the stalks finely with the shallots, garlic and celery and put to soften in a little oil over a low heat. Cook until lightly browned and soft. Chop the walnuts and sage. Combine

1–2 egg yolks
8–12 oz/250–375 g shallots
3–4 cloves garlic
2–3 sticks celery
· 4–6 oz/125–180 g breadcrumbs
8 oz/250 g Farmhouse Cheddar or a
    good Lancashire cheese
4 oz/125 g shelled walnuts
a few fresh sage leaves
salt, black pepper

with the grated cheese and breadcrumbs. Mix in the onions, garlic, celery and stalks, scraping any tasty oil from the pan. Add lightly beaten egg yolk to bind. Season with salt and pepper and then spoon onto the gills of the open mushroom caps, rounding the tops. Smaller closed mushrooms can be used – cut out the stalks, and to speed the more fiddly process of filling, put the stuffing mixture into a forcing bag.

Place in a shallow dish and pour around enough red wine to come halfway up the base of the mushrooms. Add some herbs or garlic to the wine if desired. Cover and bake for 45 minutes at gas mark 5/375°F/190°C. Take off the cover and cook for a further 15 minutes. Stock or water can be used in place of the wine.

Serve on a bed of rice, over juniper-fragranced cabbage, on rounds of toast or fried bread, with noodles or with vegetables.

Mushroom Salad

If you can find chanterelles, slice them into fine strips and then combine with the rest of the ingredients.

12 oz/375 g very fresh mushrooms,
    brown cap or button
1 tbs chopped coriander leaves
1 tbs chopped flat parsley
1 lime
2 tbs light olive or grapeseed oil
salt, pepper

Slice the mushrooms thinly. Sprinkle with the herbs and season with the salt and pepper. Squeeze the lime and pour juice over the mushrooms with the oil. Toss together and serve well chilled.

Avocados

Avocados came originally from Central America – Mexicans today consume some 166 lb/71 kg of avocado per person annually. Britons manage a surprisingly high 12 oz/375 g as opposed to the Italians' 1 oz/30 g.

These days avocados are imported from California, Kenya, Mexico and Guatemala but the bulk of them arrive from Israel where they began cultivation in the Twenties.

While avocados are best known in their savoury roles, they are very good in fruit salads too. Use the thin-skinned sweeter ones and cube them in a light syrup with melons, strawberries, kiwis, pineapples and bananas.

All three of my babies have enjoyed them, mashed, as a first food – fortunately without the fantastic side effects of John Burningham's *Avocado Baby*. Now they are older they love guacamole too, not least, I suspect, for the tortilla chips.

Avocado Gratin

Carmel, the Israeli growers, state: 'Remember, never cook an avocado'. Well, almost right: never *over*cook an avocado. The following recipe can be used as a starter, snack or a light lunch.

2 large ripe avocados – Hass or Nabal
1 large clove garlic, crushed
4 oz/125 g mature Cheddar cheese, grated
half a jalapeno chilli, finely chopped

Preheat the grill. Cut the avocado in half and scoop out the flesh. Mash it with the other ingredients then pile the mixture back into the avocado skins. Place under the hot grill for 2 or 3 minutes, till browned and bubbling. Serve immediately with toast.

Guacamole

The dip. Use it with crudités of carrot, celery, cauliflower, broccoli, peppers and turnip. Do not forget those tortilla chips if you are feeding the children too. Guacamole is essentially a purée of avocado; however, you can add some extras – try soured cream, yoghurt or fromage frais, also mayonnaise, tomatoes, red peppers and olives. Creamy blue cheese, such as St Agur, is good with the Fuerte and Ettinger varieties.

Thinned with a little more lemon or lime juice and oil, it makes wonderful salad dressing.

2–4 ripe avocados, depending on size
2 cloves garlic
1 lemon or lime
1 small onion
1 fresh green chilli pepper – how much of it you use is up to you
oil – olive or safflower
salt, pepper

Peel the garlic and onion and chop. Cut a slice from the centre of the lemon or lime and reserve. Squeeze the two halves. Cut the required amount of chilli – avoid the seeds and wash your hands. Either pound the garlic, onion and chilli to a paste in a mortar or whizz in a food processor. Mash the avocados and stir in the garlic paste, with the lemon juice. Add a little oil, if liked, to thin to the desired consistency. Season to taste with salt and pepper. Chill, well covered, until needed – but it must not stand too long as it will discolour. Decorate with the reserved lemon slice. It is said if you keep the stone in a halved avocado, it will prevent it discolouring, but I have not found this to be true; excluding air and brushing with lime or lemon juice are much more effective ways of reducing browning.

Beetroot

Beetroot has been relegated to the fourth division in Britain, rarely making an appearance except as a salad pickle, often in too harsh vinegar. Cry shame, for the beet has much more to offer. Grated *raw* beets are a fresh addition to the salad table. They can also be dressed – but take care, use a milder vinegar such as a champagne or cider, or freshly squeezed lemon or orange juice.

The green tops of beet can be used as a spinach substitute too; shred and cook briefly in butter and garlic.

Raw beets are very inexpensive; look out for the tiny ones and serve them baked in their skins and then peeled with a melted butter sauce, white pepper and salt or smetana or with a Maltaise (a Hollandaise with orange).

Baby Beets in Orange Sauce

1 lb/500 g ping-pong-ball-sized
  beetroots
4 oz/125 g shallots
3 navel oranges
1 tbs olive oil
2 tsp fecule – potato flour
¼pt/150 ml brown vegetable
  stock
salt, pepper
pinch brown sugar
squeeze of lemon
knob of butter (optional)

Scrub the beets but do not peel or trim. Boil or steam until tender – about 25–35 minutes depending on age.

Peel the shallots and chop very finely. Brown slowly in the olive oil. Pare the zest from one of the oranges with a very sharp knife or a potato peeler. Ensure there is no white pith. Cut into fine strips and blanch by pouring boiling water over them. Dry and set aside. Squeeze the oranges. Add 2 tbs stock a little at a time to the potato flour. Pour the remaining stock onto the shallots, allow to bubble up then stir in the slaked potato flour. Continue to stir over a medium heat whilst the sauce thickens. Reduce heat. Stir in the orange juice, lemon juice and seasonings. Add the prepared rinds and finish with a knob of butter if desired. Keep just warm while peeling the hot, cooked beet. Pour over the beets in a hot dish and serve.

Brassicas

Or maybe, 'of cabbages and kings'. I suppose that many have been put off the brassica family by school dinners, the unpleasant sulphurous smell of overboiled cabbage, mushy cauliflower and slimy khaki broccoli. Greens, it seems, are to be eaten only by those who have no choice and when you get to be President of the United States you are allowed to say no. Forget that. Properly treated cabbages are fit for kings, queens and members of parliament. The Member for Brent East, Ken Livingstone, raved about the following dish.

Chiffonade de Printemps

2 lb/1 kg spring greens
1 oz/30 g unsalted butter
2 tsp black mustard seeds

Wash the leaves in very cold water, shake off the excess. Cut off the stalks. Cut into strips approximately $1/4$ in/ 0.5 cm wide, across the leaves. Put the butter into a heavy-bottomed pan with the black mustard seeds and heat until they pop. Add the greens, combining with the seeds. Cover tightly and shake the pan occasionally. Cook over a medium flame for 2 or 3 minutes. Serve immediately: the greens retain bite, colour and the mustard seeds impart a wonderful added flavour.

Red Cabbage in Cider

From stir-fry to slow cook. This dish, in one guise or another, is becoming something of a classic. My recipe is full of spices, fruit and chestnuts; it is substantial enough to be eaten as a meal in its own right. Serve with fresh bread to mop up the fragrant juices.

1 medium red cabbage
12 oz/375 g red onions or shallots
3 cloves garlic
2 large Revd Wilks apples

Pour boiling water on the chestnuts and leave to stand overnight. Butter a deep-lidded casserole dish. Shred the cabbage. Finely slice the onion and chop the garlic. Cut the apples into quarters and core but do not peel. Slice up

4 oz/125 g muscatel raisins
6 oz/180 g dried chestnuts
1/2 pt/300 ml cider
2 sticks cinnamon
6 allspice berries
a few assorted peppercorns – black,
    white, pink and green
4 cloves
a little butter

the quarters. Crush the allspice and peppercorns. Drain the chestnuts. Toss all the ingredients, except the cider, together in a large bowl like a salad. Pack into the casserole and pour over the cider. If the lid does not fit very well, make a paste of flour and water and smear it around the rim. Cook slowly all day.

The cabbage is also good cold the next day as a relish.

Cauliflower or Broccoli Cheese

Here is a good example of an ordinary dish being lifted by slight variation. You can of course alter it further, using virtually any firm cheese you choose. The Stilton, though, is wonderfully rich and hard to beat. Do not overcook the cauliflower or broccoli, leave it with a slight bite.

1 large cauliflower
or
1 1/4 lb/625 g broccoli
4–6 oz/125–180 g Stilton – this is a
    good way of using any rather
    dry edges from a leftover
    Christmas cheese
1/2 pt/300 ml single cream
1/2 pt/300 ml milk
1 oz/30 g flour
1 oz/30 g butter
1 small onion
1 bay leaf
peppercorns
nutmeg
2 oz/60 g chopped shelled walnuts
or
2 tbs brown breadcrumbs
6 hardboiled quail's eggs
or
3 hardboiled hen's eggs

Peel the onion and put into the milk. Warm the milk with the bay leaf and peppercorns and a little nutmeg. Leave to infuse. Steam the cauliflower or broccoli until al dente. Drain and put into a flat dish with the peeled eggs.

Melt the butter and stir in the flour. Cook whilst stirring over a low heat until the mixture forms a ball and leaves the sides of the pan cleanly. Off the heat, beat in the strained milk a little at a time. Make sure the sauce is perfectly smooth each time before adding any more milk. Stir in half the cream. Return to the heat and bring slowly towards the boil, stirring constantly. Turn off the heat when the mixture coats the back of a spoon well. Crumble in the Stilton, stirring until melted. Mix in the rest of the cream. Check the seasonings. The sauce is unlikely to need salt as Stilton is itself quite salty. Pour the sauce over the vegetables and eggs and sprinkle on the walnuts or breadcrumbs. Place under a hot grill or in a very hot oven until lightly browned. Serve immediately with fresh crusty rolls.

Christmas Brussels Sprouts

Somehow Christmas dinner in our house would be lacking without sprouts. Button brussels tossed together with peeled boiled chestnuts are part of the festive table and I would miss them. The combination need not be reserved for high days and holy days – it makes a sustaining winter dish for many occasions.

If you wanted a wine specifically for this dish, I would offer a robust Cabernet Sauvignon, a better one from France or Australia.

1–1½ lb/500–750g brussels sprouts – tight and neat
½–1 lb/250–500g sweet chestnuts; the ratio of chestnuts to sprouts is a matter of personal taste – I like 50/50
a little hazelnut oil or knob of butter
salt, black pepper

Nick the skins of the chestnuts before plunging them into boiling water. Cook for about 20 minutes, drain and peel. If the skin is reluctant to be parted from the chestnut, return to the water for another 5 minutes. The nut meats should be virtually tender.

Trim the sprouts and drop into boiling water for 3–4 minutes; they will still be quite firm. Drain and place in an ovenproof dish with the chestnuts. Combine with a little salt, pepper and the oil or butter. Cover and place in a moderate oven (gas mark 4/350°F/180°C) until the sprouts, although retaining a bite, are cooked through – depending on size, 7–15 minutes.

Brussels, Italy

I was served sprouts cooked in tinned tomatoes once. That started me thinking, because it was almost good. A bit of tinkering and this EC dish resulted – the Low Countries meet the Med. Would that all Community conjunctions were as happy. Double the quantities for a hearty, warming main dish and sprinkle liberally with freshly grated Parmesan. Fresh block Parmesan is often cheaper, weight for weight, than the gritty, dehydrated packeted stuff. If you have supplier problems, buy a large chunk when you find it – it keeps and you will always have some to hand and never need to resort to nasty tubs or bags again. Most large towns have an Italian restaurant or a non-chain pizza house; in case of difficulty ask them for their supplier's name.

An Italian wine is preferable to a Belgian one!? Try a Barbaresco Piedmont, a full, soft, pleasant wine.

1 lb/500 g brussels sprouts
12 oz/375 g fresh plum tomatoes
8 oz/250 g shallots
4 cloves garlic
2 oz/60 g sundried tomatoes
1 tbs good pesto
olive oil
oregano
black pepper, salt
sugar
black olives (optional)

Trim the sprouts. Peel and finely chop the shallots. Peel and sliver the garlic cloves. Heat 3 tbs olive oil in a heavy-bottomed pan. Add the shallots and garlic. Cook slowly until softening. Peel and chop the fresh tomatoes. Cut the dried tomatoes into thin strips. Add both to the pan with some salt, a pinch of sugar, black pepper and some chopped oregano. Cook, covered, for 5 minutes then add the sprouts. Combine with the tomatoes. If the tomatoes are rather dry add a little stock or water. Cover and stew until the sprouts are tender. Stir in the pesto and check seasonings. Turn into a serving dish and garnish with olives if desired.

Brussels Sprouts and Walnuts

When is a warm salad not a warm salad; when is it just a vegetable dish? This question was raised recently by TV foodies. I believe the answer is simply, when it has been cooked a little longer. The following recipe is a good example – halt the cooking after 2 minutes to serve as a crunchy, warm salad or cook on to have as a vegetable. Although you could use walnut oil to cook it in, I prefer the hazelnut – there is no hint of bitterness with it.

A flinty Sancerre or another Sauvignon white would be my first choice if using the dish as a meal, supplemented by a light savoury custard or cheese and bread.

1 lb/500 g brussels sprouts
1–2 cloves garlic (optional)
3 oz/90 g shelled walnuts
2–3 tbs hazelnut oil
1 lemon
or 1–2 tbs sherry vinegar

Trim the sprouts, discarding damaged outer leaves and woody bases. Slice them, across the sprout, so that you end up with a mixture of rosettes, around the heart, and leaf strips. Break up the walnuts roughly. Heat the oil and add the walnuts and crushed garlic, if using. Stirring over a medium flame, cook until they attain that irresistible roasted-nut aroma. Add the sprouts and combine well; cook for about 1 minute before pouring over the juice of the lemon or the vinegar. If using as a salad, continue to stir-fry for 1–2 minutes, according to taste; serve immediately. Otherwise, cover, reduce heat and cook until just tender.

Season with a pinch of salt and black pepper before serving.

Sesame seeds and oil can be substituted for the nuts and a splash of tamari soy added in the place of the lemon juice.

Gingered Broccoli

I came across the conjunction of cauliflower and ginger in an Indian restaurant. I tried the idea, with and without the curry sauce, with several other vegetables but my favourites were broccoli and sugar-snap peas although the potatoes also had something going. I was amazed to see virtually the same recipe on the repeated Ken Hom series when I was channel flipping. The occasional déjà vu that you get as a cook always comes as somewhat of a jolt. A dish that you have virtually invented, then evolved over the years, suddenly appears, or a close approximation at any rate, in the pages of someone else's book. No cook works in a vacuum, we are all affected to some degree by outside influences. It is inevitable that two or more people will independently arrive at the same point. It happens in science, fashion, art and music but it is nevertheless disconcerting each time it does.

1 lb/500 g broccoli – calabrese or
white or purple sprouting
1 clove garlic
³/₄ in/2 cm fresh ginger root
knob of butter
boiling water

Break the broccoli up into small florets. Slice up the stalk into small pieces. Peel the garlic and ginger and cut up finely. Heat the butter in a pan. Add the garlic and ginger and fry gently for a couple of minutes. Put the broccoli in the pan and toss like a salad. Add enough water to just cover the bottom of the pan and cook over a medium heat, shaking the pan, until the broccoli is just tender and the water has evaporated. Do not let the pan boil dry and scorch the broccoli – add tiny amounts of extra water but do not add too much water either. Serve immediately.

Baked Cauliflower

Baked cauliflower used to mean hideously coloured 'golden crumbs'. Here it is, more elegantly, with ground almonds. If you can find the 'snowball'-type cauliflowers, about tennis-ball size, you can do individual ones.

1 large cauliflower
4 oz/125 g ground almonds
1 egg white
salt

Parboil or steam the cauliflower, keeping the head intact. Drain and place on a heatproof plate. Very lightly whip the egg white with a good pinch of salt. Brush the egg white all over the cauliflower. Immediately sprinkle thickly with the ground almonds, patting them into a thick layer. Place in a moderately hot oven (gas mark 6/400°F/200°C) until the nut crust is crisp and the cauliflower tender – about 10–15 minutes depending on size.

Roast Kohlrabi Cups

The cabbage-turnip is not immediately associated with the brassicas; however, it is not a root, but a stem swelling. Cook simply in boiling water and serve with black pepper and plenty of butter or a béchamel. Kohlrabi can be sliced fine into salads where it is rather radish-like. Young kohlrabi leaves can be chopped and braised in a little butter and stock and used to fill the roasted cups. At other times use the golden cups as a decorative and delicious way of serving elderberries, redcurrants, apple purée or other accompaniments to a rich main course.

Do not choose any kohlrabi larger than tennis-ball size and avoid any with fissures.

½ a kohlrabi per person
sunflower oil

Scrub the kohlrabi and cut in half. Either boil or steam until just beginning to soften. Cool a little and peel. Using a teaspoon, hollow out the centre to make a cup. Heat some oil in a roasting pan. Slide in the kohlrabi, turning each cup in the hot oil. Cook in the top of a gas mark 6/400°F/200°C oven for 30 minutes, turning and basting at least once, until richly browned around the edges.

Turnips can also be treated like this – do not halve but hollow out the whole small turnip. The kohlrabi or turnip could also be filled with other vegetable purées – try creamed potatoes, celeriac, parsnips, carrots or peas.

Callaloo

Callaloo, also known as Jamaican spinach or elephant's ears, deserves a mention as it makes an excellent substitute for collard greens. It comes from the taro or dasheen plant whose tubers can be baked or deep-fried. They are beautiful leaves to look at, too. They can be used to wrap parcels of rice stuffing, delicately spiced, with nuts and raisins. The parcels should then be steamed until the leaves are tender.

A Mess of Greens

You can use other sorts of leaves for this soul food dish but I like callaloo best. The original collard greens are coleworts, a non-head-forming floppy cabbage – they have a certain amount of bite to their flavour.

1½ lb/750g callaloo
1–2oz/30–60g butter
1 large yellow or Spanish onion
2 cloves garlic
salt, pepper
nutmeg (optional)

Peel and chop the garlic and onion and put it to cook slowly in the butter. When softened add the washed and chopped callaloo – chop the stalks too, they are delicious – and stir around. Cook, covered, until the leaves are quite tender. Season with salt, pepper and a little nutmeg.

Chocolate and Hazelnut Tortellini alla Panna

Ricotta Pancakes with Char-grilled Vegetables

Baked
Savoury
Custard

CLOCKWISE, FROM TOP:
*Nan, Banana Korma, Sag Bhajee,
Channa Dhall, Samosas*

Moussaka and Greek Salad

*Leek Terrine
with
Tomato
and
Red Pepper
Coulis*

Samphire

Carrots

The classic French method of cooking carrots, carrots Vichy, involves cooking them on the top of the stove until the water has been reduced away. In the first recipe the carrots are baked so the danger of them catching or burning is greatly reduced. The second requires constant attention but the vegetable is cooked in no time at all.

Plain overboiled (English style) carrots are anathema to me. Dinner table rows erupted as my sister found them so repulsive she could not bear to eat them. Strangely, my brother actually liked them and did not care for peas.

Glazed Carrots

The preparation of the carrots depends on their size. Baby carrots should merely be scrubbed and carefully trimmed. Larger ones should be cut into batons or shillings. The texture of the carrots is preserved and the honey and orange bring out the natural sweetness. The colour is deep and rich under the glaze. Alternatively, use the same method with water instead of juice and honey and sprinkle with carraway or dill seeds.

1 lb/500 g baby carrots
1 large unwaxed sweet orange
1 oz/30 g unsalted butter
2 tbs heather honey

Butter a small, lidded casserole dish. Scrub and trim the carrots, carving back the rounded ends you have trimmed off. Lay in the dish. Finely grate a little orange rind over the carrots. Squeeze over the juice of the orange. Drizzle with the honey and dot with the remaining butter. Cover and place in the oven until tender (about 30 minutes at gas mark 5/375°F/190°C. Before serving, spoon the glaze over the carrots.

Carrots and Courgettes

Using a potato peeler to make ribbons or 'vegetable tagliatelle' was something that became fashionable in the late Eighties. Other recipes I have found require you to boil the vegetables. I thought this rather a shame and devised the following recipe which not only retains more flavour from the vegetables but also has the nuttiness of the sesame oil and the optional savouriness of the soy.

4 medium carrots
4 courgettes – long thin ones
1 clove garlic
a little grated ginger root
3 tbs toasted sesame oil
1 tbs tamari soy sauce

Scrub the carrots and wash the courgettes. Trim. Run a potato peeler down the length of the carrots and courgettes, cutting each one into wafer-thin slices.

Peel and crush the garlic.

Heat the oil in a large pan or wok. Add the garlic and ginger and fry for a minute. Using a wooden fork or chopstick, stir in the vegetables. A fork is preferable to a wooden spoon as it is less likely to crush the vegetables. Fry them in the oil, stirring constantly or shaking the pan, until just tender. This takes about 3 minutes. Pour over the soy, toss and serve. Season with salt and pepper if not using soy. This also makes a pleasant salad, undercooked and well-chilled.

Celeriac

Celeriac, an ugly hairy brute of a root vegetable, is only just beginning to get the recognition it deserves in these isles. It can be chipped, boiled, roasted, mashed or fried. The flavour, like old-fashioned forced celery, is quite aromatic, slightly peppery and very savoury. It is prized for use in soups and stews. If there are any leaves on your roots they too can be used as pot herbs. Celeriac can also be used raw in salads, grated or cut in julienne.

Celeriac Batons

Simply peel a large celeriac and cut into even batons, about 1 1/2 in/2 cm long and just under 1/2 in/1 cm thick. Place in a heavy-bottomed pan with a large knob of butter and generous grindings of black pepper. Cook covered, over a low heat, shaking occasionally until soft; approximately 15–20 minutes.

Celeriac Purée

Use as a filling in a mille feuille or palmier, or as a side vegetable.

1 head garlic
white wine
1 star anise
1 large celeriac – about
    1–1 1/2 lb/500–750 g
1 egg yolk
salt, pepper
butter or *cream*
nutmeg (optional)

Break up the garlic into cloves but do not peel. Place in a small pan with wine to cover and the star anise. Simmer, tightly covered, until soft. Press the garlic through a sieve. This purée can be made, as in the potato recipe, in a slow oven. Peel and cut the celeriac into large chunks. Cook until tender in lightly salted, boiling water. Drain and mash well. Beat in the garlic purée, a knob of butter or a tablespoon or two of cream and the egg yolk. Season with salt, white pepper and nutmeg if desired.

Asparagus

The brevity of the English asparagus season means I am reluctant to do much more with them than steaming and serving with butter. The butters can be varied, with herbs or lemon, or lightly garlicked. Hollandaise (p. 240) made with lemon juice, soured cream or a butter-based sauce could be used instead but do not swamp the asparagus. I do not much care for the very fat white stems found on the Continent; I find them slightly repulsive when tinned. Do not shun the bundles of very fine green shoots, known as sprue or grass. They are normally much cheaper than the premier spears and the flavour can be good. Use especially for soup or in custards or mousses when it is almost sacrilege to purée the others.

Freshness is of prime importance. Californian or Israeli asparagus is quite nice but British is best, preferably bought direct from the producers and eaten within 3 or 4 hours at most.

Asparagus with Sorrel Butter

I love a tang with asparagus, whether it is from citrus, soured cream or, here, from sorrel. Make the butter a couple of hours in advance and cook the asparagus just before serving – never overcook and never reheat; better to eat it cold with a (lemony) vinaigrette.

1 lb/500 g bunch of asparagus
6 oz/200 g unsalted butter
small bunch sorrel
white pepper
squeeze of lemon (optional)

Pound the sorrel in a mortar until smooth. Beat the herb into the butter, seasoning with a little freshly ground white pepper and a squeeze of lemon juice. When well amalgamated, spread between two sheets of greaseproof. Chill, then cut into shapes. The butter could be chilled and then curled instead, or simply cut into cubes.

Clean and trim the asparagus. The stem should snap where it ceases to be woody. Tie into four bundles. Place the woody ends into water and bring to the boil. Steam the bundles with the bases of the stems in the water and the tips covered. How you achieve this is up to you – if you have an asparagus kettle, fine; the rest of us will improvise with inverted saucepans or foil hoods. I read once that lying the spears down in the water was just as good, so I tried it. I have gone back to the steaming rigamarole – it *is* worth the trouble. However you cook them do not overdo it; 7–10 minutes is all they normally need, but if they are exceptionally large you could add another couple of minutes.

Save the cooking water for soup made with the sprue, cream and little else.

Green Bananas

Green bananas, or plantains, make excellent, unusual vegetables. They can be simply baked with butter, black and chilli pepper; roasted; fried as below, or formed into patties.

Banana Chips

I first tried making this dish on holiday in Barbados. The hucksters sold four or five different sorts of banana, from the tiny sweet fig up to the hefty, almost astringent plantain. Use large unripe bananas if you cannot get plantains.

You can use them like croutons with the Sweet Potato Soup (p. 31).

3 or 4 plantains or green bananas
soya or peanut oil
cayenne
salt

Peel the plantains and slice, crosswise, about ⅛ in/ 0.25 cm thick. Alternatively, split the plantains into four, lengthwise, and cut into 2 in/5 cm pieces. Pour oil into a frying pan or wok to a depth of ½ in/1.25 cm. Heat until smoking. Fry a few slices at a time until crisp. Take out with a slotted spoon and place on crumpled paper to drain while frying the rest. Dust with cayenne and salt before serving.

Banana Patties

Banana patties are made in India, Africa and the Caribbean. The flavourings change but the method is virtually the same. Use to accompany curries, groundnut stew or Louisiana-style gumbos.

2 large green bananas
1 small green chilli
1 small onion
1 clove garlic
2 tsp plain flour
1–2 tbs fresh chopped coriander
*   leaves or parsley*
salt
oil

Peel the bananas and boil for 20 minutes in salted water. Very finely chop the chilli, garlic and onion. Drain and mash the bananas and work in the onion, garlic, chilli, coriander or parsley, and flour. Form into 15 balls and flatten slightly. Chill until needed, then deep-fry in hot oil until nicely browned. Drain and serve immediately.

Alliums

Where would we be without the alliums? How many recipes begin, 'peel and chop the onions and garlic'? They have such a range of flavours, from hot and pungent to mild and creamy via rich and succulent.

There are many onions, each with its own characteristics. Unfortunately, apart from spring onions, most greengrocers sell but two – Spanish and English. They may not come from either country, in fact many these days seem to be Dutch. The names mean merely mild or strong. There are also white, red, yellow and green or welsh onions, shallots, silverskins and button or pickling onions.

Garlic ought to be available, depending on the time of year, in green, pink or white. The green is fresh, the papery skin has not yet dried and the flavour is extraordinarily clean and bright. The pink-skinned garlic, often smaller in size, has a very fine flavour. I plant my garlic around the rosebushes where it is supposed to ward off blackfly. It is easy to grow. Break up a bulb into individual cloves after they have begun to sprout. Plant each clove, green tip uppermost, in early March. The new bulbs are ready for lifting when the foliage dies back in August.

Every garden surely has room for a clump of chives – the smallest of the alliums. They will grow in a terracotta pot on a reasonably sunny windowsill. They are invaluable for adding a mild oniony flavour to delicate creams, cheeses and egg dishes. The tubular leaves are useful for decoration, either cut into tiny rings (which releases the flavour) or as ribbons.

Welsh onions, otherwise known as ciboules or perpetual or green onions, are also good to grow. They can be cooked, substituted for shallots, or they can be used like spring onions in salad. The green tops can be chopped fine like chives. They grow in a clump and are non-bulb forming. To use you just pull what you need and the plant just keeps producing more.

Leeks are one of the finest vegetables. Do not boil them and serve them dripping wet in a glubby white sauce as seems to be the English habit. Leeks are best sautéed in butter with herbs or garlic or braised in wine or stock. They make an excellent cold dish in vinaigrette.

Recipes follow but interchange, where possible, the suggested vegetable. Glazed Shallots could just as easily be Glazed Red Onions. Leek Terrine could be made with welsh onions. Stuffed Spanish onions could be made with yellow ones or indeed lengths of leek, split, filled and then tied up with chives.

Glazed Shallots

The superlative flavour of shallots and their melting texture has made them in demand as an ingredient and they are rarely presented on their own. A gardening book I consulted maintained they were a flavouring and not a vegetable. I beg to differ. Their sweetness is accentuated in this dish and they look very glamorous

1 lb/500g shallots
1 oz/30g demerara sugar
1½oz/45g unsalted butter

Peel the shallots, trimming the roots and necks neatly but not quite removing. This ensures the shallots stay together in cooking. Cook in boiling water for 10 minutes. Drain and dry. Keep warm. Melt the sugar over a low heat without stirring. Then add the butter. Combine then stir in the shallots, making sure that all get coated in the glaze. Cook a further 4 minutes, stirring, and then serve.

Alternatively, the shallots can be baked in a little butter until just tender. Dredge them thickly in icing sugar and finish under a hot grill or in a very hot oven until the sugar caramelises.

Leek Vinaigrette

This dish is best made with the very slender young leeks, no thicker than your finger. These leeks are almost spurge-like, quite sappy. It is possible to see why leeks acquired the nickname of 'poor man's asparagus' – asparagus itself is very good served this way too. Try also using other dressings, including a mild mustard-based one.

1 lb/500 g trimmed leeks – save the coarser green leaves for the stock pot
6 tbs extra virgin olive oil
2 tbs champagne vinegar
handful of mint and chervil – alternatively use tarragon
salt, coarsely ground black pepper
pinch caster sugar

Cut the leeks into 3 in/7.5 cm lengths and steam until tender. Finely chop the herbs and place with the sugar, salt and pepper in a small screw-topped jar. Add the oil and vinegar and screw on the lid. Shake vigorously until emulsified. Arrange the hot leeks on a plate and dribble the dressing all over. Cool and then chill.

This dish can be eaten just warm if preferred.

Braised Leeks

Although leeks braised in red wine are good, I enjoy them more cooked in a rather sweet white. Moscatel de Valencia is a bargain Spanish white, slightly aromatic and raisiny but, due to a small acidic edge, not cloying. Alternatively use a Monbazillac or Côtes de Montravel.

The leeks could be served as a vegetable or topped with Raclette or Jarlsberg cut in fine slices and baked until the cheese is melted, with or without a pastry case. A few sliced mushrooms could be thrown in if liked.

1½ lb/750 g leeks
5 cloves garlic
1 oz/30 g butter
7 fl oz/200 ml Moscatel de Valencia
lemon thyme
salt, white pepper
nutmeg

Wash the leeks and trim. Cut into 1½ in/4 cm chunks. Peel and slice the garlic. Melt the butter in a heavy-bottomed pan. Add the leeks and garlic. Cook slowly for 10 minutes with the lid on, shaking the pan occasionally. Add the chopped herbs, salt, pepper and wine. Simmer, covered, until the leeks are meltingly tender. Reduce the liquor by turning up the heat. Serve hot.

Leek Terrine

This dish must be made in advance – there is nothing extra to hold the leeks together; it relies entirely on being pressed together for 12 hours. The leeks should be even in size, about ¾–1 in/2–2.5 cm in diameter.

The terrine can also be made with strips of courgette, briefly parboiled.

enough trimmed leeks to fill the terrine or 1 lb loaf tin – about 3–4 lb/1.5–2 kg
large vine or spinach leaves (optional)
1 large red pepper

Grill the pepper until the skin blackens and can be scraped off. Cut in half and remove the seeds. Slice into thin strips and reserve.

Wash the leeks well and cut to fit the terrine, lengthwise. Cook in a little boiling water until tender – about 8 minutes. Steam the vine or spinach leaves briefly over the leeks so they are soft and pliable but not dropping to pieces. Lay a strip of silicon paper on the base of the terrine. Lightly oil the sides. If you are using a metal baking tin, I would recommend lining it all with greaseproof. Cover the base and sides of the terrine with the leaves, overlapping them and making sure there are no gaps. Lay enough leeks to cover the base of the terrine. Squeeze them up and really force them in! Season with salt and white pepper. Add a few strips of red pepper here and there, then add more leeks. Continue this way, packing in the leeks and the pepper strips and seasoning until the terrine is full. Fold in any leaves and cover the filling neatly with some more leaves. If you have a press, place the terrine in it and screw it down. Otherwise, cut a sheet of thick cardboard to fit just inside the top of the terrine. Cover it in foil. Cover the top of the leaves with greaseproof. Place the foil-covered cardboard on top and weight it down with some jars or tins or old-fashioned weights. Leave for at least 12 hours in a cold place.

To serve, turn out and slice – use a very sharp knife or you will come to grief. Sit the slice in a puddle of soured cream flavoured with chives and garlic, or a Tomato Coulis (p. 233).

Stuffed Onions

Choose onions of a similar size. There are two farces to choose from. The first is a fairly plain one, ideal if the onions are being served as a side dish. The second is more substantial and could be cooked in a Minervois with the rest of the bottle on the table.

4 large or 8 smaller mild onions

I

3 oz/100 g white breadcrumbs
2 cloves garlic
1 tbs chopped fresh sage
¼ tsp ground cloves
salt, pepper
butter

II

4 oz/125 g mushrooms
2 tomatoes
2 cloves garlic
1 oz/30 g walnuts
4 oz/125 g Blue Cheshire
thyme
olive oil
red wine

Peel and trim the onions. Using a sharp (grapefruit) knife, hollow out the centres. Finely chop these bits of onion.

For filling I: combine onion centres with the breadcrumbs, crushed garlic, sage, cloves, salt and pepper. Pack into the hollows and place in a buttered dish. Add a little water and dot each onion with butter. Cover and cook slowly until tender – all day on a very low oven, or 2–3 hours at gas mark 2 or 3/300°–325°F/150°–170°C depending on size.

For filling II: place onion centres in a pan with the minced garlic, chopped tomatoes and olive oil. Fry until just beginning to colour. Remove from heat and add the walnuts and most of the crumbled Blue Cheshire. Season with a little thyme and pepper and pack into the onions. Lightly oil the baking dish and put in the onions. Place the rest of the cheese on top of the stuffing. Pour some red wine around the base of the onions. Cover and cook for 1 hour at gas mark 5/375°F/190°C. Remove the cover, baste and cook a further 10–15 minutes.

Prunes can be used instead of tomatoes; change the cheese to a Bleu d'Auvergne and the herb to sage. The wine could then be a vin de pays de Côtes de Gascogne.

Artichokes

Both sorts of artichokes have a delicate sweetish flavour and both come from flower plants. The Jerusalem artichoke is the tuber of a sunflower-type plant and the globe artichoke is the bud of a thistle-like plant.

The Jerusalem artichoke has nothing to do with the city of that name, being imported from the New World in the early 1800s. Its name derives from *girasole* – turn to the sun, a habit which sunflowers have. In French they are called *topinambours*. They have the rather unfortunate side effect of causing a certain amount of flatulence, but it is worth putting up with this occasionally as the flavour is very pleasant.

Globe artichokes are grown in huge numbers now in Brittany but they are also grown around the Mediterranean. The tiny ones, rarely available here, are delicious stewed à la greque and eaten whole. Artichoke hearts, preserved in brine or oil, are excellent in salads and on top of pizza. The tinned or bottled ones make a delicious purée with the addition of garlic, olive oil and a squeeze of lemon. Use it as a dip for crudités or, thinned, as a dressing for salads or chargrilled vegetables. The larger, fresh artichokes are a treat just boiled and served with seasoned melted butter for dipping the tender leaf-ends in.

Roast Artichokes with Rosemary

1 lb/500 g Jerusalem artichokes
olive or sunflower oil
few sprigs rosemary
salt flakes

Scrub the artichokes well and dry. Heat oil in a roasting tin to a depth of ½ in/1.5 cm. Turn the artichokes in the oil and add the rosemary, reserving a small sprig. Cook, turning occasionally, in a hot oven until brown and crisp on the outside and tender in the centre. Depending on the size this takes about 35–45 minutes at the top of a gas mark 6/400°F/200°C oven. Drain and serve immediately, garnished with the rosemary and a sprinkling of salt flakes.

Artichoke Purée

Thinned with more cream and a little stock this makes an excellent soup. It can also be mixed half-and-half with mashed potatoes.

The yolks of three eggs can be beaten into the purée and then their stiffly whisked whites folded through. The mixture can either be baked in a soufflé dish or ramekins or in a parbaked piecrust.

1½lb/750g Jerusalem artichokes
3tbs double cream
1oz/30g butter
white pepper, salt
nutmeg

Peel the artichokes and quarter. Cook in a little boiling water and half the butter. Warm the cream. When the artichokes are tender (this takes 15–20 minutes, depending on size), drain and mash with a fork. Beat in the cream, the rest of the butter and seasonings. Serve immediately.

Stuffed Artichokes

Look for medium-sized, fresh, tender, green-leaved globe artichokes. If the leaves are brownish or dry, pass on by. There are two recipes here; in one the stuffed artichoke is gently stewed in wine, in the other it is almost roasted in olive oil.

I

4 globe artichokes
2 shallots
2 cloves garlic
½ a lime
1oz/30g black olives
1 medium-sized tomato
1oz/30g freshly grated parmesan
2oz/60g wholemeal breadcrumbs
salt, black pepper

Wash the artichokes well. Trim the stalks and outside leaves. With a knife or scissors cut away the tops of all the leaves. Turn the artichoke around and around as you work towards the centre. Using a teaspoon or grapefruit knife remove the choke (the hairy centremost part). Drop the prepared artichokes into water and lime or lemon juice while you prepare the stuffing.

Finely chop the shallots and garlic. Skin and chop the tomato. Grate a little lime zest and chop the olives.

¼pt/150 ml *Galestro or similar*
   Italian white wine
olive oil

Combine all these ingredients with the breadcrumbs, Parmesan, a squeeze of lime juice and some salt and pepper. Pour some olive oil into the bottom of a flame-proof casserole. Set over a low heat. Spoon the farce into the artichokes, packing it in well. Put the artichokes into the oil and pour over the wine. Cover and stew for 75 minutes. Good hot, or well chilled.

II

This is a classic Italian dish with little alteration.

4 globe artichokes
3 oz/90 g white breadcrumbs
4 garlic cloves
2 tbs fresh chopped parsley
1 tbs capers or pickled nasturtium
   seeds
1 stick celery
olive oil

Prepare the artichokes as above, trimming the leaves and removing the choke. Boil in lightly acidulated water for 5 minutes then drain, upside down on a teatowel.

Press or mince the garlic. Chop the capers and celery very fine. Combine all the filling ingredients and season with salt and white pepper. Pack into the artichokes. Heat some oil in a roasting tin. Stand the artichokes in it and sprinkle with more oil. Cook in a fairly hot oven (gas mark 6/400°F/200°C), spooning over the oil from time to time, until the trimmed ends become crisp – about 30 minutes. Serve hot.

Artichokes à la Greque

Lots of vegetables can be cooked in this *court bouillon* – try cauliflower, broccoli, aubergines and button mushrooms too. Artichokes, especially the tiny ones if you can find them, are sensational. Eat barely warm or chilled, with bread and Orvieto. Quarter the tender, medium-sized artichokes. The larger ones will need to be pared down to just the hearts.

12–16 *tiny globe artichokes or 4
    medium ones, quartered*
2½ *fl oz/75 ml olive oil*
2 *shallots*
2 *cloves garlic*
1 *lemon – 2 tbs white wine vinegar
    can be used if preferred*
½ *pt/300 ml water*
small bunch of herbs tied together
    – *parsley*
    – *fennel, stalk as well as leaves*
    – *lemon thyme*
    – *lovage*
    – *a bay leaf*
1 *tsp coriander seeds*
1 *tsp white and pink peppercorns*
salt

Wash and trim the artichokes.

Peel and very finely chop the shallots and garlic. Simmer them in the olive oil until soft but not coloured. Pare a small amount of lemon zest and reserve. Squeeze the juice and add to the oil with the water, the herbs and the lightly crushed coriander and pepper. Season with a good pinch of salt. Simmer for 20 minutes. Add the artichokes and cook 8–12 minutes depending on size. Take out with a slotted spoon and stand on a deep plate. Strain over the cooking liquor and strew with some fresh herbs if liked and the lemon rind cut into find shreds.

Parsnips

Parsnips are one of the consolations of winter in this country. Sweet and rich, they are best after the first frost, as are brussels sprouts. They are excellent baked with lemon juice and a little honey, like the Glazed Carrots (see p. 185). Mashed with butter, cream and nutmeg they are superlative; I could eat a whole dish. Try substituting Ricotta for the butter and cream occasionally.

Roast parsnips in olive or sunflower oil, placing the peeled, halved vegetables into *hot* oil. They can be baked or fried in butter and black pepper. They make a good soufflé and have an affinity with all manner of spices, making them at home in a curry.

Parsnip and Potato Galettes

Choose slightly waxy potatoes for these crisp golden cakes. Made slightly thinner they can be used to sandwich a mousseline of broccoli or other delicate creamed vegetables; or use with a cheese-based filling.

2 medium potatoes
2 large parsnips
2 oz/60 g butter
salt, black pepper
nutmeg or *pinch ground cloves*

Peel and *finely* grate the parsnips and potatoes. Rinse, drain and dry thoroughly between two teatowels. Place into a bowl and sprinkle over a generous grinding of sea salt, a grating of nutmeg and some freshly ground black pepper. Melt the butter and pour all but a tablespoon over the grated vegetables. Mix well with a fork.

Brush two heavy baking sheets with the remaining butter. Spread the mixture out to a thickness of 1/8 in/ 0.25 cm. Draw a wide-bladed knife through the mixture, marking it into 3 in/7.5 cm squares. Push the edges back slightly making a gap of 1/2 in/1 cm between each square. Alternatively, use crumpet rings to form rounds. Bake at the top of a gas mark 5/375°F/190°C oven for 6–7 minutes. Take out the trays and turn the galettes carefully with a fish slice to brown the other sides.

The galettes can also be made with small parsnips and potatoes, sliced paper-thin on a mandolin and laid in concentric circles. This is altogether more time-consuming but is quite attractive.

Salsify

Salsify is delicious roasted in the oven in sunflower oil or in olive oil to which a couple of sprigs of lavender have been added. Cut the peeled salsify into 2 in/5 cm lengths and turn into hot oil in a flat roasting tin. In a hot oven it will take about 20 minutes for the salsify to cook through and turn golden. Drain and serve.

Salsify can be shallow-fried in a little butter – for an added dimension dip the lengths into milk and then into dried fine breadcrumbs before frying. Dish up very hot with twists of lime.

Potatoes

No longer humble, the potato has begun its renaissance. Old varieties are being reintroduced in the major supermarkets, even up here in the North, and new varieties are arriving. It seems unfortunate that price is the prime mover, but at least now that we have to pay for them as a 'serious' vegetable rather than a filling staple we are paying more attention to their preparation, even when treating them simply.

Roasting can be done with skins on or off, parboiled or not; the oil can be varied – sesame, olive or nut; herbs or garlic can be added, wine can be sprinkled on. Baking can be a similar adventure, with skins merely scrubbed or smeared with oil or butter, or crusted in salt, or wrapped in brown paper with herbs and they can be served with butters, herbed or otherwise, pesto, tapenade, yoghurt, cream, purées and all manner of cheeses.

Soft and creamy, crisp and crunchy, a whole book could be written on potato recipes. I will have to content myself with just a few here, and others elsewhere in the text.

Pink Fir Apple and Prunes

Pink Fir Apple potatoes have a curious, knobbly, elongated shape and a superlative flavour. In this recipe they are slow-cooked but do not break down. They take up the richness of the prunes and the aroma of the thyme.

1½ lb/750g Pink Fir Apple
    potatoes
8 oz/250g stoned prunes
12 oz/375g small shallots
3 tbs sunflower oil
7 fl oz/200 ml water
3 tbs Pineau de Charente (optional)
several sprigs of thyme
a few pink peppercorns
salt

Scrub the potatoes and dry. Peel and trim the shallots, quartering any large ones. Heat the oil in a flameproof casserole. Fry the shallots until colouring. Pour over the Pineau. Add the prunes, potatoes, water, herbs and seasonings. Combine and bring to the boil. Cover tightly and cook slowly until the potatoes are tender. This is better done in the oven but can be satisfactorily done on the hob. It will take between 1–2 hours – do not try and rush it otherwise the flavours will not develop so well and the potatoes could drop to pieces.

Garlic and Potato Purée

Because the garlic is cooked slowly on its own first it is mild and creamy, combining well with the earthy graininess of the mashed potatoes.

1 head garlic
1/4pt/150ml white wine
sprig fresh rosemary
2lb/1kg potatoes – Maris Bard, for choice
1oz/30g butter
2–4 fl oz/75–100ml top of milk or single cream

Put the unpeeled garlic in a small, lidded casserole with the rosemary and the wine. Bake very slowly until the cloves are meltingly soft; you could leave it all day in an Aga or on an S setting. Leave to cool. Peel the garlic and rub through a fine sieve.

Scrape or finely peel the potatoes and plunge immediately into boiling, lightly salted water. Cook steadily on a medium heat until soft but not dropping to pieces.

Drain and mash with the butter, cream and garlic purée, seasoning with a little freshly ground white pepper. *Don't* use a food processor to 'mash' the potato – it doesn't, it spoils the texture, making it glutinous and sloppy. If you need extra muscle-power use the paddle or 'K' beater on a mixer in 'pulse' bursts.

Serve immediately; avoid having to re-heat.

Lemony Potatoes

Best made with new potatoes, but it is possible to cut large ones into chunks. Oranges can be substituted and when the potatoes are less good than hoped for, a dash of cinnamon can be added to the (wholemeal) crumbs.

1lb/500g small new potatoes, e.g. Jersey Royals
1 lemon

Scrape or scrub the potatoes and boil until just tender. Drain and place in an ovenproof dish. Grate the lemon rind and mix into the breadcrumbs with plenty of fresh

2 tbs soft white breadcrumbs
black pepper, sea salt
1 oz/30 g unsalted butter

ground black pepper and a little salt. Squeeze the lemon and sprinkle the juice over the potatoes. Scatter over the breadcrumb mixture and dot with small pieces of butter. Bake at gas mark 7/425°F/220°C for 10–15 minutes, or place under a low grill until nicely crisp on top.

Potatoes in Red Wine

The potatoes develop a jewel-like crust; turn them at least once during cooking to make sure it is even. Choose even-sized potatoes, about the shape of a size 1 egg. Thick-skinned potatoes will need to be peeled.

8 medium King Edward potatoes
8 cloves garlic
olive oil
robust red wine – from the South
    of France, a gutsy vin de pays
    from the Ardèche would do
    very well
savory or rosemary

A large cast-iron or heavy earthenware lidded casserole dish is the best receptacle for this dish. Peel the garlic. Scrub or peel the potatoes. Dry. Heat oil to the depth of ½ in/1.25 cm in the base of the casserole. Add the potatoes and garlic and turn about in the oil. Add ¼ pt/150 ml red wine (careful it does not spit at you) and the herbs. Cover and place in a fairly hot oven (gas mark 6/400°F/200°C for about 50 minutes or until soft in the centre, removing to turn and baste every so often. Add a little more wine if necessary.

Potatoes and Onions in White Wine

Anton Mosimann, I note, prepares potatoes in a similar way to this. A slightly different texture and flavour is obtained by layering the slices in a deep dish, rather like Pommes Dauphinoises.

1 lb/500 g Kerrs Pinks or Désirée
  potatoes
3 or 4 large red onions
a little oil
white wine – I like a sweetish
  Bordeaux
several sprigs of lavender
coarse sea salt, black pepper

A heavy flat dish or roasting tin is required. Cover it in a film of oil. Scrub the potatoes and dry. Cut in half, lengthways, with the grain. Cut each half into $\frac{1}{8}$ in/ 0.25 cm slices. Peel and trim the onions. Cut in half from top to bottom, then slice as the potatoes, keeping the onion layers together.

Lay a row of overlapping potato slices on top of the oil. Keep the straight (cut) end underneath. Lay a row of onion slices beside it, with the cut end of the onion at right angles to that of the potatoes. Fill the dish with alternating rows of potatoes and onions. The overall effect, with the colour of the onions, is a mass of Art Deco borders. Pour over enough wine to just cover. Sprinkle with some freshly ground black pepper and lay on the lavender. Cover with a baking sheet or foil. Cook in a moderate oven (gas mark 5/375°F/190°C) for 20 minutes, then uncover and cook until the wine is reduced away and the potatoes are cooked and browned – another 40–45 minutes. Sprinkle with a little coarsely crushed sea salt just before serving.

Potatoes, prepared as above and laid on top of sesame oil and sprinkled with sesame seeds before roasting, are also very good.

Samphire

Glasswort, sea asparagus and marsh samphire are all the same plant. A vivid green, succulent (in both senses) looking plant, it is leafless with many jointed branches. It grows wild on the salt marshes of Britain's coasts from the Wash, round the South up to the West of Scotland and all around Ireland. It is an annual plant and should not be confused with the rarer rock samphire (a.k.a. sea fennel) which is a perennial.

The samphire is high in soda and was formerly much used in soap and glass making. It can be difficult to find fresh – there are but a few characters who go 'samferring' now, but open markets and fishmongers in East Anglia are good places to try (Swaffham or Beccles, particularly). You can sometimes find it pickled, deliciously crunchy and piquant. It is easy, if you find a good supply, to pickle your own. It won't keep long fresh so buy double and pickle half. Pickled samphire will keep all winter; the season for fresh is from May until the end of August.

Samphire has been used in Nouvelle Cuisine as minute decoration, a little criss-cross on the plate. While it is undeniably attractive, samphire is better consumed in larger quantities to appreciate its unique sea-side flavour.

Boiled Samphire

1 lb/500 g samphire
2 oz/60 g unsalted butter
white pepper
a quarter of lemon

Wash the samphire very well in lots of cold water. Pick off any floppy bits and discard. Tie into four bundles and trim the roots, but do not remove entirely. Lay the bundles in a large flat pan of boiling water. Cook no longer than 9 minutes. Overcooking will lose the lovely colour as well as impairing the flavour.

While the samphire is cooking melt the butter, season with the lemon and fresh ground white pepper. Divide between four small dishes and set on warm plates. Drain the samphire and place a bundle on each plate. Remove the string and serve.

Dip the stems in the butter, holding the root end. Pull the fleshy part of the stem from the woody stalk with your teeth. A bit messy, but delectable.

Pickled Samphire

1 lb/500 g samphire
1 large lemon
white wine vinegar

Clean the samphire in plenty of cold water and remove the roots completely. Place in a pan with the juice of the lemon and enough cold water to cover. Bring to the boil and cook for 10 minutes. Drain and pack into sterilised jars. Cover with cold vinegar and seal. (Ensure your lids are non-corrosive.)

Tomatoes

Unfortunately, tinned tomatoes have made rather too many appearances on vegetarian menus in the past, responsible for that unpleasant uniform brick colour. They do have their uses and the quality variations between brands are enormous. Price is no guide – look for tomatoes packed in tomato juice for a richer flavour.

The best way to get good tomatoes is to grow your own – or live next door to someone who does.

It is hard to beat the flavour of tomatoes slowly fried in butter – with garlic and herbs if desired – and served on toast. If this sounds too simplistic for dinner, dress it up slightly. Make the toast into croustades – fit slices of bread into greased bun tins, corners sticking up like handkerchief points. Bake them at gas mark 6/400°F/200°C until crisp and browned, while frying tiny cherry tomatoes slowly in butter. Spoon two or three tomatoes into each croustade, decorate, if you must, with a sprig of herbs or a dusting of Parmesan. Use as canapés or as an accompanying vegetable.

Plain grilled tomatoes dotted with butter are good, but when you also sprinkle on a layer of light muscovado sugar before placing them under the hot grill, then you have something extraordinary. Sweet and savoury seem to be playing leapfrog in each mouthful.

I have yet to find a flavoursome large tomato commercially available. For several years I grew Marmandes, a big knobbly fruit with an excellent flavour. I went to Spain and had beautiful salads containing the same tomato. But bitter disappointment when I bought the Dutch-grown ones. The tomatoes were very large but with negligible flavour. If you have no access to good big tomatoes, make the next dish with smaller ones. A bit more fiddly perhaps but then life is Shirley long enough to stuff tomatoes *and* mushrooms.

Stuffed Tomatoes

For a special brunch, serve scrambled eggs made with cream, butter and truffles in scooped-out baked tomatoes. A light lunch could be raw hollowed-out tomatoes stuffed with goat's cheese, mint and garlic. For a more substantial meal use the filling below and serve on a bed of rice or fresh ribbon noodles.

1–4 tomatoes per person depending on size

Cut the tops off the tomatoes and scoop out the flesh. A rounded teaspoon, a parisian baller or a grapefruit knife

bunch spring onions
2 cloves garlic
6 oz/175 g Single or Double
    Gloucester
2 slices white bread
marjoram
olive oil
salt, black pepper
1/4 pt/150 ml plain yoghurt
    (optional)

are all suitable tools. Chop the flesh. Sprinkle the insides of the tomatoes with a little salt and stand upside down on a rack.

Finely chop the spring onions, including some of the green part, and the garlic. Put to fry in 3 tbs olive oil. Cut the bread into small cubes. When the onions have softened add the bread and fry until golden. Remove with a slotted spoon and place in a bowl. Add the grated cheese, tomato pulp and finely chopped marjoram. Combine well with a fork and season with the pepper. Pack carefully into the tomato shells. Stand the filled tomatoes in a lightly oiled dish. Either replace the tomato tops or spoon on a layer of yoghurt. Bake in a moderate oven (gas mark 4–5/350°–375°F/180–190°C) for 20–30 minutes depending on size. Serve immediately.

Tomato Ragoût with Polenta

A hearty, substantial dish with echoes of a Bolognese. Instead of the polenta you can, of course, serve the ragoût with pasta. An apt wine would be a Barbera d'Asti – choose one a few years old to avoid the astringency found in the younger wines.

1 1/2 lb/750 g deep red plum
    tomatoes – if you cannot get
    good tomatoes use a proportion
    of good tinned ones
12 oz/375 g red onions
2 small sweet red peppers
5 cloves garlic
3 sticks celery
4 oz/125 g black olives
1 oz/30 g dried porcini
2 carrots
1/4 pt/150 ml dry red wine
olive oil

Bring the water to the boil with 1/2–1 tsp salt. When it is boiling, sprinkle in, while stirring, all the polenta. If you have a wooden spatula that is ideal, otherwise use a wooden spoon. Stir constantly until it is smooth and thick. Cook over a gentle heat for 20 minutes, stirring frequently. Beat in a good knob of butter and 1–2 oz/30–60 g freshly grated Parmesan. Turn out onto an oiled surface and spread to a thickness of 1 in/2.5 cm. Allow to cool completely.

Peel and slice the onions and crush the garlic. Begin to fry in a little olive oil in a large pan. Cut the peppers into

parsley, including the stalks
oregano
basil
salt, pepper
brown sugar
small piece lemon rind
butter
Parmesan cheese
1¼ pt/740 ml water
8 oz/250 g fine yellow polenta
    (cornmeal)
pine nuts (optional)

strips, discarding the seeds. Finely chop the carrots and celery. Add the peppers, celery and carrots to the pan when the onions have softened. Continue frying, shaking or stirring occasionally.

Roughly chop the tomatoes. Finely chop the oregano and parsley and quarter the olives. Add the tomatoes to the pan and cook, stirring, for 5 minutes. Stir in the oregano, parsley, lemon rind and olives. Add the red wine and the procini. Season well with salt, black pepper and a pinch of sugar. Bring to the boil then turn down and gently simmer for 1½ hours until thick and rich. If it is still very liquid, turn up the heat to reduce.

Cut the cold polenta into crescents or lozenges and arrange them around the edge of a large heatproof platter. Dot with a little butter and dust with more Parmesan. Place in a hot oven (gas mark 6–7/400°–425°F/200°–220°C) for 10 minutes, until nicely browned. Take out and spoon the ragoût into the centre and scatter over the torn basil.

Baked Tomatoes

A very simple but delicious way of preparing tomatoes. Serve with bruschetta and fresh cheese or a cheese soufflé.

3–5 tiny tomatoes per person
mixture of herbs, including thyme,
    marjoram or oregano, chives,
    lemon balm and lovage
salt, white pepper
butter
greaseproof paper

Wash the tomatoes carefully (do not nick the skins). Cut the greaseproof into 12 in/30 cm squares. Butter the centre of each paper then lay on a little bunch of herbs. Stand 3–5 tomatoes on each. Sprinkle with salt and pepper. Bring the four corners of the paper into the centre and twist them together to seal. Bake at gas mark 4/350°F/180°C for 25 minutes. Allow each person to open their packet at the table to savour the herb fragrance.

Stewed Green Tomatoes

An unusual vegetable, halfway to being a relish. The acid content is high, so cook slowly. You may like to add some spices or chopped fresh or dried dates, making it rather chutney-like. It is very good with bubble and squeak or the Double-Ovened Chestnut Soufflés (p. 142).

1 lb/500 g green tomatoes
1 mild onion
1 oz/30 g butter
brown sugar to taste
salt, pepper

Quarter the tomatoes and sprinkle with a little salt. Stand 30 minutes. Scrape off the salt. Mince the onion and fry in the melted butter until beginning to colour. Add the tomatoes, stirring them about. Cook, covered, over a low heat until the tomatoes are almost soft. Season to taste with sugar, salt and pepper. Allow to cook, uncovered, a further 5 minutes after adding the sugar. Can also be eaten cold.

Turnips

As with many of our homegrown crops, turnips have been in the wilderness for years. Only the advent of the 'New British' cooking has returned them to the restaurant table. I do not care for the huge woody specimens but the small purple or pink-topped ones are delicious. If you are a gardener, serve the first pullings, cooked quickly in butter and water, dressed with the first peas. Raw in a winter salad, they are peppery and crisp.

They can be cooked slowly in milk in the bottom of the oven or boiled and mashed like potatoes. Bake the very small ones with a little knob of butter, black pepper and a tiny sprig of rosemary, all wrapped up in a paper parcel – see Tomatoes (p. 208).

Do not forget their use in the stock pot. In vegetarian cuisine, where there is no gelling from stock bones, the turnip's high pectin content is useful.

Mustard-Glazed Turnips

Serve with rich, eggy or creamy dishes as an excellent contrast. Good, too, with pies and pâtés.

By coincidence I find that the best turnips in France come from Meaux, just like the mustard.

1 lb/500 g baby turnips
2 tbs wholegrain Meaux mustard
2 tbs honey
*a little oil – sunflower, soya or
    sesame*

Scrub and trim the turnips. Parboil briefly. Drain and stand in a roasting tin. Make a paste of the mustard and honey and brush it over the turnips. Pour a little oil into the base of the roasting tin. Place at the top of a gas mark 6/400°F/200°C oven for 15 minutes then place on a lower shelf until cooked through (another 10 minutes maximum).

Turnip Salad

Somehow that does not sound too enticing. A Salat de Navet, perhaps? A rose by any other name . . .

8 oz/250 g baby turnips
1 small lime
1 butterhead lettuce
1 thin carrot
salt, white pepper
1 tbs walnut or hazelnut oil

Wash and dry the lettuce and arrange on a large plate. Pare the skin from the turnips and cut them into julienne strips. Do this rather than grating in a food processor. Scatter over the lettuce. Using a potato peeler, run the blade down the carrot to make curls. Decorate the edge of the salad with these. Sprinkle quite liberally with salt, white pepper and the lime juice. Drizzle over the nut oil and serve.

Legumes

Contrast the savoury earthiness of lentils against the intensely sweet delicacy of new peas – the range of flavours and textures from legumes is huge. There are always some in season. Mangetouts and fine beans have become the frozen peas of the more expensive restaurant. This is not to say they should be avoided but their over-use in that milieu should be checked. Fresh peas or beans in the doldrums of winter can be most welcome, whether they come from Guatemala or Kenya, but they should not cause us to abandon our own seasonal vegetables.

Broad Beans in Soured Cream

Excellent made with the first picking of beans, so small and tender the whole pod can be eaten. Later the beans can be shelled and peeled and served in the same sauce. Cooked, cold chick peas are also good in the soured cream; the mint gives them a lightness not normally associated with pulses. Serve them in barquettes made of hollowed cucumber or blanched courgettes. The broad beans can be served as a vegetable or as a main dish – in the latter case, double the quantities.

1 lb/500g young broad beans
2 oz/60g unsalted butter
¼pt/150 ml soured cream
good handful mint or lemon balm
1 clove garlic
a few chives
½ a lime
salt, white pepper

The beans need little attention before dropping into boiling water for 10 minutes. Trim the stalk ends and check for blemishes. While the beans are cooking, push the garlic through a press. Melt the butter with the juice of the lime, the garlic, salt and pepper. Finely chop the herbs and add to the butter. Drain the beans and cover in the butter sauce. Place in an ovenproof dish and spoon over the soured cream. Bake at gas mark 4/375°F/180°C for 15 minutes. If having cold, halve the amount of butter, pour it over the warm beans and cool. Then combine with the soured cream.

Peas and Lettuce

A very French dish, but the English used to eat cooked lettuce. It is ideal for the first peas, not enough to eat on their own (except raw by the handful), and the tender cabbage-type lettuces. Certain cut-and-come again varieties are also suitable. If the peas are older they will need a little initial cooking before adding the lettuce.

8 oz/250 g tiny fresh peas
2 Tom Thumb lettuces
1/2 tsp caster sugar
white pepper
1/2 oz/15 g unsalted butter

Wash the lettuces, shake dry and cut into strips. Melt the butter. Add the lettuce and the peas and season with the sugar and a little pepper. Cook covered for a bare 5 minutes. There should be enough moisture in the lettuce to steam the peas. If, extraordinarily, there is not, add a tablespoon, but no more. Serve, sprinkled with chopped herbs if desired.

Stir-Fried Mangetouts and Almonds

Mangetouts require minimal cooking and scant water to preserve their colour and juicy crispness. Ginger root could be used judiciously instead of the garlic. Sesame oil could be substituted, with a dash of soy for a more Chinese slant.

The same method can be used for green beans. If preferred the nuts can be dry-fried and a little water added with the lemon juice to cook the vegetables.

12 oz/375 g mangetouts
1 clove garlic
2 oz/60 g flaked almonds
juice of 1 lemon
1 oz/30 g butter
black pepper

Top and tail the mangetouts, stringing any as necessary. Peel and finely slice the garlic and fry with the almonds in the butter until they are beginning to colour. Add the mangetouts and lemon juice and cook quickly, stirring (use a chopstick or a wooden fork) or shaking continuously until the mangetouts are just cooked but still crisp, about 2 minutes. Serve immediately.

Hummus

Good hummus on warm pitta bread is delicious. It should not be dried out and crusty around the edges as it is in many delis but creamy with a tahini tang and fragrant with garlic and olive or sesame oil. It is very easy to make – indeed, using a tin of precooked chick peas is preferable to most commercially available hummus. A food processor makes light work of the mashing.

8 oz/250 dried chick peas – also
    sold as garbanzos
4 cloves garlic
3 tbs tahini – sesame seed paste, it
    looks like anaemic peanut
    butter
olive or sesame oil
1 lemon
salt, pepper
coriander leaves (optional)

Soak the chick peas overnight. Boil in water until tender. If you want a mild garlic flavour also cook the peeled cloves of garlic in the water. Drain, reserving the cooking water.

Purée or mash. Beat in the tahini and the crushed garlic. Thin to desired consistency with the oil and cooking liquor. Add a squeeze of lemon and salt and pepper to taste.

Stir in chopped coriander leaves if using and chill well.

Flageolet Beans

One of the most delicate of the dried beans, flageolets are a very pretty pale green inside. Their texture means they are an ideal salad vegetable and like all pulses they absorb the flavours of oil, vinegar and herbs wonderfully. I have been unable to find them fresh but they are available tinned and make a pleasant purée with oil and garlic. Flavour with fresh chopped mint and serve as for hummus.

8 oz/250 g dried flageolet beans
1 bay leaf
1 lemon
4 or 5 cloves of garlic
a little dill weed
thyme
parsley
marjoram or *basil*
7 tbs olive oil
salt, pepper

Soak the beans overnight then drain and boil in fresh water with 1 tbs oil, the bay leaf and a little lemon zest. Boil for ½–1 hour, until the beans are just tender. Drain and immediately dress with the rest of the oil, the juice of the lemon and the minced herbs and garlic. Sprinkle with salt and pepper and allow to cool. Chill before serving.

Rice

Staple of most of the world's population, rice should be a pleasure, not a hardship, to eat. Plain boiled rice can accompany many dishes, not just curries. Choi, a Korean student who lived with us briefly, was puzzled by my beautifully cooked, each grain separate, rice. To him, as a Korean, as with half of China and all Japan, well cooked rice is sticky and rather glutinous. The rice used in Japanese and Korean cookery is shorter in grain but that which is labelled pudding rice here is not correct: look for Japonica rice. Elsewhere in the Far East, long grain rice is used.

Rice Salad

Rice salads usually leave me cold, particularly those with frozen peas and tinned sweetcorn but this one rises above the ordinary

8 oz/250 g long-grain rice
3 tbs sesame or peanut oil
1 lemon
3 'fig' bananas
1 red pepper
1 bunch spring onions
1–2 cloves garlic
1/2 small green chilli pepper
1/2 tsp turmeric
1 tsp garam masala
1/2 tsp ground coriander
1/2 tsp ground ginger
coriander leaves
1/2 tsp salt
generous grinding of black pepper
pinch of sugar

Boil the rice in water until just tender. While it is cooking prepare the other ingredients, as they need to be added while the rice is hot. Very finely chop the chilli pepper, spring onions and garlic. Grill the red pepper and remove the blackened skin. Remove the seeds and chop the flesh into small dice. Cut the bananas into small pieces. In a small jar, combine the zest of the lemon, its juice and all the spices, salt, pepper and sugar. Add the oil and shake all together.

Mix the hot rice with the onions, pepper, bananas and dressing. Allow to cool and then stir in the finely chopped coriander leaves.

Chopped hardboiled eggs could also be added, if liked.

Savoury Rice Pudding

Rice pudding may be able to make a comeback on the tails of New British cooking, if it can live down the tinned varieties. This would be most just, as a good rice pudding is nothing to sneer at and should not be relegated to the nursery table.

This savoury version is adapted from an Eliza Acton recipe. It is made to be turned out, like a cake, and served in wedges. Alternatively make smaller ones in ramekins.

Use as a side dish with ragoûts and stews or as a main course accompanied by a rich sauce, the Madeira (p. 223) perhaps, and some plain green vegetables.

3¹/₂oz/110g pudding rice
1 pt/600ml full cream milk
2oz/60g butter
3 eggs
1 bay leaf
3 tbs grated Parmesan
2oz/60g fine dry breadcrumbs
salt, black pepper
nutmeg

Place the rice and milk in a saucepan with the bay leaf. Simmer gently for half an hour, adding 1¹/₂oz/45g of the butter after 15 minutes. Towards the end of the cooking you will have to stir quite frequently to prevent sticking. You should now have a soft, creamy mass. Remove the bay leaf. Season it well with salt, pepper and nutmeg. If desired, some extra Parmesan or other strong, finely grated cheese can be added here – this is especially recommended if serving with a tomato-based sauce or stew. Allow to cool.

Well grease a deep dish or tin with the remaining butter. Combine the crumbs with the Parmesan and scatter thickly over the buttered surface. Separate the eggs and beat the yolks into the cooled creamed rice. Whisk the egg whites until stiff and fold through the rice mixture. Spoon carefully into the prepared dish and bake for 1¹/₂ hours at gas mark 1/275°F/140°C. When it is golden and quite firm, turn it out and serve.

Tricolour Rice

This was not originally conceived as one dish, but three separate ones. Serve in a moulded ring, one colour on top of another, or on individual plates, a spoonful of each arcing across the top of the plates. Change the rice type to make rice balls or pyramids, using either Japonica or American Rose – they both have short grains and are sticky. Form into balls with wetted hands. Any of them can be used as farces for stuffed vegetables (particularly red, green and yellow peppers but also aubergines, mushrooms, onions, etc.), vine leaves or pitta breads. The yellow and green rices are particularly good cold, dressed with a vinaigrette.

The colours are clearer if you use white rice, and a shade subtler if you choose brown. There are some good brown rices around but some are very husky. The unpolished American Long Grain is good and it is now possible to get a brown Basmati. Basmati's fragrance here is squandered, so use Patna or the American Long Grain.

Yellow

6 oz/180 g rice
1/2 lemon
1 bay leaf
1 oz/30 g butter
few strands saffron or 1/2 tsp
    turmeric

Red

6 oz/180 g rice
1/2 pt/300 ml tomato juice
2 shallots or one red onion
1 tsp paprika or 1/4–1/2 tsp cayenne
1 oz/30 g butter

Green

6 oz/180 g rice
2 spring onions
1 oz/30 g parsley or parsley and
    coriander
2 cloves garlic
1 oz/30 g butter

Yellow: Soak the saffron in a little hot water. Melt half the butter in a pan. If using turmeric, fry it gently before adding the rice. Stir the rice in the butter. Pour on twice the volume of boiling water. Add the saffron, bay leaf and the juice of the lemon and stir around once. Cover tightly and turn down to low. Cook for 15 minutes (20 if you are using brown rice but 10 if you are using Basmati). Turn off but do not uncover for another 5 minutes. Remove the bay leaf. Then add some tiny strips of lemon peel and the rest of the butter. Stir lightly with a fork, fluffing up the grains. There should be no water to drain and the rice should be perfectly cooked.

Red: Very finely chop the shallots or onion or put through processor. Fry gently in half the butter and the cayenne – if using paprika, though, do not add it until the end. Add the rice and cook for 1 minute, stirring. Pour on the tomato juice and 2 fl oz/60 ml boiling water. Bring to the boil, stir once, cover and reduce the heat to a simmer. Turn off after 15 minutes but leave covered for the next 5. Stir in the remaining butter and paprika.

Green: Place the herbs, spring onions and garlic in a food processor or mortar and pestle and purée. Fry the purée in half the butter for a minute, add the rice and cook a further minute, stirring. Pour on boiling water to twice the volume, stir once then cover and reduce the heat. Cook 15 minutes but leave the lid on for the extra 5 minutes. Fork through the rest of the butter.

If moulding, butter the ring or basin well. Individual ones can be done most effectively in darioles or ramekins. Pack the hot rice in layers, cover and stand in a warm place for 3–4 minutes before turning out.

Spiced Rice

Fruity, fragrant and quite beautiful. As an alternative to the pomegranates, stir in some fresh cranberries 7 minutes before the end of cooking. Pistachios can be substituted for the almonds.

10 oz/300 g long grain rice
3 shallots
1 clove garlic
1 oz/30 g butter
4 cloves
2 tsp ground cinnamon
2 tbs afghan raisins
2 tbs sultanas
2 oz/60 g almonds
1 orange
1 pomegranate
salt, pepper

Blanch and skin the almonds. Peel and finely chop the garlic and shallots. Pare the rind from the orange and cut into fine strips. Pour boiling water onto the strips and allow to stand 5 minutes before draining. Squeeze the juice from the orange.

Melt the butter and add the cinnamon and cloves, fry for half a minute then stir in the garlic and shallots. Cook, stirring, for a couple of minutes then add the rice and almonds. Stir to coat all the grains in the butter. Allow to heat through but do not fry. Pour on the orange juice and enough boiling water to double the volume. Stir, cover and turn down the heat. Cook for 10 minutes, stir in the raisins and sultanas and cover and cook until all the liquid is absorbed and the rice is tender. Stir in the pomegranate seeds, orange rind and salt and pepper before serving.

10
Sauces and Other Accompaniments

This section contains a few extra sauces and adornments not included in the main recipes. Some, the fondues for example, are dishes in their own right. Use sauces judiciously to complement and flatter. A good sauce can make a good meal better, but it cannot rescue a disaster. There are few occasions when the sauce should swamp the food.

The optional extras are just that – but worth thinking about. Use them as accents and contrasts: bringing out flavours, pointing up textures and showing off colours. Home-made pickles and relishes are like fresh bread, petits fours and home-made jam – they show that you care, that you are serious about quality and pay attention to details.

Madeira Sauce

This dark rich sauce was originally devised to be a filling, with the mushrooms, for savoury pastry horns – cornucopias. I then realised that the strained sauce was so good it deserved to be served on its own.

The sauced mushrooms need not just be served in the pastry horns – they are delicious with rice, in the batter saucers (p. 129), with noodles, or in any ordinary pie crust.

12 oz/375 g mushrooms – brown cap or field
2 oz/60 g dried mushrooms, including some morels
1 oz/30 g stoned prunes
8 oz/250 g shallots
3 cloves garlic
1 oz/30 g butter
¼ bottle Madeira, not Malmsey but Verdelho or Bual
1 oz/30 g dried chestnuts
vegetable stock
sage
salt, pepper

Soak the chestnuts for at least 3 hours, then cook them slowly, with some herbs, in enough stock to cover. You can do this in a covered pan on the top of the stove or in a casserole. Cook until tender (about 1 hour). Pour ½ pt/ 300 ml boiling water onto the crumbled dried mushrooms and allow to stand.

Peel and finely chop garlic and shallots. Cook in butter slowly until soft. Wipe mushrooms and chop. Add to pan. Cook 10 minutes. Cut up prunes, chestnuts, and sage. Stir into the shallots and mushrooms with the dried mushrooms and their soaking water. Season with salt and black pepper. Cook, covered, for a further 20 minutes. Add Madeira, take off heat and allow to stand an hour if possible.

Bring sauce to simmering boil, stirring occasionally; reduce by a third. Strain and check seasonings.

Spiked Cream

Use to raise the status (and calories and cholesterol, unfortunately) of humble baked apples or stewed fruits. Better, in my opinion, than traditional accompaniments to Christmas pudding and mince pies. Brandy, Rum, Calvados or Marsala all work fabulously but there are other possibilities – try Grand Marnier, a little orange rind, a dust of cinnamon and orangeflower honey to serve with a dark chocolate sponge.

½pt/300 ml double cream
2 tbs brandy
1–2 tbs heather honey
1 cardamom pod
3 allspice berries

Split the cardomom pod and scrape out the seeds. Crush them well with the allspice. Place in a small saucepan with the brandy and honey. Heat but do not boil. Allow to stand until quite cold, then strain.

Whip the cream until beginning to mound, then whip in the brandy and honey in a thin, steady stream. Continue whipping until softly peaking. Do not over-whip. Serve.

Pickled Pineapple

Peter Piper picked a peck of pickled pineapples? Well he might have done had he tried them. Although I had been familiar with pineapple relishes and chutneys, it was not until I went to Mauritius that I came across a plain pickle. Mauritius is a rare place with a glorious convergence of cultures and their cuisines. French, Indian, Creole and Chinese happily coexist and their kitchens as well as their lives are richer for it.

3 or 4 small pineapples
1 pt/600 ml distilled malt vinegar
4 oz/125 g golden granulated sugar
4 cloves
6 allspice berries
8 white peppercorns
2 tsp black mustard seeds
¼ tsp salt

Place the vinegar and sugar into an enamel or stainless steel pan. Add the cloves, allspice, peppercorns and salt and bring slowly to the boil.

Meanwhile peel and slice the pineapple crossways, a little under ½ in/1 cm thick. Cut each slice into quarters. Pack into clean jars, sprinkling with mustard seeds. Boil the vinegar hard until reduced by a third and strain over the pineapple. Cover and seal. Leave in a dark place for 5 weeks before using.

Alternatively, you can add the pineapple to the pan and simmer in the vinegar until softened. Take out and pack with the mustard seeds, while reducing the vinegar. In this case, tie the cloves, allspice and peppercorns in a muslin bag.

Pear Sauce

The same method can be used for making apple sauce. Baking is preferable to boiling, the sauce being less likely to 'catch' on the bottom. Subtle spicy flavours can be added instead of the blackcurrants – cardamom, cinnamon or ginger all work well; try also scenting it with vanilla.

If you want to keep some sauce, double the quantities, pack into clean jars and sterilise in a hot water bath (bain marie).

1 lb/500 g slightly underripe
*   Williams pears – windfalls are*
*   ideal*
2 oz/60 g blackcurrants
1–2 blackcurrant leaves
½ oz/15 g butter
4 tbs water
sugar
1 tbs Crème de Cassis
or 1 tbs blackcurrant or raspberry
*   vinegar*
black pepper

Roughly chop the pears; do not skin or core but remove any bad bits. Place into a casserole with a tight-fitting lid. Add the blackcurrants, leaves, butter and water. For the sweet version add 2 tbs sugar and the Crème de Cassis. For the savoury, add the vinegar, only ½ tbs sugar and a generous grinding of pepper. Cover and cook slowly until soft and pulpy. This can be as long as all day in the slow oven of an Aga or it can be 1–2 hours at the bottom of a cool oven.

Rub through a sieve and check seasonings – particularly the sugar and vinegar. Reheat if necessary over a low flame.

The cooled sweetened sauce is delicious swirled through fromage frais or yoghurt. It can be combined with equal quantities of whipped cream or custard for a fool.

The savoury sauce teams well with fritters, cheeses, stuffed mushrooms and egg dishes.

Peach and Ginger Sauce

Fécule, simply starch in English, is used to thicken this fruit-based sauce. For transparent or less pulpy sauces I would use arrowroot, but here potato flour or cornflour is acceptable. The benefit of these alternatives to wheatflour is the minimal cooking required, thereby retaining the fresh flavour of the fruit.

Once again, with small alterations this sweet sauce can be used for savoury purposes – with fritters, cheese or egg dishes and, like the more common plum sauces, to accompany Chinese food.

4 large ripe peaches
¼pt/150ml water + 1tbs
2tsp potato flour
1 large nobble of preserved ginger
a little ginger syrup or sugar

Scald the peaches and peel. Cut in two and remove the stones. Cut into regular small chunks. Chop the ginger into fine shreds and place in a small pan with the peaches and ¼pt/150ml water. Cover and bring to the boil. Simmer briefly until the peach pieces are about to disintegrate. Remove from the heat. In a tea cup, mix the potato flour with the tablespoon of water. Stir the slaked starch into the peaches. Return to the heat and, stirring constantly, allow to bubble and thicken. Sweeten with ginger syrup or sugar to taste. Serve hot or chilled. The sauce can be turned into a pudding itself by folding through the cold mixture some fromage frais or petit suisse and cream.

A sweet wine could be substituted for the water, to great effect.

Marbled Fondue

This is little more than chocolate and alcohol – use it as a sauce over ice-cream or sponge pudding, or as dip for soft fruits, especially strawberries and cherries. If you can beg or borrow a silver chafing dish for this fondue, it will look stunning. To serve individual fondues, take a trip to the beach. Gather a few flat pebbles. Heat the pebbles in the oven. Place the hot stones in earthenware dishes and stand ramekins on top for the fondue.

You can choose to do just a plain or a white chocolate fondue but the marbled effect is lovely.

8 oz/250 g plain, bitter, chocolate
8 oz/250 g white chocolate
4 tbs white rum

to serve:

1–2 lb/500 g–1 kg fresh fruit:
*   strawberries, cherries, bananas,*
*   pineapples, lychees, kiwis –*
*   anything that will go with*
*   chocolate and sit on the end of a*
*   fork*
¹/₂ pt/300 ml double cream
4 oz/125 g shelled hazelnuts

Toast the hazelnuts in a dry pan until lightly browned. Cool and then grate finely.

Whip the cream until mounding.

Prepare the fruit, cutting any large ones into bite-sized chunks.

Set a pile of cream, a pile of grated nuts and a pile of fruit on each plate.

In two separate bowls over hot water melt the plain and white chocolates. Beat half the rum into each. Spoon the chocolates into either the ramekins or the fondue pan, from opposite sides. Swirl together very lightly, using a skewer. As the fruit is dipped in it will marble more. Keep barely warm.

After dipping in the chocolate, dip the fruit in the nuts, in the cream, and then into your mouth.

Cucumber or Banana Raita

Raita is a welcome balm after a mouthful of fiery curry. Plain yoghurt is often served with perhaps a decorative smattering of toasted cumin seeds or a dust of paprika. The addition of cucumber enhances its cooling properties. Banana seems able to counteract the eyewatering effects of cayenne.

The success of the raita depends on the quality of the yoghurt. If you are not making your own and have no Middle Eastern or Indian shop nearby, the best widely available alternatives are the strained Greek or full cream goat's milk varieties. Those from mythical Dales and Vales are best avoided here – the consistency is wrong and the flavour too sharp.

Before the energy-consciousness-raising times of Heath's three-day week and Callaghan's winter of discontent, making yoghurt at home was easy. Pilot lights in ovens and feeble cylinder jackets for immersion tanks meant a steady background heat was always available. Now electronic ignition and sprayed-on solid-foam casings save fuel but reduce the yoghurt maker's options. There are 'yoghurt makers', of course, and gardeners' propagators give a good ambient temperature (put the milk in a bowl first – not directly into the seed tray!). Aga-ists and Rayburners are a breed apart but those with storage heaters can also count themselves lucky, at least in this regard. Other methods of keeping the milk just warm include the heating of bricks, wrapping in blankets and easiest of all, using a wide-necked thermos flask.

Whilst you are actively encouraging one bacterium to grow, you certainly do not want any uninvited guests – be scrupulous about cleanliness of bowls and utensils. A pint of full cream UHT milk makes life easy: merely warm it to blood heat and stir in the starter. This can be either a small pot of good quality 'live' plain yoghurt or a packet of yoghurt 'culture', available from health food stores. Leave in your chosen warm place for 12 hours, by which time it should be lovely and thick, clean on the tongue but not sour. Some of your own yoghurt can now be used as the starter for the next batch. It can become a habit. My mother used to make yoghurt every evening. One of the best things about her yoghurt, left in the oven overnight with the pilot light for company, was the slight crust it formed on the top.

Although raita is best known as an accompaniment to curry, there is no reason why it should not be served at other times. It makes a delightful starter and a pleasant side dish for a summer meal. Try it as a cold filling for hollowed-out tomatoes or courgettes. Good, too, with Middle Eastern food, cutting the richness of aubergine in an Imam Bayaldi or contrasting the spiciness of a Bulgar Pilaff.

1 pt/600 ml plain yoghurt
1 large cucumber
or 4 small 'fig' bananas – 2
    ordinary ripe ones will do if
    necessary
1 tsp cumin seeds
1 tbs chopped coriander leaves
small sprig of mint
pinch cayenne
garam masala
salt, black pepper

Toast the cumin seeds in a small pan. Allow to cool and then crush or grind in a mill. Pare the green rind from the cucumber. (If liked, you can reserve some fine strips to decorate the top of the finished raita.) Slice cucumber thinly and place in a bowl. For the banana version, peel and cut into small chunks and put into a bowl. Add the yoghurt, cumin, finely chopped coriander and mint leaves, ¼tsp garam masala, a pinch of salt and a good grinding of pepper. Carefully combine with a fork. Chill well and sprinkle with a tiny amount of cayenne to decorate, just before serving.

Fondue Hollandaise

This is a totally inauthentic recipe – I have never heard of the Dutch making fondue and I am not sure they would use cider if they did. However, my excuse is that it tastes very good, is much cheaper to make than the Neufchatel, and for those who feel guilty about these things it is a lower-fat fondue – not that that is saying much! What else can you do with Edam for grown-ups?

1 lb/500 g Edam cheese
1 tbs flour
½ pt/300 ml dry cider
1 tbs Calvados
1–2 cloves garlic

Cut the cheese into small cubes and dust with the flour. Wipe the garlic around the pan and heat the cider until almost simmering. Sprinkle in the floured cheese while stirring continuously. When all is stirred in and melted and the sauce is smooth, beat in the Calvados.

Keep warm while dipping chunks of bread into the cheese. Try also crudités: celery, mushroom, tomato, onion, apple, cauliflower, grapes.

Crème Anglaise – Custard

Do not try cooking custard in a pan directly over heat, you are bound to come to grief. Ignore all other claims on your attention for the 10 minutes or so it takes to thicken. Flavour with vanilla, a few slivers of lemon or orange peel, geranium leaves, angelica stems or coffee beans. Infuse the cream with the flavour by heating the cream and then keeping warm for 15 minutes before proceeding.

Double the quantities to make a good old-fashioned trifle. Place a layer of sponge cake in the base of a glass dish. Cover thickly with raspberries and sprinkle liberally with Marsala. Scatter over crushed amaretti. Cover with a layer of sliced peaches and pour on the custard. Chill well, for at least 12 hours. Whip some cream and spread or pipe over the trifle. Decorate with toasted, flaked almonds and berry fruits.

6 egg yolks
1 pt/600 ml single cream
1–2 oz/30–60 g caster sugar
1 vanilla pod (or see above)

Heat the cream with the vanilla pod in the top of a double boiler. For a more pronounced vanilla perfume, slit the pod. Beat together the egg yolks and sugar in a basin. When the cream is very hot, but not boiling, pour onto the egg yolks in a steady stream, beating continuously. Strain back into the double boiler and cook, *stirring all the time*, until the mixture thickens enough to coat the back of a spoon. This is very important. Do not allow the base of the top of the double boiler to touch the water below and keep the water simmering, not madly boiling. If you do not possess a double boiler, fit a heatproof basin over a pan.

Chocolate Custard

Use this rich Crème Anglaise variation with baked pears, tarts, pastries and cakes. If you are a serious chocaholic, try a Chocolate Trifle. Lay a chocolate sponge in the base of the dish, covering it with strawberries, sprinkling with Kahlua and then placing sliced pears on top before covering with the chocolate custard. Chill, then top with whipped cream and decorate with chocolate curls.

6 egg yolks
1 pt/600 ml single cream
1–2 oz/30–60 g caster sugar
3½ oz/110 g very dark chocolate –
   at least 67% cocoa solids

Heat the cream in the top of a double boiler. For a mocha custard, infuse it with a few slightly crushed coffee beans. Beat together the egg yolks and sugar in a basin. Break the chocolate into small pieces and place in a small basin over hot water to melt. When the cream is very hot, beat gradually into the egg yolks. Strain back into the double boiler and cook, *stirring all the time*, until the mixture thickens enough to coat the back of a spoon. Pour a little hot custard onto the melted chocolate, mixing well. Then scrape the chocolate into the rest of the custard and combine smoothly.

The custard can be poured into ramekins, chilled, and eaten like chocolate mousse.

Coulis

The controversy over why mayonnaise is so called raged for decades. Carême believed it should be magnonaise, from *manier*, to stir. *Larousse Gastronomique* favours a derivation of *moyeu* – old French for egg yolk. Others credited it either to the towns of Mahon or Bayonne. The etymological difficulties in cookery terms are legion. What meant something in one era can mean something quite different in the next. This is apparent in the word 'coulis', or cullis. Today it appears to mean a fresh-tasting sauce of vegetable or fruit, barely cooked, if at all. According to *Larousse*, formerly, coulis were meat juices that ran out in cooking and 'now' (actually 1961) 'coulis (or cullis) is none other than what we call today veal stock (*fonds de veau*)'. The same source admits that some authors apply the term to rather liquid purées (as I shall). The dictionary, by the way, tells us that cullis means gutter, from *couloir*, to run. The etymology at least, is clear.

The first recipe is for Tomato and Red Pepper Coulis. (The nomenclature associated with 'peppers' is odd, too, with all their aliases.) The second is a sweet one – Apricot and Orange Coulis.

Tomato and Red Pepper Coulis

The coulis can lend a vivid splash of colour to a pale egg dish such as a savoury custard. It contrasts beautifully, both to the eye and the palate, when served with rice-stuffed vine or spinach leaves. It can be used hot or cold and can be further enhanced by the addition of chopped fresh basil, mint, oregano or chives.

12 oz/375 g ripe, red,
  well-flavoured tomatoes –
  homegrown Alicante can be
  delicious
2 medium-sweet red peppers
  (capsicums)
1 small lemon
dash of hot chilli pepper sauce
or 6 black olives
pinch sugar
sea salt, black pepper

In a flame, or under a hot grill, blacken the pepper skins. Remove the crisp paperiness by scraping under cold water. Split, and discard the seeds and any white pith.

Chop the tomatoes roughly and put in a small pan with a tablespoon of lemon juice and a little of the lemon zest. Cook until just pulpy – this does not take long but depends on the type and ripeness of the tomatoes. Push through a fine sieve with the peppers, or purée in a food processor. Splash in a drop or two of distilled hot pepper sauce or stir in the slivered or chopped olives. Season well with a pinch of sugar, sea salt and black pepper. Chill or reheat to serve.

If too thick, it can be thinned slightly with a little tomato or lemon juice. Other delicious alterations to the consistency (and flavour) could be made with olive oil, vodka, dry sherry or vinegar. Do not overdo it though or you may end up with ketchup instead!

Apricot and Orange Coulis

Ideal for November to March, the coulis is made with dried fruit and fresh oranges. Dried peaches, available in some health food shops and delicatessens, are more delicate and could be teamed instead with the sweeter satsumas or clementines. The coulis can be served with sponge pudding, cheesecake, baked custard, rice pudding, mousses and so on.

It can be adapted for a savoury role by adding browned shallots a little stock for simmering the apricots in, a tablespoon or two of vinegar, and reducing the sugar and adding seasonings. It could then be used with couscous or curry.

6 oz/200 g unsulphured dried apricots
2 very large oranges
¼ pt/150 ml water
sugar or honey

Put the apricots and water in a small covered pan and bring to the boil. Simmer for 10 minutes. Remove from the heat then add the zest from 1 orange and the juice from 2. Transfer to a china or glass bowl, cover and leave to stand in a cool place for at least 8 hours. Purée either in a liquidiser or through a sieve – the latter gives a better result but is more time-consuming. If necessary, sweeten with sugar or honey. Thin with more juice if required.

Caramelised Clementines

Italian restaurant cooking has long included caramelised oranges on its dessert menus. I prefer to use tiny clementines; they have no pips and their flavour is excellent. (The flatter satsumas are not a good idea as they tend to fall apart too easily.) They make a good savoury accompaniment if the caramel is made with white malt vinegar and rosemary leaves are sprinkled over the top. Use fine shreds of ordinary orange peel as it is almost impossible to find unwaxed clementines.

8 clementines
7 oz/200 g granulated sugar
3½ fl oz/100 ml water
fresh orange peel, with no pith

Cut the orange peel into thin shreds. Blanch in boiling water and drain. Peel the clementines, with your hands not a knife. Remove any 'hairy' bits of pith but do not break up into segments.

Combine the water and sugar and put onto a low heat to melt. Cover and bring to the boil. Uncover and heat until the syrup reaches the hard crack stage – a drop in cold water will make brittle threads – and it has begun to colour: 310°F/155°C. Take off the heat and put in the clementines and the peel. Use a fork to carefully turn them about so they are all coated in the glaze. Keep the pan warm by standing it over boiling water.

Lift them out and pile neatly on a plate. Chill before serving.

Grilled Nectarines

Not only nectarines respond well to this treatment. Peaches, pineapples, mangoes and tomatoes have all been successfully tried. Use them as an accompaniment to white cheeses (the grilled goat's cheese especially), light egg dishes, salads, curries or tajine.

For mangoes, cut lengthwise, along the flat of the stone, without peeling. Score the flesh with parallel diagonal lines, ½in/1cm apart. Turn the mango 'inside out'. The flesh will then stand up on the convex curve. To do this, hold it skin-side down, gently folding the edges underneath until the middle pops upwards. This is a very simple procedure – don't worry.

In a hurry, smear fruit with wholegrain mustard and sprinkle with sugar – not as good but still nice.

4 ripe but not squashy nectarines
2 tbs clear honey – acacia is best
2 tsp balsamic vinegar
black mustard seeds

Peel and halve the fruit. Lay cut-side down on an oven-proof dish. Combine the honey and vinegar. Brush over the nectarines. Sprinkle liberally with mustard seeds. Place under a hot grill until the seeds pop. Serve immediately.

Elderberry and Port Sauce

Although I have specified port, this rich savoury sauce is equally good with a soft, well-rounded claret. The sauce is highly recommended for the Christmas dinner table when, of course, there will be no fresh elderberries. Bottling the fruit in October is simple and, I believe, preferable to freezing. Do not pick until the fruit clusters hang down on the bushes. Either pack the berries into stone jars and cook in a slow oven, or in heavy glass jars (e.g. Kilner) and stand in boiling water. In each case, layer the berries with a little sugar and cook until the juices run. Seal whilst hot and store in a cook dark place. Elderberries can then be used for sweet and savoury dishes – try adding a couple of tablespoons to an apple pie mid-winter.

*8 oz/250 g fresh or bottled
  elderberries*
7 fl oz/200 ml ruby port
3 shallots
1 cinnamon stick
2 cloves
1 oz/30 g unsalted butter
light muscovado sugar
black pepper

Peel and finely chop the shallots. Soften and then brown them in a little over half the butter. Add the elderberries. If fresh, allow the berries to pop before adding the port. Preserved berries should be added with their bottling liquid and the port. Add the cinnamon, cloves, and a liberal grinding of black pepper. Cover and simmer gently for 20 minutes. Turn up the heat and reduce sauce by half. Strain into a clean pan and check seasoning, adding sugar to taste. Cut the remaining butter into small cubes. Bring the sauce back to the boil. Remove from the heat and, adding the butter bit by bit, move the pan around and around to swirl the butter in. Serve immediately. Do not stir or reheat.

Cheese Fondue

The Alpine regions, Swiss, French and Italian, all have their own versions of fondue, the ultimate cheese sauce. The Swiss use Gruyère and/or Emmenthal in a Neufchatel Fondue and the French, Franche Comté. Both melt the cheese in white wine. The Italians use Fontina and cook it with eggs and milk to make a cream.

My parents, like many couples in the Sixties and early Seventies had fondue dinner parties. As with most things that come into vogue, in time it became terribly *un*fashionable to eat fondue. It is a shame that the acceptance of an authentic dish depends on the vagaries of fashion.

8 oz/250 g Gruyère
8 oz/250 g Emmenthal
1 tbs plain flour
1 tbs Kirsch
½ pt/300 ml dry white wine
2 cloves garlic

Cut the cheeses into small cubes and dust with the flour. Cut the garlic cloves in half, lengthways, and rub around the saucepan. Pour in the wine and heat to just below a simmer. Stirring with one hand, sprinkle in the floured cheese with the other. Add in a slow, fairly continuous stream, stirring all the time. As you stir and the cheese melts it will form a rich smooth sauce. When all the cheese is added, beat in the Kirsch.

Traditionally it is now kept warm, over a spirit burner, while diners dip in chunks of crusty bread. Alternatively, serve it over cooked vegetables such as leeks, broccoli or cauliflower. Or spoon it into croustades or pastry shells.

Beurre Bourguignon

I adapted this velvety sauce from the classic French beurre blanc. However, I find it reminiscent of stroganoff. Its echoes of Mitteleuropa are derived from the smetana. Very cheap, so-called 'cooking wines' are often best avoided – they bring their faults with them into the pot.

Very large flat mushrooms, sprinkled with oil and balsamic vinegar and then baked or grilled, are superb accompanied by this sauce and lots of fresh crusty bread for mopping plates. Try it also on wide ribbon noodles with stir-fried florets of broccoli and shiitake mushrooms.

3 medium English onions
2 cloves garlic
1 tsp olive oil
2 large brown cap or field mushrooms
8 fl oz/240 ml Burgundy – do not panic, it need not be a classified growth. The bottle simply labelled 'Bourgogne', with no specific commune or vineyard, is sufficient for these purposes.
5 fl oz/140 ml vegetable stock
sage
salt, white peppercorns
4 oz/125 g unsalted butter
2 tbs smetana or cultured soured cream

Peel and finely chop the onions and garlic. Put into a pan with the bare minimum of oil. Cook over a low heat until beginning to brown. Slice the mushrooms and add to the pan. Pour on the wine and stock. Add a few sprigs of roughly torn sage and 3 crushed peppercorns. Season with a pinch of salt. Bring to the boil and simmer for 30 minutes. Turn up the heat and reduce by half. Strain into a clean pan and boil away until only 8 tablespoons of liquid remains. Cut the butter into small dice. Off the heat, stir in the smetana or soured cream. Allow to warm through and then, on a very low heat, whisk in the butter, a little at a time. Check seasoning. Keep warm until needed in a bain-marie – do not boil.

Hollandaise Sauce

Hollandaise is one of those egg/emulsion sauces that traditionally frighten home cooks. This is a great pity as it really is not at all difficult to make – whichever way you choose. As with many classic sauces, the classic sources give you wholly conflicting advice. To heat in a double boiler, over a flame, or indeed not to cook the eggs at all. Basically a hollandaise contains egg yolks, butter and lemon juice or vinegar. Balsamic vinegar gives a deep rich colour and a mellower flavour. Lemon juice – or lime – is especially good over broccoli or asparagus. Substitute orange and you have a maltaise, which is recommended over fennel or celeriac.

I give two methods: the first can be made in a liquidiser or by hand. It is very simple. It achieves good results, but it can be bettered – see method two.

For people completely unconcerned with their cholesterol level, try combining 1/4pt/150ml whipped double cream with 1/2pt/300ml hollandaise to give a mousseline. It doesn't taste as if it is bad for you, and after all, the asparagus season is very short.

A good handful of fresh herbs, finely minced and then squeezed through muslin is another excellent way of flavouring the sauce. Parsley and chervil respond best to this treatment.

A birch whisk is the ideal implement for this sort of sauce making.

Method I

4oz/125g unsalted butter
2tbs lemon juice or balsamic
*   vinegar*
3 egg yolks
Salt, pepper – cayenne is an
*   optional extra*

Whisk together the egg yolks, seasonings and lemon juice, or place in a liquidiser and run the blades for a few seconds.

Melt the butter in a small pan and heat until bubbling. Do not allow it to brown. Drip the hot butter onto the egg yolks whisking it in all the while. How fast you can go depends on how well you can whisk. Add it steadily, without stopping, beating continuously. When all the butter is whisked in and the sauce is thick, serve immediately or keep warm for a short while over hot water. If using the liquidiser, switch on and pour the hot butter in a thin stream onto the eggs. The sauce should be ready by the time the butter is all added, but if not, run a few seconds longer.

Method II

4 oz/125 g unsalted butter
1½ tbs lemon juice or *vinegar –*
 either balsamic, white wine,
 sherry or champagne
4 tbs boiling water or *light,*
 wine-based stock
3 egg yolks
salt, pepper

If you are feeling brave you can cook the sauce over a direct (low) flame, but the less intrepid might be well advised to stick to the double boiler. Melt the butter and keep warm. Combine the lemon juice or vinegar with the water or stock in a small pan. Season with salt and pepper. Bring to the boil and reduce by half. Strain into a double boiler and, when cooled to blood heat, beat in the egg yolks. Heat, stirring continuously until the mixture begins to thicken. Turn off the heat and gradually whisk in the butter. Serve at once.

In either of the recipes, if the mixture does begin to curdle, all is not lost. Beat it, little by little, into a fresh egg yolk.

Beurre Blanc

Beurre Blanc, unless you are to cheat and add a little cream to it, is delicate and needs to be served as soon as it is made. The cream will allow it to be held, over hot water or in a vaccum flask, until required.

Although a myriad of variations are possible, essentially the sauce consists of white wine and vinegar reduced with finely chopped shallots and finished by whisking in unsalted butter.

¼ bottle medium dry white wine
8 oz/225 g unsalted butter
1 shallot
2 tbs white wine vinegar
salt, pepper

Peel and very finely chop the shallot. Place in a pan with the wine and vinegar. Bring to the boil and boil hard until only 4 tablespoons of liquid remain in the pan. Strain into a clean pan if a perfectly smooth sauce is required. If you need to keep the sauce a little while, now add 2 tbs double cream and allow to bubble. Move to a minimal heat. Cut the butter into small dice. Whisk in the butter, a bit at a time. Do not allow the sauce to boil. As you whisk, the mixture will thicken. When all the butter has been added, season and serve. Unbelievably good with tiny or quartered stewed artichokes.

Try Pineau de Charente, simmered with the shallot and mushroom peelings, to accompany Stuffed Mushrooms (p. 172). Lime and ginger – use six limes and one lemon with some grated ginger – can go with barquettes of courgettes filled with oyster mushrooms.

Rum Butter

I have adapted this recipe from one my friend Lesley passed me some years ago. I have no idea where hers came from. I much prefer this version to the rather sickly butter cream of the usual brandy butters, despite the alleged attendant salmonella risks. Perhaps it is the traces of Caribbean ancestry but I invariably use dark rum and not brandy in all my Christmas baking.

The recipe can be used throughout the year as a delectable filling for cakes, crêpes or biscuits. Increase the rum, freeze in individual moulds like a parfait, and serve with a hot prune or mincemeat sauce as an ingenious alternative to Christmas pudding.

6 oz/200 g best unsalted butter
6 oz/200 g golden caster sugar
3 tbs maple syrup
1 egg
3 oz/100 g ground almonds
1 tbs dark rum
½ pt/300 ml double cream

Beat the butter until pale and light. Beat in the syrup and then the sugar. Whisk the egg and brandy together in a small bowl or cup. Gradually beat this into the creamed butter mixture. Then sprinkle in the almonds and, stirring vigorously, incorporate them. Slowly add the cream, beating continuously until all is incorporated and it is light in texture. Keep cool.

Blackcurrant Reduction

Clean and fresh-tasting, a blackcurrant reduction is ideal served with pâtés or creamy white cheeses or batters. It is used to great effect with the Choux Swans (p. 92). Increase the sugar content and use as a sweet sauce for ice cream, pancakes, mousse, etc. I prefer to sieve my sauce, enjoying the clarity of an unthickened fruit sauce but this, of course, gives a smaller quantity. Here, as elsewhere, less can certainly be more.

Fine lines of a contrasting reduction, a yoghurt, or a cream could be piped across a puddle of the sauce and then feathered or, more simply, just briefly swirled together.

Liqueurs or cognac can be added.

The same method applies for other fruit: elderberries, bilberries, redcurrants, cloudberries, raspberries, blackberries, gooseberries, lingonberries. Bottled and frozen fruit can be used out of season. If using bottled fruit, be cautious about adding sugar.

1 lb/500 g plump ripe
    blackcurrants, topped and
    tailed
golden caster sugar
¼pt/150 ml water
few sprigs mint (optional)

Put the fruit, water and mint, if using, in a heavy-bottomed pan. Cover and bring to the boil. Simmer for 20 minutes – the fruit should then be soft and pulpy. All the currants will have popped. Pour the fruit into a sieve over a clean pan. Press with the back of a wooden spoon to extract as much juice as possible but do not work the fruit through the sieve. Sweeten the extracted juice to taste. Bring it slowly to the boil and then boil hard to reduce by half or a third depending on your taste. Watch the pan (do not let it scorch).

Serve hot or cold.

Gooseberry Relish

Make this relish when the gooseberries are green – the thinnings from dessert varieties can be used. It is increasingly difficult to buy properly ripened gooseberries. In the rush for earlier markets, many growers are picking the fruit while still immature. The gooseberry that can be eaten raw is becoming a rarity in our shops.

Over the moors at Egton Bridge they hold a Gooseberry Show every August, where the fruits are huge – and ripe. Single gooseberries can weigh 2 oz/60 g each, the size of an egg!

The relish can be used with curries, egg dishes and cheeses. It is excellent with grilled goat's cheese on bruschetta. The best goat's cheese I have had came from Bramfield in Suffolk. Clean, fresh, almost grassy, it was soft, creamy and delicate. The nearest cheese to it is the Sussex Slipcote – a sheep's cheese.

To make bruschetta, cut thick oblique slices from a ciabatta (a baguette will do *in extremis*). Grill, then rub with a split clove of garlic and dribble with the darkest, fruitiest olive oil. Pile on some goat's cheese and place under a hot grill until lightly browned. Serve immediately with the following relish, hot or cold.

12 oz/375 g green gooseberries
3 oz/90 g golden granulated sugar
1 tsp Meaux mustard
1/4 tsp allspice
1 shallot
3 tbs water
1/2 oz/15 g unsalted butter
   (optional)
small bunch chives
black pepper

Peel and very finely chop the shallot and simmer, covered in the water, until tender. Top, tail and halve the gooseberries. Add to the pan with the mustard, sugar and spice. Heat gently, stirring until the sugar has melted. Cook over a moderately high heat for 5–7 minutes, stirring continuously. The gooseberries should not have broken down completely and the mixture should be thick. Beat in the butter and most of the chopped chives, reserving a few to sprinkle on the top.

Herb Vinegars

Most people are familiar with tarragon vinegar, having seen the leafy strands like biology specimens lined up on supermarket shelves. Many of these mass-produced herbed vinegars seem to miss the mark – either they simply do not use enough herbs or the vinegar is of inferior quality. Malt vinegar will not do. Some I have tried seemingly have seen just the one sprig of tarragon suspended therein.

The recipe below can be used for all sorts of herbs – marjoram, fennel, dill, thyme, mint, basil and, of course, tarragon, but do try the lavender. It is particularly good over salads of cucumber or stawberries. It is also said to be therapeutic in cases of headache. Herbs can also be used in combination – try fennel and mint or, more traditionally, sage and thyme. Once again, experiment and find exciting new combinations. Chervil and . . .?

This method is also good for making a delectable flower vinegar from either rose, calendula or violet petals – unsprayed, of course. Dark, old-fashioned, deeply scented roses combined with champagne vinegar would be an epicurean treat over a delicate summer salad.

Both vinegars and oils are excellent ways of keeping herbs for winter use that do not freeze or dry particularly well, such as chives or mint.

Those brown- or gray-glazed Victorian stoneware jars beloved of Seventies interior decorators have a real purpose here. If yours have already exited via the car boot sale, use glass jars, but protect from the light to preserve the colour of the vinegar.

Lavender Vinegar

lavender, including only a few flowers – for other herbs, pick just before flowering
white wine vinegar

Lightly crushing the leaves between your fingers, half fill a large jar with lavender. Top up with vinegar and cover. Steep for 6 weeks then strain into clean small bottles. Add a nice sprig of lavender, stalk first, to each bottle before sealing.

Garlic Vinegar

Great on salads and in curries and for sprinkling over pizza; I like to make this vinegar with green garlic but it can also be made with the more widely available dried. Some chopped chives in the finished vinegar are both decorative and tasty.

4 oz/125 g garlic
2 pt/1 l white wine vinegar

Mince or finely chop the garlic and place in a jar with the vinegar. Cork. Steep for a fortnight, inverting the jar night and morning. Strain into clean bottles, adding some chopped herbs if desired, and seal.

Fruit Vinegars

In the Aladdin's caves of good delis and upmarket food halls the shimmering ruby and topaz of the bottled fruit vinegars command high prices. Yet it is simple indeed to make flavoured vinegars. They can be used in many ways. A little in a tall glass topped up with water or soda makes an excellent, thirst-quenching drink. As the basis for sweet and sour coulis, relishes, or similar sauces they are invaluable. They can be used for flavouring puddings. Try them drizzled over steamed or grilled vegetables. Their addition to salads lends an extra dimension and they are also useful as a fillip for soups and sauces. Some are said to be a remedy for coughs, colds and sore throats. Most soft fruit can be used – strawberries, raspberries and blackberries being the most common. Try, too, spiced peaches, plums, currants and cranberries.

I give the two following recipes as blueprints – the methods are basically the same. The first is a quite sweet vinegar, the second a more powerful brew. Experiment with whatever fruit you have, adding spices as you desire. While you may not use fruit vinegars much at the moment, when you have a tempting array in the cupboard you will be inspired to be creative with them.

Strawberry Vinegar

2 lb/1 kg ripe, full-flavoured
    strawberries – essential not
    only for the taste but of course
    the colour of the finished
    vinegar
2 pt/1 l white wine vinegar
2 lb/1 kg golden granulated sugar
    or less
optional extras: ¼ pt/150 ml
    brandy
2–3 dried red chillies

In a large bowl – on no account should it be metal – crush the strawberries with the back of a wooden spoon. You are not trying to mash them, just bruise them. If using the chillies, slit lengthwise and lay on the fruit. Pour over the vinegar and cover with a cloth. Allow to steep for 4 days in a cool but not cold place. Stir two or three times a day.

Strain, preferably through muslin, into an enamel or stainless steel pan. Add the sugar, using between 8–16 oz/250–500 g sugar for each pint/600 ml of liquid. The enormous variation is a matter of taste – I prefer the lesser amount normally, but there have been occasions on which the more syrupy vinegar has proved its worth. If you want it primarily for use as a cordial, use the greater amount.

Warm the liquid, stirring, until the sugar has dissolved. Bring to the boil and boil for 10 minutes. Add the brandy, if required. Pour into warm, sterilised bottles. Screw down the top or stopper with a clean cork and seal with melted paraffin wax.

Peach Vinegar

2 lb/1 kg ripe peaches – bargains can be found in supermarkets and on stalls in high summer by purchasing punnets of Italian peaches. They are often on the small side and are less than perfect for the table, but most useful here or in chutneys.
2 in/5 cm fresh root ginger
1 fresh green chilli
2 dried red chillies
5 black peppercorns
12 allspice berries
2 sticks cinnamon bark
8 coriander seeds
2 pt/1 l white wine vinegar

Wash the peaches. Scald with boiling water and remove skins. Quarter, and place skins and flesh in a large glass or glazed earthenware bowl. Cut the ginger into four equal pieces and bash with a rolling pin. Add to the peaches. Cut the chillies, red and green, in two from top to bottom and place in the bowl. Roughly crush the spices, except the cinnamon, in a pestle and mortar.

Push the cinnamon bark into the peaches and scatter over the other spices. Pour on the vinegar and leave to stand, covered, for 6 days. Stir two or three times a day.

Strain and bottle. Alternatively, sugar can be added as in the previous recipe and the vinegar boiled up before bottling.

Flavoured Oils

Another way of creating more flavour in a salad apart from the fruit and herb vinegars is to use a flavoured oil. Very popular in Mediterranean cooking are the simple conjunctions of olive oil with herbs. Use over plain boiled pasta, pizza, focaccia or bruschetta and also on rice and vegetables. Peppers add pungency, garlic gives earthiness and other spices impart exotic resonances. True gourmandism must surely call for truffle-scented oil. The parings of truffles can be used very profitably for this purpose.

Flavoured oils come into their own at barbecues, brushed over split baby aubergines, courgettes and peppers.

Exact quantities are not necessary, merely a decent *glass* bottle of olive oil, to which you add a combination of the following before sealing and allowing to steep for 6 weeks. Shake the bottle from time to time and keep in the dark. You can then strain into clean bottles and reseal, if liked. Use any of these herbs, singly or combined:

basil
thyme
oregano
chives
mint
fennel
lavender
rosemary
savory
tarragon
parsley, including stalks
zest of lemon
chopped garlic
dried chillies
fresh green chillies
sundried tomatoes
peppercorns – green, pink, white or black
coriander – leaves, stalks and seeds
allspice

In almond or other light oil try also:

cinnamon bark
flowers – hibiscus, rose and jasmine
vanilla pod
ginger

11
Ices, Mousses and Creams

T his chapter contains some of my favourite recipes. Ices, in all their forms, are not difficult to make. If you have never attempted to make your own before, be warned – it is impossible to settle for synthetics again. Ice cream will have to mean ice cream, not ice non-milk vegetable fat. Weight or cholesterol watchers can choose granitas or sorbets. Do not reserve the ices just for the summer – Muscovites buy ice creams even in the depths of winter. Try other fruits and vegetables too – avocado will make an excellent parfait, feijoa a great sorbet. Serve iced fruits with fresh fruits. Contrast hot with cold, serve with fruit pies or sauces or try a Baked Alaska.

If you have an electric ice cream maker, follow the manufacturer's instructions as models vary.

Vegetarian jellies do not set as well or as clear as gelatine ones. Consequently there are only a few recipes where I have used gelozone.

Carrot, Orange and Ginger Sorbet

A starter or between-course palate-cleanser. The richness of colour of this fragrant ice comes from a light muscovado sugar and excellent carrots. Serve in cucumber cups, drizzled with a little spiced yoghurt. The Chinese are said to have invented ice cream centuries ago; their influence is still here too with exotic soy and root ginger flavouring this delightful sorbet.

The antecedents of this sorbet are obvious – the soup of the same name – it is one example of how the creative process can work.

1 lb/500 g well-flavoured carrots,
    coarsely grated
1 onion, chopped
1½ in/3–4 cm peeled root ginger,
    finely chopped
3 sweet oranges
2 tbs light oil
2 tbs dark soy sauce
7 oz/200 g muscovado sugar
7 fl oz/200 ml water
2 egg whites
salt, pepper

In a heavy-bottomed pan with a close-fitting lid put the oil and the onions. Cook slowly until softening without colouring. Add the ginger and soy sauce, stirring over the heat for a couple of minutes. Grate the rind from one orange and squeeze the juice from all. Add to the pan with the grated carrot and mix well. Cover tightly and cook over a gentle heat until the carrot is soft.

Make a syrup by dissolving the sugar in the water and heating until 230°F 110°C. Place the carrots in a food processor or liquidiser and pour on the syrup. Blend until very smooth. Pass through a sieve into a large bowl.

Cool, then chill well. Whisk the egg whites with a pinch of salt until stiff. Season the carrot mixture well and fold through the egg white. Freeze until mushy. Scrape out of the bowl and beat well. Return to the freezer and freeze until firm. Allow to soften for 30 minutes in the fridge before serving.

Celery and Apple Sorbet

A scoop of sorbet served surrounded by a fan of red Worcester Pearmain slices would make a delightful start to an Autumn dinner party. Serve with small warm cheese-and-onion croissants and a good traditional medium dry sparkling cider.

1 small head celery
2 large Bramley apples – a little
    under 2 lb/1 kg in weight
2 egg whites
8 oz/250 g fromage frais
chervil or flat parsley
sugar
salt, pepper
Calvados (optional)

Wash and roughly chop the celery, including the leaves, and place in a pan with a little water. Bring to the boil and simmer 10 minutes. Cut up the apples and add to the celery. Cover and cook until soft. Push through a sieve. Cool. Chop the herbs; there should be about a tablespoon. Stir into the purée with some sugar, salt and pepper to taste. A little Calvados could be added. Place in the freezer and freeze until slushy. Beat well. Fold in the fromage frais. Whip the egg whites until stiff, then fold them through. Return to the freezer. When beginning to solidify again, take out and beat. Do this twice before freezing until firm.

Soften slightly in the fridge before serving.

Cucumber and Mint Ice

A sauce of spiced yoghurt drizzled over this cooling ice looks and tastes divine. Into ¼pt/150 ml plain yoghurt beat 1 tbs good tomato purée, a crushed clove of garlic and 1 tsp ground roasted cumin seeds.

Save the peel from the cucumber and wind into roses, securing the bottoms with 'pins' of thyme stalk or part of a cocktail stick. Use to decorate the ice, with small sprigs of mint.

As an excellent palate cleanser, serve a small scoop in a chilled glass with a teaspoon of Grappa over it.

Try a light, zesty wine such as the unusual dry English, Avalon Seyval, from Somerset. Alternatively go for a fizz: somehow it seems in the nature of ices to be rather frivolous, so bubbles are appropriate – a Sekt maybe.

2 medium or 4 small, sweet
    cucumbers
1 large lemon
1 tsp sea salt
2 tsp caster sugar
white pepper
good handful mint
2 egg whites

Remove the ends of the cucumbers and pare the skin. Cut up roughly and then whizz in a food processor until smooth. Finely grate the lemon and squeeze it. Add the zest and juice to the cucumber purée and season with the sugar, salt and white pepper. Strip the mint leaves from the stalks and chop finely or put through a herb mill. Stir into the cucumber and then place in a flat, covered dish. Freeze until firming but still a bit mushy.

Whisk the egg whites until stiff. Beat the semi-frozen cucumber hard and fold through the egg white. Return to the freezer. Refreeze until slightly firmer. Scrape back into the food processor and process until smooth again. Return to the freezer and freeze until firm. Allow to soften in the fridge for 30 minutes before serving.

Mexican Chocolate Cream

The slightly grainy cream is good on its own or over pears. It is not overly sweet and the wine you choose should not be either. Try a Château de Pocé Touraine from the Loire, which has the sort of slightly sweet pear taste of the Chenin Blanc grapes.

1¾pt/1l full cream milk
2oz/60g sugar
1 stick cinnamon
6oz/200g plain dark chocolate
2tbs fine cornmeal
2 egg yolks

Melt the chocolate, with a quarter of the milk and the cinnamon, in a double boiler over simmering water. Add the sugar and stir well. In a separate bowl, beat the egg yolks with the cornmeal. Add the hot chocolate milk to the egg yolks, a little at a time. Beat in well. Add the rest of the milk and return to the heat. Cook, while stirring continuously, as the mixture thickens. Allow to just simmer, still stirring, for 2 minutes. Remove the cinnamon stick. Turn into individual ramekins and top with a swirl of whipped cream and a grating of chocolate when thoroughly chilled.

Fruits of the Forest Bombe

If you cannot find a forest handy for berry gathering, you could call this bombe, less romantically, Soft Fruit Bombe. Any of the ice creams are good to eat on their own. Chocofreaks might like to use very dark chocolate, melted with a little white vegetable fat, to coat the pudding basin before building up the ice cream layers.

To drink with the Bombe I would recommend an Angas Brut Rosé, a fizzy pink wine, delicate and fruity from the same area in Australia as the liqueur Muscat previously mentioned.

1 pt/600 ml double cream
8 egg yolks – use the whites to
    make sorbets or mergingues
1 lb strawberries – preferably tiny
    wild ones
12 oz/375 g cloudberries or
    raspberries, wild if possible
4 oz/125 g bilberries or blueberries
appropriate liqueurs, e.g.:
    Crème des Fraises
    Cloudberry liqueur
    Crème aux Framboises
    Crème aux Myrtilles
    1 vanilla pod
8 oz/250 g caster sugar

Slit the vanilla pod and put it with the cream in the top of a double boiler and heat until the cream is steaming. Have ready the egg yolks beaten with 4 oz/125 g of the sugar. Pour the hot cream onto the yolks in a steady stream, beating all the time. Strain back into the pan and cook, stirring continuously, until the mixture coats the back of the spoon. Stirring in a figure of eight, or elliptically across the middle of the pan, like a 'Spirograph' pattern, is better than just stirring around and around. Allow to cool.

Meanwhile, prepare the fruits separately. Top and tail the bilberries or blueberries and place in a small pan over a gentle heat until they begin to pop. Add the Crème aux Myrtilles and sugar – not too much, retain the sharp clean edge of the fruit. Cool.

Hull the strawberries. If cultivated ones, purée with about 1 oz/30 g sugar. Stir in 1–2 tbs Crème des Fraises. Put tiny wild strawberries in a bowl with the sugar and liqueur and crush lightly with the back of a spoon whilst combining.

Push the cloudberries or raspberries through a sieve, discarding the pips. Add the liqueur and sweeten the purée to taste.

Pour half the custard over the strawberries and fold through. Place in the freezer in a covered tray. Of the remaining custard, pour one-third over the blue/bilberries and two-thirds over the cloud/raspberries. Gently combine the fruits and custard and put them in the freezer. As the mixtures begin to harden, stir them from time to time. When the strawberry ice cream is about the consistency of commercial 'soft-scoop', pack it around the sides and base of a deep pudding basin or mould. Aim for an even layer, smoothing it out with the back of a spoon. Replace in the freezer, freezing until firm. Then cover the strawberry layer with the same of cloud/raspberry icecream. Freeze again before filling the centre with the bil/blueberries. Press each ice cream firmly onto the other. Pack down tightly, cover and freeze. Allow to stand 30 minutes in the fridge before serving. Dip the basin in hot water briefly and then invert over a plate. Cut in wedge slices like a cake. This will be easier to do if the knife is dipped in hot water too.

If you have not got the patience for the layering as described above, simply put the bilberry ice cream flat into the base of the basin (this will be the top when inverted), followed by the raspberry ice cream and then the strawberry. The turned out dome will show bands of colours like a Neapolitan block.

Layered Mousse

To show this mousse off to its best advantage you will need tall glass flutes. If you have none, use whisky tumblers, increasing the number of cherries in the bottom to three.

Chocolate and wine really do not go together – instead serve a small ice-cold shot of Maraschino, which could be used instead of the rum in the mousse if preferred.

4 oz/125 g dark chocolate
4 oz/125 g white chocolate
1 tbs espresso
3 tbs white rum
4 egg yolks
5 egg whites
2 oz/60 g unsalted butter
8 large black cherries
1/4 pt/150 ml double cream

Stone 4 of the cherries and place 1 in the base of each glass. Pour 1/2 tbs rum over each cherry and allow to stand, covered in a cool place, for 12 hours.

In two separate bowls over hot water melt the 2 chocolates. Add the remaining rum to the white chocolate and the espresso to the bitter. When the chocolates are completely melted, beat 2 egg yolks and add 1 oz/30 g butter into each. Beat very well until quite smooth. Whisk the egg whites until stiff. Fold half into each mixture. Do it gently and do not stir or beat.

Place a spoon of dark mousse on top of the cherry, then some white, then some dark, and so on until the glass is full. Do not try to press down or smooth. Gently tap the glass to settle the contents if necessary. Chill well for 4 hours. Whip the cream and pipe a rosette in the centre of the glass. Top with a cherry, retaining its stem if possible.

Tomato Mousseline

The secret of success with this mousseline is in the tomatoes. As with so many other recipes, I favour Gardners' Delight because it is the best readily available tomato. When the new 'flavour-improved' designer fruit come onstream in my local stores I will possibly change my practices. Failing any good homegrown supplies the cherry tomato reigns supreme.

Fromage frais with cream is available in large tubs in the chilled cabinets of big supermarkets. I prefer it here to negligible fat variety or to the creamy strained Greek yoghurt. Those alternatives can be used and, indeed, so can whipped cream, but balance is best served by the 8% fat fromage frais – not too sharp, not too rich.

Wine is mildly problematical; try an Italian red, a Valpolicella or, on a different taste plane, a German white, a Spätlese Riesling. Either works, up to a point – I would be inclined to wait for the next course for wine if having the mousseline as a starter.

The mousseline, although it mounds and will 'spoon', is not, in these proportions, going to set very firm. You can increase the gelozone and/or add egg yolks, but this is detrimental to the flavour and texture. Better to retain the delicacy and serve in ramekins or cucumber rings than to turn out an inferior mousse. Surround the ramekin with a salad of thinly sliced, peeled cucumber, sprinkled with caster sugar, chopped apple mint, lime juice and white pepper.

2 lb/1 kg cherry tomatoes
2 tbs gelozone
2 tsp olive oil
2 cloves garlic
10 oz/300 g fromage frais with
*   cream (8% fat)*
pinch of salt, black pepper
sugar

Put the garlic through a press and into a heavy-bottomed pan with the oil. Place over a very low heat to soften slightly. Cut the tomatoes in half and add to the pan. Cover and cook slowly until the tomatoes have all broken down. Push the pulp through a sieve into a clean pan. Season to taste with salt, a pinch of sugar and plenty of black pepper. If the tomatoes are a little on the insipid side, a twist of lime could help and some freshly chopped herbs. Cool a little before sprinkling over the gelozone whilst whisking. Reheat, still whisking, until steaming and thickened. Cool, whisking occasionally. Fold through the fromage frais. Check seasoning, spoon into ramekins, then chill well.

If using cucumber rings, chill the mixture and fill the rings just before serving. To make the rings, cut a large cucumber into 2½in/6.5cm lengths. Stand the pieces upright on a board. Insert a very sharp knife vertically into the flesh ⅛in/0.25cm in from the skin. Keeping the same distance from the skin, hollow out the flesh. It is possible to carve the centre out in one piece which can then be sliced for the previously mentioned salad. Ensure the base of the ring stands flush against the plate before spooning in the mousseline.

Raspberry Brulée

A very easy dessert. Most soft fruits can be used. Chop larger fruits into bite-sized pieces. Peaches and strawberries are particularly good. Frozen fruit can be used at a pinch, but tinned are best avoided. In the depths of Winter try a combination of clementines and cointreau.

1 punnet raspberries
1 lb/500g fromage frais with cream
  (find this in a large tub on the
  supermarket dairy shelf)
a little brandy or fruit liqueur
demerara sugar

Preheat grill to very hot. Divide the fruit between 4 heat-proof ramekins and drizzle the brandy or liqueur over. Spoon the fromage frais over the fruit and level the top. Cover each with a ¼in/7mm layer of sugar and place under the grill until the sugar caramelises, allow to stand a minute or two then serve.

Wensleydale, Garlic and Three Herb Cheesecake

For a delightful summer luncheon, serve this savoury cheesecake with a green or fruit-based salad. The Avocado, Tomato and Orange Salad (p. 59) is an admirable companion for it. Endless variations are possible in the combinations of herbs used. Just try to use fresh herbs, chop them finely and do not be heavy-handed. Green garlic if available would be best.

A luscious Orvieto or a crisp Chardonnay both work remarkably well here.

4 oz/125 g crushed wholemeal biscuits
2 oz/60 g melted butter
8 oz/250 g Yorkshire curd or cottage cheese
4 oz/125 g grated Wensleydale cheese
1/4 pt/150 ml plain yoghurt – Greek set sheep's milk is very good
3 eggs, separated
2 large cloves garlic, crushed
salt, freshly ground black pepper – there is no substitute
fresh herbs: a mixture of chervil, lovage and a hint of mint is good, but experiment, although you should avoid rosemary in this instance, it is a little too insistent. (When chopped, there should be a scant tablespoon, but this would vary according to taste and the herbs used.)

Add the biscuit crumbs to the melted butter, mixing well. Lightly grease a loose-bottomed 8 in/20 cm deep cake tin. Press the biscuit mixture into the base of the tin.

Beat together the egg yolks and yoghurt, add the cottage cheese and beat again. Stir in the garlic, Wensleydale cheese and herbs and season with a little salt and a generous grinding of black pepper. Whisk the egg whites until stiff then fold into the cheese mixture very gently.

Spoon the mixture over the biscuit base and bake at gas mark 3/325°F/170°C for 45 minutes until set and lightly browned. Allow to cool in the tin for 10 minutes, if serving warm. Run a knife around the edge to loosen, then slip the sides off. To serve cold, chill in the tin. We prefer it cold the following day.

For a truly splendid buffet centrepiece, double the quantities given, bake it for 1 hour in a 12 in/30 cm tin at gas mark 2/300°F/150°C and chill well. Decorate with fine slices of truffle or, less extravagantly, with the chestnut or brown cap mushroom. Glaze with a champagne or white wine jelly using 2 tsp agar-agar to 1/2pt/300 ml wine. Heat only half of the wine with the agar-agar; when thick whisk in the rest, spoon over the cheesecake and return to the refrigerator.

Serve unmoulded on a platter strewn with borage and sweet cicely flowers, pale nasturtium petals and feathery fennel and curly or frisée endive leaves.

Kiwi Sorbet

The kiwi could have been made for sorbet. The fruit's clear green flesh is beautiful iced. The only additions are sugar syrup and egg whites – the flavours are clean and fresh.

A light sparkling wine, even on the dryish side, such as one of the Germans (Henkletrocken or Kellertreppchen) or the better known French (Veuve du Vernay) would do the sorbet justice. A grown-up version of an ice-cream soda could be tried if guests aren't too sniffy!

6 large ripe kiwi fruit
7 oz/200 g caster sugar
14 fl oz/400 ml water
2 egg whites

Dissolve the sugar in the water and bring to the boil. Boil 5 minutes and cool. Peel the kiwi fruit and place in a food processor or blender. Purée with the sugar syrup and freeze until mushy. Whisk the egg whites until they form soft peaks. Beat the semi-frozen mixture and then fold through the egg whites. Return to the freezer for 30 minutes before scraping the mixture back into the food processor bowl and whizzing to break down all lumps. Return to the freezer and repeat the processing in 20 minutes. Cover and freeze until firm.

The sorbet will need to soften slightly before serving.

Peach Parfait

Another very easy iced cream. Serve with a warm reduction of raspberries flavoured with a crème aux framboises liqueur. Although the recipe says to freeze in moulds, you can, of course, freeze in a covered container and serve in scoops. Remember to transfer to the fridge for half an hour before serving to soften slightly. Apricots and mangoes can also be used.

A well chilled bottle of Muscat de Beaumes de Venise would be most welcome here.

4 ripe peaches
4 eggs
4 oz/125 g golden caster sugar
½ pt/300 ml double cream

Scald the peaches and skin them. Halve and stone them. Either work through a sieve or purée in a food processor. Separate the eggs. In a bowl over hot water, beat the yolks and sugar until very light, thick and creamy. Whisk the egg whites until stiff and whip the cream until mounding. Fold the purée through the egg yolks, then fold in the cream. Lastly fold in the egg whites. Spoon into individual metal moulds and freeze until firm. Alternatively, freeze in a ring mould and fill the centre with raspberries when turned out.

Petites Terrines

U se 'baby Hovis' loaf tins to set these jellied layers of tender fresh vegetables. If you do not feel extravagant enough for truffles, use snippets of good black olives. The visual effect will be similar, but of course the flavour won't be the same.

Good old Châteauneuf du Pape, mellowed over five years or so, is a big enough wine to cope with the truffle and Calvados.

1 tinned black truffle
4 quail's eggs
1 pt/600 ml good clear vegetable stock
1 tbs Calvados
1–2 tsp gelozone (agar-agar powder)
8 oz/250 g thin leeks
4 oz/125 g baby carrots
8 oz/250 g fine courgettes – yellow if possible

Line the tins with wetted greaseproof paper. Chill. Clean and trim the vegetables. Cut into even strips ¼ in/0.5 cm wide and simmer in the stock until just tender. Remove with a slotted spoon and cool. Hard boil the eggs, 4–5 minutes, then plunge into cold water. Peel and slice. Finely slice the truffle.

Sprinkle the gelozone over the stock and whisk in with the Calvados. Heat until thickened.

Spoon a little stock into the bottom of each tin and arrange the egg and truffle slices. Chill the tins, keeping the remaining stock warm. Layer in the vegetables when the tops are set, moistening with stock as you go. When the tins are full, chill well until set. Then turn out and surround with ribbons of sweet red pepper, charred under a flame then peeled. Serve with good bread.

Pineapple and Cream Cheese Sorbet

I can almost forgive the old-bat-out-of-hell impersonation of the cook/owner of a Suffolk wine bar as I got some of the idea for this ice after trying her Mascarpone and Geranium Sorbet. It was *the* best thing on the menu by far. The other influence was probably those tubs of cottage cheese and pineapple pieces in the chill cabinet at the supermarket. They are almost nice. This is wonderful: the freshness of pineapple with a little more body than most sorbets. Good on its own or served in a coupe with contrasting ices – blackcurrant, strawberry or kiwi; but stunning as a Baked Alaska-type pudding. Save the pineapple's greenery. Mould the ice into a pineapple shape, freezing hard. Stand on a round of sponge cake, top with the leaves and pipe with a thick coating of meringue rosettes to resemble the pineapple's exterior. Dust with icing sugar. Cover the leaves with foil and pop into a very hot oven for 2–3 minutes. Remove the foil and serve straight away.

A lightish fizzy wine, as in a sweet Vouvray or an Italian spumante, is good with many ices.

1 medium-sized ripe pineapple – it will smell *ripe, also a leaf pulled from the crown will come away easily*
8 oz/250 g cream cheese
7 oz/210 g golden granulated sugar
14 fl oz/420 ml water
2 tbs Kirsch
2 egg whites

Dissolve the sugar in the water and boil hard for 5 minutes. Peel the pineapple and roughly chop. The top could be sliced off and the flesh cut and scooped out, with the pineapple's skin left intact. The empty shell can then be used to serve the finished sorbet. Place the fruit in a food processor bowl and pour over the hot syrup. Process with the Kirsch until smooth. Cool, then freeze until mushy. Process again briefly, incorporating the cream cheese. Whip the egg whites until softly peaking and fold through. Place in the freezer again and stir from time to time until firm. Allow to soften slightly before serving.

Rhubarb and Ginger Sorbet

When a combination works it makes sense to try it in different guises. I therefore make no apology for repeating myself in the sorbets after the soups. If you have a favourite pairing, attempt something more unusual with the familiar. Apple and cinnamon need not only be in a pie – a soup or a jam or a terrine are all possibilities. The creative process in cooking is not just a matter of an inspirational bolt from the blue, but sometimes it is a matter of evolution. At times it may be difficult to recall, or even know, the actual progenitors of an idea as the evolving takes so many twists, turns and tangential diversions. You do not have to be specially gifted, just open and prepared to experiment. You should never feel too tied to a recipe – if you are cooking, you are in control.

Rhubarb makes a good cleansing sorbet that could be used between courses, as a starter or, a little sweeter, as a fresh pudding. Ginger wine, with or without the enrichment of frothy egg yolks (à la zabaglione), makes a good accompaniment to the sorbet as dessert.

I am hestitant to recommend a wine to partner the astringency of rhubarb, tempered though it is with the sugar. I would be inclined to serve it without any as a starter and with an equable sweet wine for the pudding. An odd but wonderful Romanian dessert wine to turn up in a local supermarket has been the Tamaioasa.

It is a nice and extremely pretty idea to make a couple of sorbets and serve them in small ovals of contrasting colours in a glass coupe or on a white plate. The green of the Kiwi Sorbet (p. 262) is a stunning counterpoint to the pink of the rhubarb and the flavours are excellent together.

1½lb/750g young pink rhubarb
root ginger
14floz/420ml water
7oz/210g golden granulated sugar
    (+ 1–2oz/30–60g extra to
    taste for the pudding sorbet)
3 egg whites
1 dried chilli and a few black
    peppercorns (optional, for the
    starter)

Wipe and trim the rhubarb. Bruise the root ginger with a blunt instrument. Layer the ginger, sugar and rhubarb in a deep bowl and leave overnight.

Place the contents of the bowl into a pan with the water and the chilli and peppercorns, if using. Slowly bring to the boil, and boil for 5 minutes. Pass through a sieve, removing the chilli, ginger and peppercorns.

Cool quickly, then freeze until mushy around the edges. Whisk the egg whites until softly peaking. Scrape the almost frozen rhubarb into a bowl and beat hard. You could whizz in a food processor for a few seconds, if you prefer. Fold in the egg whites, combining so no lumps of white bubbles are showing. Return to the freezer. When firming around the edges, turn into a bowl again and beat. Repeating this process once more will give a smoother sorbet but it is not essential – the graininess of the larger crystals that occurs with less churning is pleasant in a sorbet but unwelcome in an ice cream. Freeze until firm.

Allow to soften for 30 minutes in the refrigerator before serving. Whilst semi-frozen the sorbet can be piped or moulded for an extra decorative effect.

Burnt Cream with Rhubarb

At the other end of the year, use lightly stewed and quartered quinces. Guava makes an unusual alternative. The cream, of course, is a classic English dish, dating back to the eighteenth century. The French call it either crème brulée or crème au miroir.

Drink small glasses of well-chilled ginger wine. Usually thought of in terms of Christmas and log fires, it is most pleasant as a pudding wine.

1 pt/600 ml double cream
4 free range eggs
1 lb/500 g long, thin, deep pink
  sticks of forced rhubarb
golden granulated sugar

Wipe the rhubarb and cut it into ½ in/1 cm pieces, place in a pan with a minimum of water and stew until just soft. Divide between 6 ramekins, reserving a little.

Heat 16 fl oz/480 ml of the cream. Beat the eggs with 3 tbs sugar. Pour the hot cream onto them, beating all the time. Strain into a heatproof bowl. Cook over hot water until the custard coats the spoon thickly. Spoon over the rhubarb, chill.

Cover the surface evenly with a layer of sugar and place under a hot grill until caramelised. Cool, top with a spoon of the remaining cream that has been whipped and a piece of rhubarb.

Tomato and Stilton Ice Cream

A pretty pinky-red ice cream. Serve in cucumber cups as the Mousseline (p. 259), or in tomato lilies or on a green bed of salad leaves moulded in copper shell tins.

When I first tried out savoury ices, at the beginning of the Eighties, people were amazed; these days they are more blasé. I used the recipe for an early competition entry. The local radio station thought it a huge joke, especially in a tourist trap village like ours where every other shop sells 'homemade' ice cream. I was the novelty item on the news. If you would like to be frivolous with the ice cream, make savoury cones out of thinly rolled cheese pastry wrapped around a cream horn mould. Serve the ice cream in scoops in the cones and top with a cherry ... tomato.

Try the ice cream with a white Corbières, served well chilled.

1 lb/500 g good red tomatoes,
*   roughly chopped*
1 lemon
1–2 tbs vodka
pinch cayenne pepper
2 free range eggs, separated
4oz/125 g Stilton
1/2 pt/300 ml double cream
salt, pepper
sugar

Squeeze the lemon juice into a pan. Add the chopped tomatoes, skin and seeds, and cook until soft and pulpy. Sieve into a clean pan, stir in the vodka and season with a pinch sugar, a pinch cayenne, sea salt and freshly ground black pepper. Beat in the egg yolks and cook over a low heat until the mixture thickens; if you are faint-hearted, cook it in a double boiler. Stir constantly. Take off heat. Crumble the Stilton into the tomatoes, stirring well until it melts into the mixture. Cool.

Whip the cream until it just holds its shape. Spoon into the Stilton/tomato mixture, gently combining. Whisk the egg whites until they form soft peaks. Fold through the tomatoes. Freeze in a flat container; when mushy scrape into a bowl and beat well. Return to the freezer until almost firm, beat again. Either freeze in moulds or in a covered box. Allow to soften slightly before serving.

Mascarpone and Amaretto Baskets

Attractive, hedonistic fare. A rich fruity end to a light dinner. The baskets can be obtained from any good deli or, better still, made by shaping the still-warm almond tuiles or brandy snaps around the bottoms of 1 lb jars after they come out of the oven. These can be made a dozen or so at a time, and keep well in an airtight container.

Alternatively, coat the back of 4 savoy cabbage leaves with a fairly thick layer of melted chocolate. When cold, carefully peel off to leave a beautifully textured half shell to cradle the peach.

Serve with a well chilled Taltarni Brut Taché, a pretty pinky sparkling wine from Australia. It sets the peaches off wonderfully.

8 oz/250 g Mascarpone
2 oz/60 g lexia raisins, chopped
2 oz/60 g blanched almonds,
* chopped*
1 tsp zest sweet orange
2 large Italian peaches
4 baskets of Almond Tuile or
* brandy snap*
Amaretto (almond liqueur)

Soak the raisins, almonds and zest in a little Amaretto ovenight. Scald the peaches and peel. Halve them and poach gently in a little water and Amaretto. Cool. Before serving beat the macerated raisins and nuts into half the Mascarpone and divide between the baskets. Top with a peach half, cut-side down. Pipe the remaining Mascarpone around each peach and serve.

Summer Pudding

The ingredients for this old-fashioned recipe may sound rather unprepossessing but if you have never tried a summer pud you really haven't enjoyed summer's bounty to the full. Don't be fooled by frozen commercial imitations, accept no substitute: make your own. Double or clotted cream is the essential accompaniment.

The choice of wine will ultimately depend on the fruit used but a Blanquette de Limoux, a soft, slightly buttery sparkler would be quite a good choice for a pudding where strawberries predominated.

white bread, preferably a milk loaf – at our baker's this is a fine, white, cylindrical loaf
a mixture of strawberries, raspberries, currants (red, black or white), loganberries, blueberries, mulberries, etc. Early in the season, lightly stewed rhubarb can also be added. Use in any combination (the amount varies to fill available basins – approx 1½ lb/750 g).
honey to taste
2 tbs Crème aux Myrtilles
lemon geranium leaf (optional)

Slice the bread to about ¼ in/1 cm thick. Fit into individual pudding basins, overlapping the slices, using the crusts to make a pattern. Cover the bottom and sides ensuring there are no gaps. Top and tail currants, hull strawberries and raspberries, etc. In a saucepan, heat the currants with the geranium leaf until they start to pop. Add berries and heat briefly until their juices start to run. Sweeten to taste with a *little* honey. Strain off juice and add the crème aux myrtilles.

Brush the bread all over with the juice. Pack the fruit tightly into the pudding basins. Pour over any remaining juice. Cover with more bread slices. Sit a weight on top. Leave in a cold place for at least 4 but preferably 8–12 hours.

When ready to serve, slip a palette knife around the basin, cover with a plate and invert pudding onto the plate.

Top with a rosette of double cream into which a little honey and 1 tbs Crème aux Myrtilles has been beaten.

Filled Cake

A prosaic title for a gorgeous unexpected pudding. An ordinary-looking chocolate-covered cake is cut open to reveal a pink and creamy centre, studded with strawberries or cherries.

I like a soft but less sweet white wine with chocolate. The Tokay d'Alsace or Pinot Gris succeeds where many others fail. A *Hungarian* Tokay is not the same at all.

If you have to 'plate' the pudding to serve, make it in a loaf tin. Better, though, to cut the cake at the table to allow the surprise of the filling to be enjoyed by all.

4 eggs
6 oz/175 g golden caster sugar
3 oz/75 g plain flour
1 oz/25 g cocoa
8 oz/250 g small strawberries or
    stoned black cherries
4 oz/125 g raspberries
12 oz/375 g Mascarpone or other
    cream cheese
¼ pt/150 ml soured cream
icing sugar
Crème de Framboises
8–10 oz/250–300 g dark chocolate
1–2 oz/30–60 g white chocolate
    (optional)
½ oz/15 g white vegetable fat

Warm a large mixing bowl by filling it full of boiling water and allowing it to stand whilst you grease and line an 8 in/20 cm round springform cake tin and an 8 in/20 cm square one. Pour away the water and quickly dry the bowl. Whisk together the eggs and the caster sugar in it, until the mixture is very thick and the trail from the whisk sits on the surface. Sift in the flour and cocoa. Fold it through very gently. Pour half into each tin and bake about 18–20 minutes at gas mark 5/375°F/190°C. It should feel firm and springy. Turn out onto a rack to cool.

When cold remove the lining paper. Clean the round tin and reline. Split the round cake and trim any crispy edges. Fit the top half of the cake into the base of the tin. Sprinkle all over with liqueur – fruit juice can be used if preferred. Halve the square sponge and trim into strips to fit around the sides of the cake tin. Pour some liqueur onto a plate and dip the strips in it before fitting in the tin.

Sieve the raspberries, sweeten to taste with icing sugar. Beat the Mascarpone and beat in the soured cream. Whip until thick. Fold the raspberry purée through the cream. Spoon some onto the sponge base, scatter over some strawberries or cherries and cover with more filling mixture. Continue in this way until all the fruit and cream cheese has been used up. Cover with the remaining sponge round and sprinkle with a little more Crème de Framboises. Lay a flat plate on top and weigh it down. Chill overnight.

Melt 8 oz/250 g dark chocolate with the white fat. The best way to do this is in a basin over hot water. Stir to combine. Remove the cake from the tin. Pour over the chocolate, spreading it evenly over the sides and top. Allow to set and serve.

If desired, the top can be decorated with chocolate frills, dark or white or both, arranged like an exotic bloom with overlapping petals working in to the centre of the cake. Chocolate leaves could be moulded instead and placed like a garland around the edge.

To make the frills or caraque, spread melted chocolate over an ungreased, smooth surface to thickness of a little under ¼ in/0.5 cm. Kitchen laminate worktop, marble, or the back of a baking tin will do. Leave to just set, then, working fast, scrape the chocolate using the side of a pallete knife or a wallpaper stripper held at an angle of 45°. Beware, the frills are very delicate; move with the point of a knife.

Leaves are simple to make. Merely brush melted chocolate over the upper side of clean, unsprayed garden leaves. Rose and apple leaves work particularly well. Leave to harden on a sheet of greaseproof before peeling off the green leaf.

Blackbottom Cheesecake

The base of this creamy exotic cheesecake is very dark, sticky, fudgey chocolate. The cheesecake is a light but rich mixture of double cream, soured cream and cream cheese flavoured with passionfruit. The cream is topped with 'flowers' of fresh strawberries and set off with a crescent of strawberry purée. Make the bases using crumpet rings for individual servings. A guest at my house once proposed to this ultimate chocolate confection!

A sweet-but-not-sweet wine to serve with it is the Coteaux de Layon, Château du Breuil.

2oz/60g dark chocolate, at least
    47% cocoa solids but preferably
    60% +
1 tbs espresso coffee
2oz/60g golden granulated sugar
1 large free range egg
2oz/60g unsalted butter
dash of dark rum
¼pt/150ml double cream
¼pt/150ml cultured sour cream
4oz/125g cream cheese
8oz/250g deep red fragrant
    strawberries
2 passionfruits

Break up the chocolate and place in a bowl over hot water, with the sugar and the coffee and rum. Warm, stirring until the chocolate has melted. Using a large whisk, off the heat, beat in the butter in small pieces a little at a time until well combined. Then whisk in the egg.

Butter the insides of 4 crumpet rings and stand them on a baking tray lined with baking parchment. Spoon the mixture evenly between the rings and bake at gas mark 3/325°F/170°C for about 40 minutes. Cool and chill.

Beat the soured cream and cream cheese together. Halve the passionfruit and scrape into a sieve. Press the fruit through into the cream cheese, and beat in. Whip in the double cream until the mixture is quite stiff. Unmould the chocolate bases onto serving plates. Cover with a thick, even layer of cream/cheese mixture and top with thin slices of overlapping strawberries with their pointed ends radiating out like flower petals. Purée the remaining strawberries and sieve. Place a crescent of strawberry purée beside the cheesecake, piping fine lines across it with a little of the cream/cheese mixture and serve.

Marsala and Brown Bread Parfait

Who would have thought wholemeal bread could be frivolous? Made in individual pudding basins, this iced cream makes a good substitute for Christmas pudding. It *is* rich but it is also light – dress it up with a Marsala-laced hot mincemeat sauce.

Grandma introduced me to the rather unfashionable delights of Marsala on an excursion to Vipiteno in the Italian Tyrol at the tender age of fifteen. Heavy, sweet but not cloying and with more than a hint of almonds, it speaks of puddings immediately you open the bottle. Its untrendiness means it can be difficult to find – try Malmsey if you are stuck, or Amaretto. Dark rum also can be recommended.

An equally good variation is to use Kahlua, the Mexican coffee liqueur, instead of the Marsala and to add slivered chocolate to the bread before folding in.

Another alternative is to add a little orange peel and cinnamon to the crumbs halfway through toasting and to serve a frozen ball of parfait on a circlet of caramelised orange slices.

Let your imagination run free in the drinks cabinet – I am sure there are many other interesting possibilities. The recipe is a cinch as, unlike a true ice cream, there is no egg custard to fret about and no churning to be done. Make it, freeze it, eat it – three steps to heaven indeed.

I would sip Marsala too whilst eating the ice, but I'm hooked on it – saner mortals may prefer a marginally lighter sweet wine, probably one of the heady Muscats. The Australians make some extraordinary Muscats; try the Victorian ones from Brown Brothers or a Yalumba liqueur Muscat from Rutherglen of the Barossa Valley.

4 eggs
4 oz/125 g golden granulated sugar
3 oz/90 g wholemeal or maltmeal
 bread
4 tbs Marsala
¹/₂ pt/300 ml double cream

Reduce the bread to small crumbs – either in a food processor in short bursts, or by grating, or with a fork dragged over the surface. (The latter method will not work on sliced, plastic-bag 'bread'.) Spread the crumbs out in a roasting tin and sprinkle over half the sugar. Place under a medium grill and toast, turning the crumbs about often, until nicely browned. Allow to cool. Separate the eggs. Stiffly whip the whites, then whisk in the remaining sugar. Beat the cream until just beginning to mound. Whisk the egg yolks until thick and pale, beat in the Marsala. Fold the cream through the egg yolks, then gently stir in the crumbs and finally fold in the egg whites. Do not stir but *fold*, ensuring all is properly combined. Spoon into small pudding basins or into a large shallow container and freeze until firm.

Before serving, allow to soften half an hour in the fridge.

Granita with Melons

Watermelon is refreshing but many find the seeds a nuisance. My sister, when we were children, patiently threaded hers to make necklaces – it was the Sixties, beads were in. You could find yourself with enough raw materials to start a cottage industry once you have tried this Granita. The pink of the watermelon ice contrasts superbly with the pale greens and golds of the cantaloupe, ogen and charentaise melons. Galia and honeydew melons can be substituted if necessary.

The granita can be used simply as a bed on which to serve the other melons if you do not have the time to arrange it as below.

Serve with a chilled Loupiac.

1 watermelon
1 charentaise melon
1 cantaloupe melon
1 ogen melon
black peppermint or ordinary mint
1 lemon
12 oz/375 g sugar
water

Cut the watermelon in half from top to bottom. Scrape out all the flesh and push through a sieve. Reserve the rind. You need 1 pt/600 ml puréed watermelon. Dissolve 8 oz/250 g sugar in ¼pt/150 ml water. Add a strip of the lemon peel. Bring slowly to the boil and boil for 5 minutes. Cool, strain and then combine with the watermelon. Freeze in flat trays. Less coarse ice crystals will be formed if you beat the ice as it becomes slushy.

Using a parisian baller or a well-rounded teaspoon, scoop the other melons into balls. Place in a dish. Dissolve the remaining sugar in 2½fl oz/75 ml water and bring to the boil. Boil for 5 minutes then add some finely chopped mint and the juice of the lemon. Pour all over the melon balls and leave in a cool place.

To serve, soften the ice slightly. Cut the watermelon rind into wedges no thicker than 1½in/4cm across the centre. Stand the rinds on plates and pack a crescent of the ice into each. A few tiny black peppermint leaves can be laid on top to resemble the seeds, if desired. Place a little pyramid of melon balls beside the watermelon 'slice'. Spoon a little of the syrup over them.

Summer Fruit Terrine

A fresh raspberry jelly holds summer fruits in elegant layers. Made in a terrine dish or a lined loaf tin, when set it is sliced and laid on a plate puddled with cream or yoghurt feathered with Crème de Cassis. All the fruit must be ripe and perfect. The choice of fruit is dependent on availability but avoid banana and pineapple. Banana discolours and pineapple inhibits setting.

A sparkling Chardonnay, with apricotty overtones, either a French or an Antipodean, is an apt and appealing partner. If the fruit you choose is rather acid, lots of currants and blueberries, you may prefer, by way of contrast, a richer more puddingy wine – one of the Italian Moscatos still provides the fizz, with greater sweetness.

1½lb/750g raspberries
3 tbs gelozone
4oz/125g sugar
good selection of summer fruits
(about 2lb/1kg): peaches
apricots
strawberries
greengages
plums
blackcurrants
redcurrants
Doyenné
d'été pears

If using currants, top and tail and 'pop' over a gentle heat. Cool. Crush the raspberries and press through a sieve to extract the juice. Place in an enamel or stainless steel pan. Sweeten to taste with the sugar. Sprinkle over the gelozone and whisk in. Heat until steaming and thickened, lightly whisking all the time. Remove from heat but keep pan warm over hot water. Line a loaf tin or terrine with wetted greaseproof or silicone paper.

Prepare all the fruit, stoning, peeling, slicing or quartering. Spoon enough raspberry jelly into the terrine to cover the base. Lay overlapping slices of your first chosen

cream or *yoghurt*
Crème de Cassis

fruit. When the layer is complete, dribble over more raspberry jelly and then add more layers of fruit and jelly. The fruit is not suspended in jelly, rather the jelly acts as the most delicate of mortars. Be firm but gentle with the fruit, evenly layering it and packing the tin full. Finish with a layer of jelly. Cover with greaseproof or silicone paper. Cut a piece of cardboard the size of the top of the tin. Place it on top of the paper and weigh it down. If you have a pâte press use that. Chill well for about 12 hours. Dip in hot water and slip a knife around the edges before turning out and slicing. A very sharp knife makes the job so much easier.

Spoon cream onto the plate and run several fine lines of Crème de Cassis across it. Gently drag a toothpick or skewer over the surface of the cream at right angles to the Cassis, tracing lines about 1 in/2.5 cm apart. Alternate the dragging from left to right and from right to left. Other feathering patterns are possible – spiralling the Cassis and dragging in and out to the centre is very effective. If this sounds too much of a faff, just marble the Cassis into the cream using the back of a teaspoon. Lay the slice of terrine on top.

Strawberry Cheese Streusel

Not a cheesecake, not a crumble. Something different, delicious hot, warm or chilled. The fruity strawberries go exceptionally well with the mild, tangy Lancashire cheese. A soft white wine, a Jurançon with its honeyed spiciness perhaps, would be great.

8 oz/250 g Lancashire cheese, finely grated
½ pt/300 ml cultured soured cream
4 oz/125 g caster sugar
2 eggs, lightly beaten
1 lb/500 g fresh strawberries, hulled and quartered
1 tbs arrowroot
8 oz/250 g plain flour
4 oz/125 g butter
2 oz/60 g demerara sugar
1 oz/30 g porridge oats
2 oz/60 g digestive biscuit crumbs
miniature of Cointreau or Grand Marnier (optional)

Rub the butter into the flour, stir in the oats, demerara and crumbs, combining well. Press two-thirds of the mixture into the bottom of a lightly greased, deep, straight-sided pie dish 9 in/23 cm in diameter. Toss the strawberries in the arrowroot, then place in the dish on the base. Drizzle over the liqueur if using. Beat the cream and caster sugar together, then beat in the eggs. Stir in the cheese and spoon over the strawberries. Sprinkle with the remaining crumble mixture and bake at gas mark 3/325°F/170°C for 40 minutes until firm to the touch.

Alternatively divide between 4 ramekins and cook for 20–25 minutes. Serve hot or warm with cream.

If serving cold, the cake can be turned out and cut into wedges. Decorate it with piped cream and tiny strawberries with the green tops left on.

Autumn Pudding

First cousin to the more traditional Summer Pudding, made with windfall and hedgerow harvests, this is a pudding for free, almost!

Failing a sweetish country wine – I once was given a most remarkable parsnip one (yes, really) – use one of the cheaper Muscats.

enough wholemeal or granary bread to line a heatproof pudding basin
enough fruit to fill it: apples, pears, plums, damsons, blackberries, blaeberries (bilberries)
brown sugar
butter

Butter the pudding basin and sprinkle thickly with the brown sugar. Slice the bread fairly thickly and remove the crusts. Use to line the basin. Peel and roughly chop apples and pears, stone damsons and plums, wash berries. In a large saucepan, cook gently until beginning to soften. Sweeten to taste and pack into the lined basin. Top with buttered bread, butterside up. Sprinkle well with more brown sugar.

Bake at gas mark 5/375°F/190°C for 40 minutes

Allow to stand for 10 minutes, then turn out on a plate. Serve with cream, custard or ice cream.

Caramelised Pear and Ginger Pudding

An old-fashioned sponge pudding with a dark fruity top, ideally served with a Crème Anglaise (p. 231). Made in ramekins to be turned out on individual plates, this is a warming and comforting pudding.

Serve with a glass or two of Malmsey.

dark muscovado sugar
3–4 pears, preferably the firm
  Conference
crystallised ginger
4oz/125g unsalted butter
4oz/125g soft brown sugar
4oz/125g self-raising flour
2 eggs

Well grease the ramekins. Shake some dark muscovado sugar all over the insides, covering well. Peel and thinly slice the pears. Arrange in overlapping slices over the base and sides of the ramekins. In the centre of the base place a nugget of crystallised ginger.

Beat the butter until light and then beat in the soft brown sugar. Gradually beat in the eggs. Fold in the flour and spoon over the pears. Stand in a roasting tin of water and bake at gas mark 4/350°F/180°C for 20 minutes. Allow 3–5 minutes before running a knife around and turning out.

Serve on a plate, puddled with the Crème Anglaise.

12
Breads

Pictures of bread queues in the former Soviet Union showed that at least they had something worth queuing for. The success of sliced factory bread in this country is a mystery to me. Are flavour and texture such unimportant criteria in the choice of food today?

The French will buy their bread two or three times a day to ensure its freshness – the British buy theirs in plastic bags, stuffed full of 'improvers' so it 'feels' fresh for days.

Recipes are given for German, Indian and Italian breads as well as the classic French brioche and croissant. Also included in this chapter are Christmas cake and pudding. Cornbread, muffins and soda bread are not very time-consuming and add interest to soups and stews or make tea time a bit special. Freshly baked cinnamon-flavoured rolls for breakfast are worth getting out of bed for.

Even if you do not intend to become a regular home baker do try making bread at least once or twice. It is a very satisfying activity and you might find it therapeutic. You will certainly eat better bread.

Soda Bread

As Irish as potatoes and Guinness, soda bread needs no yeast or kneading. Traditionally it is shaped in a round, with a slashed cross on the top. This is either to bless the bread or to let the Devil out, depending on which bit of lore you like to believe. If you cannot get buttermilk, try half-and-half milk with yoghurt or soured cream. Carraway seeds scattered over the top before baking, although maybe not authentic, are to be recommended. I prefer the fine-milled wholewheat flour, but this a matter of taste. White flour is inappropriate, though.

The bread can be used warm or cold, with plenty of unsalted Irish farm butter – if you can get it before the intervention stores do.

1 lb/500 g wholewheat flour
1½ tsp baking soda
2 tsp cream of tartar
1 tsp salt
½ pt/300 ml buttermilk or milk and
* soured cream*
1–2 tbs molasses
1 oz/30 g white vegetable fat

Melt the white fat with the molasses. Sift the flour, salt and cream of tartar together. Mix the soda into the milk and then pour into the flour with the fat and molasses. Combine with a few brisk strokes and scrape onto a floured surface to shape into a round approximately 10 in/25 cm in diameter. Place on a well seasoned, thick baking sheet and cut a cross in the top. Bake at gas mark 6/400°F/200°C for 30 minutes.

Barmbrack

Another Irish tea-time treat. Van Morrison lyrically (as ever) recalling his early Belfast years (as often) includes barmbrack in his evocative list of winter foods in *Sense of Wonder*. For years I believed that Barmbrack must originally have been leavened with yeast as in 'barm', but no. It is in fact a corruption of the Irish *bairigen breac*, meaning speckled cake. My dictionary states that a Barmbrack is a currant bun, but I have always known it sliced thin from a loaf. Mrs Lange of Slingsby, who makes the best afternoon tea in North Yorkshire, serves it thus, but she calls it Bara Brieth. Her recipe came from a cousin in Wales. To my knowledge Bara Brieth *is* yeasted. Mrs Lange's mother made a plainer, less fruity loaf she called Bara Brith that was yeasted. A woman at the *Irish Times* confirmed that, certainly these days in Ireland, Barmbrack is sold in a loaf. Perhaps Cassell's meant 'bun' in the sense of Scottish Black Bun?

Further research uncovered two more recipes, both exactly the same but one called Lincolnshire Dough Bread and the other Irish Barnbrack (*sic*). As in the oral tradition of songs and stories, recipes too, evolve. One culture borrows from another, names are interchanged and corruption (in the nicest possible way) is rife. What follows is my childhood memory of what was termed 'barmbrack', followed by Bara Brieth as experienced from North Wales/Cheshire and with reference to Dorothy Hartley in *Food in England*.

1 lb/500 g plain flour
2 tsp baking powder
8 oz/250 g currants
4 oz/125 g afghan raisins
4 oz/125 g sultanas
7 oz/210 g soft brown sugar
1 tbs treacle
1 egg
1/2/300 ml freshly brewed or cold
    tea

Combine the dried fruit, sugar and treacle in a bowl and pour over the tea. Leave to stand at least 12 hours.

Sift the flour and baking powder. Lightly beat the egg and mix into the fruit. Stir in the flour, combining well. Spoon into a well greased loaf tin and bake for 1½ hours at gas mark 4–5/350°–375°F/180°–190°C. Allow to get quite cold before slicing. The barmbrack keeps very well – I think, like most fruited cakes, it improves with a bit of age.

Bara Brieth

1 lb/500 g granary *bread flour* – *this lends an agreeable maltiness*
1/2 oz/15 g *dried* fermipan *yeast*
4 oz/125 g *white vegetable fat or butter*
1 *egg*
8 oz/250 g *mixed dried fruit, including peel*
4 oz/125 g *brown sugar*
good pinches of ground cinnamon, allspice and salt
1/2 pt/300 ml *boiling water*

Mix together the fruit and spice and pour over the boiling water. Stand in a warm place and allow to cool to blood heat. Sift the flour and remove the whole cracked wheat grains – if there are quite a number add a bit more flour. Sift again with the salt and yeast. Rub in the fat. Pour on most of the soaking water from the fruit to make a soft dough. Add it all if necessary, and some. Flours can vary in absorbency by as much as a fifth, so precise volumes of liquid are not possible. Adding too little is preferable to too much – you can always add a little more. Knead the dough well. When the dough is smooth, knead in the dried fruit, folding and rolling them in. Shape into a loaf and put in a well greased loaf tin. Leave to rise then bake at gas mark 7/425°F/220°C for 15 minutes, then reduce the heat to gas mark 5/375°F/190°C and continue baking for another 45–60 minutes until firm and browned. Turn out and cool on a rack. Serve thinly sliced and buttered.

Fruit Cobbler

The fruit cobbler can be large and overflowing or small and dainty. The recipe illustrates the communal version. The individual ones can be made in deep ramekins with scones cut no bigger than old pennies and ⅓in/1 cm thick. Lay on the top of the previously cooked fruit, each overlapping the other slightly, to cover. Brush with milk and sprinkle with a little sugar. Bake at gas mark 5/375°F/190°C for 10 minutes or until risen and browned.

Many fruits are suitable, either on their own or in combination. With the vagaries of the English summer – heatwave followed by hailstorms – hot soft fruit is more than suitable. There have been many Wimbledons, cold and grey, when spectators would have been delighted to swap strawberries and cream for Strawberry Cobbler. In the Autumn and Winter use damsons, blackberries or elderberries with apples and pears.

8 oz/250 g plain flour
1 tsp baking powder
3 oz/90 g butter
1 egg
4 oz/125 g golden caster sugar
4 tbs plain yoghurt
a little milk
1 lb/500 g strawberries
8 oz/250 g blackcurrants
1½ tsp arrowroot – not necessary
*   for drier fruit such as apples,*
*   pears, etc*

Top and tail the blackcurrants and place in a saucepan over a gentle heat to pop. Hull the strawberries and quarter any very large ones. Dust with the arrowroot, turning the fruit about in it so they are covered. Stir the strawberries into the currants, off the heat. Sweeten to taste with caster sugar – do not overdo it, the topping is sweet too. Place in a deep pie dish.

Sift the flour with the baking powder. Rub in the butter. Stir in 2 oz/60 g caster sugar. Beat the egg and yoghurt together and mix most of it into the rubbed-in mixture to form a soft dough. Add the rest of the egg/yoghurt if the mixture is too dry.

Turn onto a lightly floured surface and scarcely knead, just enough to get rid of the cracks. Pat out gently to a ½in/1.5 cm thickness – roll if you must, but with the most delicate of strokes. Stamp out rounds with a straight (not fluted) 2 in/5 cm cutter. You could also cut diamond lozenges or simple wedges. Cut down through the dough in a single motion – do not drag the knife. In any case, lay the scones onto the fruit, overlapping them like roof tiles. Brush with a little milk and sprinkle with some sugar. Bake at gas mark 6/400°F/200°C for 20 minutes, covering the top with greaseproof after 10 minutes if browning too fast. Serve with cream (double or clotted), ice cream, yoghurt or a good custard.

Avocado and Mozzarella Loaf

This loaf, eaten after a clear soup, would be a very good lunch in the garden. Make sure the avocado is soft and ripe otherwise the filling does not meld. If you are in a hurry just cut the loaf into two rather than three layers. Variations in the loaf are possible, using combinations of different flours and meals or by adding seeds to the basic dough.

A good Normandy cider, clean and dry and well chilled, would complete the al fresco lunch picture.

1 lb/500 g flour – a mixture of ½ wholewheat and ½ plain is suggested
4 oz/125 g butter
1 tsp celery seeds, toasted
1 egg
½ pt/300 ml buttermilk or soured milk
1 medium onion
1 tsp grated zest of lemon
3 tsp baking powder
1 large or 2 small avocados
6 oz/180 g 'baby' mozzarella – these are the small rounds sold in liquid contained in plastic bags at the supermarket or in a large bowl at the Italian deli

Sift together the flours and the baking powder. Rub the butter into the flours and stir in the lemon rind and the celery seeds. Peel the onion and grate it into the flour. Combine well. Beat the egg into the milk and add to the flour, mixing just enough to make a very soft dough. Do not beat. Add a little more milk if you have very absorbent flour. Turn into a well-greased loaf tin and bake at gas mark 6/400°F/200°C for 15 minutes; reduce the heat to gas mark 4/350°F/180°C for another 25 minutes until firm, well-risen and brown.

Have ready the peeled stoned avocado and the mozzarella both in thin slices.

Allow the loaf to stand 5 minutes then split horizontally into three layers with a sharp knife. Quickly cover the cut layers with slices of avocado and cheese. Season with a little salt and a generous amount of black pepper and reassemble the loaf. Place on a baking sheet and return to the oven for 5 minutes. Serve immediately, decorated with chopped black olives if liked.

American Muffins

It is not hard to see a connection between Irish soda bread and American muffins. The secret with American muffins is in the mixing – you hardly do any at all, just the barest minimum to combine wet with dry ingredients. A good muffin is very light with a tender crumb. They are so easy they are ideal for those awful mornings when you find last night's midnight munchies have left you no bread for breakfast. With savoury additions – sundried tomatoes, chopped olives, cheese, fried onions or mushrooms – they take the place of bread with salad, soup, mousse or stew. Equally at home for morning coffee or afternoon tea.

Bilberries are more difficult than most fruit to gather in quantity, but just a few can be thrown into a sweet muffin batter as can other berry fruits, dried fruits and citrus peel. Tiny wild strawberries, just a handful will suffice, in a soured cream muffin will give you a delectable breakfast. Seeds and nuts can be sweet or savoury. Flours can be varied and spices added. Curry powder and finely chopped dried apricot went into a muffin made with yoghurt and gave an excellent accompaniment for the Curried Parsnip Soup (p. 23). Prune and cinnamon ones married with the Chestnut, Mushroom and Red Wine Soup (p. 37). Serve them soon after baking, preferably still warm. If you do have to reheat – this works for scones too – lay the muffins on a baking sheet, sprinkle with cold water, cover with an inverted cake tin and put in a hot oven for 5 minutes.

8 oz/250 g self-raising flour – if using wheatmeal, increase the liquid slightly
1/2 tsp baking soda
good pinch salt
good pinch cream of tartar
1–2 tbs sugar – depending on other flavourings or honey or molasses. If using honey or molasses beat in with the wet ingredients
either: 1 egg
1 oz/30 g butter
1/4 pt/150 ml milk or buttermilk
or: 1 egg
1/3 pt/200 ml soured cream or yoghurt

Sift together the dry ingredients, adding any required spices. Melt the butter, if using. Either beat together the egg, milk (or buttermilk) and butter or the egg and yoghurt (or soured cream). Have ready any other additions as suggested above. Combine the ingredients with a fork or a palette knife. Do not try to rid the mixture of lumps. Do not beat, just stir very briefly, turning one mixture into the other. Spoon the rough batter immediately into well-greased bun tins. Do not overfill – a little over half full is ideal. Place in a hot oven (gas mark 6/400°F/200°C) for 20 minutes until well risen and browned.

Croissants

There is no one thing in cooking that defeated me for so long as making a good croissant. Repeatedly I tried as many recipes as I could find but the results were miserable – too greasy or flabby or hard, or once, shudder, slimy. Eventually, courtesy of somewhere between Anne Willan and the Brothers Roux, I achieved my goal. The procedure is much the same as the rolling, buttering and folding in puff and flaky pastries. Early misguided attempts with wholemeal flour have put me off ever considering an alternative flour again. Strong enough unbleached plain flour is unlikely to be British – homegrown wheat is too soft. The oven must be very hot. Croissants must be made with butter, unsalted and preferably Norman. The butter must be kept cold. They should ideally be eaten on the same day as making. Use leftovers the next day for stuffing, see the next recipe, or freeze for the same purpose later.

1 lb/500 g strong plain flour
2 tsp salt
1½ tsp sugar
½ oz/15 g fermipan yeast
6 oz/180 g unsalted butter
1 egg + 1 yolk
warm water – about ½ pt/300 ml

Sieve together the flour, salt, sugar and yeast. Rub in 1 oz/30 g of the butter. Make a well in the centre and tip in most of the water and one lightly beaten egg. Work together until a soft dough is formed – add a little more water if necessary. Knead on a floured surface until the dough has become smooth and elastic and firm. Roll out to about 20 × 8 in/50 × 20 cm. Lay on a sheet of floured greaseproof and fold into three. Pop into a bag and place in the coldest part of the fridge. Cut the butter up into small cubes. Dust them lightly with flour and keep ice-cold. Take out the dough and unfold it. Dot a third of the butter over two-thirds of the dough. Do not take the butter too close to the edge – leave a ½ in/1 cm border all the way around. Fold the unbuttered third over half the buttered dough and fold that over on itself, enclosing all the butter. Seal the edges by pressing together with a rolling pin. Wrap again and chill for 30 minutes

Turn the dough through 90° so that the shorter edge is towards you and then roll the dough out to 20 × 8 in/50

× 20 cm again. Proceed as before with another third of the butter. Fold, wrap and chill again. Repeat once more with the remaining butter and then roll, fold and chill another couple of times.

Finally roll out to a rectangle 20 × 10 in/50 × 25 cm. Using a sharp knife cut into 8 squares, 5 × 5 in/12.5 × 12.5 cm. Cut each square into two triangles. Beat together the remaining egg yolk with a tablespoon of water and brush each triangle with it. Avoid the very edges. Roll up the triangle towards the point. Lay on a baking sheet with the point underneath. Gently curve the two ends in to form the classic crescent. Space the croissants apart well and allow to prove, slowly, *not* in a warm place. Room temperature or a little below is better. This takes about an hour. It is possible to leave them overnight in the fridge for a breakfast baking; expect minimal loss of quality. Brush with a little more of the egg and water and bake at gas mark 7/425°F/220°C for about 17 minutes.

Stuffed Croissants

A good use for less than perfect croissants or brioches, whether shop bought or a bit stale. Useful when in a rush, a very quick supper dish when you feel too tired to lift more than a finger. Two fillings are suggested but many others elsewhere in the book could be used. Spinach with feta is very good, cheese and onion with or without a splash of wine, mushrooms and soured cream, any leftover pâté or vegetables – the list is limited only by one's imagination and larder.

If you have a good source of croissants then keep some frozen for emergency meals. Served with a salad or stir-fried vegetables, it is a meal in less time than it takes to queue for a burger.

8 croissants or small brioches – if the croissants are very large ones, either double the filling quantities or halve the number of croissants, depending on how ravenous people are

Filling I

6 oz/180 g Lancashire cheese, grated
1 large or 2 small avocados
2 cloves garlic, crushed
dash of cayenne pepper
salt

Filling II

1 large red onion
4 oz/125 g mushrooms
2 cloves garlic
1–2 oz/30–60 g stoned prunes
sage
oil
salt, pepper

I: Peel, stone and mash the avocado with the garlic. Stir in the cheese and the cayenne. Season to taste with salt.

II: Peel and chop the onion and garlic and fry in a little oil, over a medium heat, while chopping the mushrooms. Add the mushrooms to the pan and fry until the juices run. Meanwhile cut up the prunes and finely chop some sage. Stir into the mixture, adding a dash of brandy if liked. Season to taste with salt and pepper.

Using a sharp knife, slit the long edge of the croissants (or cut the top of a brioche). Divide the filling evenly and spoon into the split croissants. Place on a baking sheet and place in a moderate oven (gas mark 4/350°F/180°C) for 8–10 minutes.

Cornbread

Not far from baked Italian polenta is American cornbread. A stalwart of the soul food canon, it appears in various guises as one travels through the Southern states and on into Mexico where, without any frills of butter, milk or eggs, it is flattened to make tortillas.

There are Johnny Cakes, Hoe Cakes, Zephyrs, Corn pones, Dodgers, Puffs, Hush Puppies, Muffins or Sticks. It can be cooked in a big square tin in the same way as Yorkshire pudding or glamorised into the gritty-textured soufflé-like Spoonbread (see p. 143). Mrs Beeton's recipe, American Bread, is more like the latter.

Mine are via the ladies of St John's Guild, Montclair, circa 1925 – quantified and barely adjusted. My grandmother, having left Trinidad with my grandfather, married him in New Orleans cathedral and spent her honeymoon on the train to New York. She acquired this now sadly disintegrating compendium of food and invaluable advice as a new bride. As well as wonderful recipes, some with undeniable hints of the antebellum South, the book is full of hints on how to 'humanize cow's milk' or wash feather pillows, or how to drive nails into hard wood without bending, and how to care for the sick. To cure earache, the ladies suggest a strong solution of tobacco dripped into the ear or a small roasted onion or garlic clove could be popped in instead. As for growing pains, the child's legs should be wrapped in wrung-out hot salty towels – in bed – and then swaddled in warm dry thick flannels.

Virginia Cornbread

With acknowledgements to Mrs S. Beasley who must be at least a hundred if she is still with us.

1 lb/500 g fine yellow cornmeal
4 oz/125 g plain flour
¾ pt/425 ml buttermilk
2 eggs
1 tsp baking powder
1 tsp baking soda
1 tbs melted butter
boiling water
good pinch salt

Grease a deep square tin and put in a hot oven – gas mark 6/400°F/200°C. Combine the cornmeal, flour and salt. Pour about ¼ pt/150 ml of boiling water over it to moisten through. Beat in the eggs. Dissolve the soda in the buttermilk and beat that in vigorously with the melted butter. Pour into the preheated tin and bake for 20–25 minutes. Serve hot, cut into squares.

Christmas Pudding

One of the hardest things about writing this book was quantifying ingredients in recipes I had only ever made by eye. This pudding was the worst offender. For years I had added a little bit of this, some of the other and, oh yes, that too. To get it all down on paper was daunting. The list of ingredients, by its very length, may put you off if you have never made a Christmas pudding before, but do not worry: the method is easy. Approximately half the population eat shop-bought puddings. Given the quality of most of them, this is a national tragedy. The long boiling time does put people off but a pressure cooker will halve that. My friend Polly used to make all her extended family's puddings, cooking them in an old wash boiler. The smell that pervaded her cottage for days was heavenly.

Other dried fruits can be used. Cubes of dried mango and papaya as well as pineapple are now to be had. Dried cherries, pears, peaches, bananas, apricots and apples have all been incorporated in my puddings over the years. Before vegetable suet became available, I used to use melted butter in both the pudding and the mincemeat. This has quite a good flavour but suet gives a more authentic texture.

Here, then, is a Christmas pudding with no animal fats but tasting every inch a traditional pudding. Serve with cream, custard, hard sauce, ice cream, whatever, and enjoy it. A wicked treat on Boxing Day is to fry thin slices in butter and serve dusted with sugar.

12 oz/375 g raisins – preferably a
    mixture of lexias and afghans
8 oz/250 g currants
8 oz/250 g sultanas
2 oz/60 g stoned prunes
2 oz/60 g stoned fresh or dried
    dates
4 oz/125 g dried figs
3 oz/90 g shelled pecans
3 oz/90 g shelled walnuts
2 oz/60 g dried pineapple chunks
2 oz/60 g white glacé cherries
2 oz/60 g red glacé cherries – the
    natural coloured ones are best
2 medium apples

In a large bowl combine all the dried fruits, roughly chopping the figs, dates and prunes. Break up the nuts and add to the fruit with the cherries. Finely grate the lemon rind over the mixture and chop the peel. Grate the apples and carrots, cut up the clementine segments and squeeze the juice from the lemon. Do not discard the empty lemon halves. Add all this fresh fruit to the dried, combining well. Mix together the sugar and spices and sprinkle all over the bowl, stirring in. Pour on the alcohol or fruit juice – about $\frac{1}{4}$–$\frac{1}{3}$ pt/150–200 ml. Cover and leave to stand for at least 12 hours, but preferably 24–48.

2 medium carrots
1 lemon
2 clementines
1 large piece of candied citron peel
4 oz/125 g breadcrumbs – a
*   mixture of wholewheat and*
*   white if possible*
3 oz/90 g vegetable suet or melted
*   butter*
5 eggs
3 oz/90 g dark muscovado sugar
2 tsp ground cinnamon
1 tsp freshly grated root ginger
1 tsp ground cloves
good pinch black pepper
rum, brandy, stout, Marsala or
*   fruit juice*

Butter a couple of pudding basins, have ready some string, greaseproof paper and foil.

Combine the breadcrumbs and suet then stir them into the soaked fruit. If using melted butter stir in separately before the breadcrumbs. Beat the eggs and stir well into the mixture. Have a wish. Ensure that the mixture is not too stiff – if it is, add more rum or whatever. If it is too sloppy, add a few more breadcrumbs. It should be soft and dropping. Spoon into the basins, packing in well. Fill right to the top. Cover with a sheet of buttered grease-proof, with a pleat down the centre to allow for expansion. Pleat a double thickness of foil over the top and tie around with the string. You will make life easier for yourself if you make a handle of string across the top for lifting out the steamed pudding.

Place the covered puddings in a large saucepan with water coming halfway up the basin. Add the reserved lemon halves to the water and bring to the boil. Cover the pan and top up with boiling water from time to time. Boil for 6 hours. Cool and store in a cool dry place until Christmas.

On Christmas Day, boil as before for an hour. Remove foil and paper and invert the pudding onto a deep plate. Warm a little rum or brandy in a small pan, set light to it and pour over the pudding. You can do this operation at the table, with a ladle over a candle flame. It looks more impressive if you don't singe your eyebrows!

Christmas Cake

The cake should be made, ideally, six or more weeks before Christmas. I have given up thick royal icing and now prefer a luscious arrangement of candied fruit. In good years I prepare this myself, in more normal hectic years the deli is a good place to find the wonderful French boxed, bursting with mirabelles, marrons, prunes, cherries, peaches and so on. In the teeth of strong opposition, I still cling to my marzipan around the sides of the cake. Crimped along the top edge, it forms an elegant frame for the shining fruit. I think it is well worth making marzipan and a recipe follows.

6 eggs
12 oz/375 g butter
4 oz/125 g muscovado sugar
8 oz/250 g caster sugar
15 oz/480 g plain flour
3 lb/1.5 kg mixed dried fruit,
    including: muscat raisins
              sultanas
              currants
              cherries
              pineapple
              papaya
              mango
              apricot
4 oz/125 g pecans
4 oz/125 g walnuts
4 oz/125 g almonds
1 lemon
1 lime
1 orange
1/4 pt/150 ml Amaretto or Marsala
1 vanilla pod
2 tsp ground mixed spice –
    cinnamon, ginger, cloves

Leave the dried fruit, nuts and the grated rinds of the lemon, orange and lime to stand, covered, overnight with the Amaretto and the juice of the lemon, orange and lime.

Sieve the flour with the spice. Grease and line a 10 in/25 cm round cake tin. Wrap the outside in a double thickness of brown paper.

Beat the butter until soft and light. Slit the vanilla pod and scrape the tiny beans into the butter. Beat in both sugars very well until almost fluffy. Break an egg into a cup and whip lightly with a fork. Pour into the creamed butter and sugar, beating it in well. Repeat with the other eggs. The success of the cake will depend on this procedure. Do not add too much egg at once, and incorporate well before adding any more. Do not allow it to curdle. *In extremis* you can add a tablespoon of the measured flour to stop the mixture separating, but beating well is the real answer.

Fold in the flour and the fruit, alternately, in small amounts. Hands are really the best tools here – they allow you to get under the mixture more easily and you are less likely to find pockets of dry ingredients. When all is amalgamated, pack into the prepared tin. Slightly dish the top of the cake mixture instead of levelling. This means that when it does rise (only a bit) it won't form an unsightly Vesuvius in the centre.

Bake at gas mark 3/325°F/170°C for 1 hour, reduce to gas mark 2/300°F/150°C and cook for a further 1½–2 hours, covering the top if necessary to prevent over-browning. My former oven required me to keep a large roasting tin full of water on a lower shelf to prevent the cake burning on the bottom. This was because the source of heat was across the base of the oven. It used to be common to stand rich fruit cakes on a tray of sand to diffuse the base heat.

Use all your senses to tell when the cake is ready. The smell is unmistakeable, it will stop 'singing' (true; listen to a cake that is not fully cooked and you will hear a hissy, 'whee!' noise), and when a bright skewer is inserted in the centre it will come out clean. The crust should be a rich brown, smelling of sugar and spice and everything nice. Turn the oven off and leave the door ajar. Allow to get completely cold before removing from the tin. Store well wrapped. I like to feed my cake with some more alcohol, dribbling it over the top and allowing it to soak in.

Marzipan

St Mark's pain (as in bread, not dolour), March Pane (as in window, frosted *or* bread), massepain, marciapane or marzipan is a pliable paste of almonds, sugar and egg white. Its etymology is unclear and its origins hotly disputed, with Greeks, Turks, Romans, Arabs and nuns all queuing up to lay claim to its invention.

I like marzipan a lot, more so because of the almond deprivation I suffer in my house. I have to admit to sneaking chunks from the cake covering and scoffing it straight. Many Continental pâtisseries make intricately decorated marzipan cakes, glazed and baked, sometimes gilded and often studded with shining fruit. The paste is so easily worked, like infants' playdough, that all manner of tiny fruits and vegetables are fashioned out of it for petits fours. Vegetable colours can be kneaded into the marzipan or painted on after shaping. Let your imagination go. Cocoa powder can be dusted on as the earth on carrots and potatoes and a clove can be the stalk of an apple or pear. My sister, as a child, was given a marzipan alligator so beautifully crafted that he stayed as a permanent resident in the refrigerator for a decade or more. I own up to eating my pig (was someone trying to make a point?) rather more promptly.

Small cakes can be made in heart moulds, lined with marzipan and filled with finely chopped figs, apricots, almonds and amaretti. Turn them out and place under a hot grill for a minute or so to caramelise the marzipan slightly.

Use the paste too for stuffing dates or prunes – a Christmas task delegated to us as children – or for Simnel cake come Easter.

Homemade marzipan is so much better than the lurid blocks available commercially. Do try it.

12 oz/375 g shelled almonds
6 oz/180 g caster sugar
6 fl oz/175 ml water
1 tbs Kirsch or 2 tsp rose or
    orangeflower water
1 egg white
6 oz/180 g icing sugar

If the almonds are not already blanched – it is better if they are not – pour boiling water over them and allow to stand for a couple of minutes. The skin should then slip off easily. Nick the end and pop the kernel out. Leave the unpeeled ones in the water. Any bashful ones should be coaxed out of their coats by a second scalding. Dry well and place in a food processor with the Kirsch or orange-flower water. Alternatively grind finely in a mincer and work in the flavouring.

Dissolve the sugar and water in a small pan over a low heat. Bring to the boil, without stirring, and boil until the soft ball stage. This means a little of the syrup dropped into cold water can be gathered into a malleable ball; it happens at 234°F/100°C if you have a sugar thermometer. Pour the syrup into the ground almonds and process or work until a smooth paste is formed. Allow to get completely cool. Whisk the egg white until the foam just starts to peak. Work into the almond paste. Then add the icing sugar, a little at a time, until a soft pliable mass is formed. Ensure that the mixture is kept as cold as possible. Wrap in waxed or greaseproof paper, place in a tin and keep in a cool dry place until required.

Knead lightly before use on a surface dusted with icing sugar. Use either sieved apricot, plum or peach jam or a scarcely beaten egg white to brush the cake before covering with the marzipan.

Cheese and Onion Plait

Fragrant with dill seeds and a rich oniony crumb, the plait has a golden egg glaze sprinkled with cheese during the last 5 minutes of baking. Vary with herbs – sage or thyme are excellent – or use garlic, chives or leeks instead of onions. Also good baked as rolls; these should take between 10–15 minutes to bake depending on size.

1½ lb/750 g strong plain flour
1 large onion
*2 oz/60 g cheese – Farmhouse
    Cheddar or a Gloucester*
½ pt/300 ml milk
2 eggs
2 tsp dill seeds
½ tsp dry mustard powder
½ tsp ground cloves
1 tbs sugar
½ tsp salt
black pepper
4 oz/125 g melted butter
½ oz/15 g dried yeast

Peel the onion and either chop very finely or grate. Place in a saucepan with the milk, butter, sugar, ground cloves and dill seeds. Bring almost to the boil then remove from the heat and leave in a warm place for an hour. It should then be at about blood heat, just warm.

Sift the flour with the salt, mustard, a little black pepper and the yeast. Beat one of the eggs and add it to the milk mixture. Make a well in the centre of the flour and tip in the milk. Bring all the flour into the liquid gradually, working it to a smooth dough. Leave to rise under an inverted greased bowl for about an hour. It should have doubled in size. Punch the dough back sharply in the bowl and knead again briefly. Divide into three equal pieces and roll each into a long sausage, slightly fatter in the middle than at the ends. Plait the 'sausages' together. Some find this easiest by joining all three at one end and braiding like a pigtail to the other end. Bakers seem to prefer laying two in an X and then the third length through the centre. Then from the middle each half of the loaf is worked separately. Right goes to the left over the centre, left goes over to right, followed by left going under the centre to right, and vice versa. The whole loaf is turned and the other end plaited.

However you have achieved your plait – and you could just twist the lengths together – carefully pick up the loaf and lay it on a floured baking tin. Cover and leave to prove for 30 minutes. Beat the remaining egg with a pinch of salt and brush the plait all over before placing in a hot oven (gas mark 7/425°F/220°C) for 25 minutes. Grate the cheese. Take out the loaf, brush again with the egg and sprinkle with the cheese. Return to the oven for a further 5 minutes. Serve warm or cold.

Brioche

A good brioche is rich, yellow and feather-light. Its crust looks like a deep brown leather – it should not feel just like that, though. Delicate flavourings, a swirl of spice or a scattering of finely grated orange rind for example, can be added just before shaping. Brioches have their own special shaped tins that are deep and fluted. If you do not have one use a 1 lb coffee tin or a small deep cake tin.

Brioches, because of their lightness, are best accompanying clear delicate soups rather than the heavier ones. Leftover individual brioches are very good stuffed. The large ones can be toasted or fried in butter and dusted with cinnamon and sugar.

8 oz/250 g plain flour
8 oz/250 g strong white flour –
*   ensure there is no added*
*   vitamin C*
6 oz/180 g soft unsalted butter
5–6 eggs
1 oz/30 g fresh yeast or a little
*   under half that, dried fermipan*
*   yeast*
1/2 pt/300 ml milk
2 oz/60 g golden caster sugar
salt

Scald the milk and allow to cool to blood heat. Sift the flours and a pinch of salt together. Take out 4 oz/125 g of the flour and place in a bowl (and add the dried *fermipan* yeast if using). Cream fresh yeast with the sugar and stir in the warm but not hot milk. Pour onto the 4 oz/125 g of flour and combine. Leave in a warm place until the yeasted mixture has doubled in size.

Cut the butter up into small pieces. Beat 4–5 eggs (the more eggs the richer the dough) one at a time into the yeasted mixture, using the side of your hand or a electric mixer's dough hook. Work in the remaining flour and butter, a little of each at a time. Beat until no longer sticky. Cover and allow to rise for 4 hours or so. Knock the dough back by pushing down sharply in the bowl, and shape. For a classic shaped loaf, fill the greased tin with two-thirds of the dough reserving the rest to make a ball for the characteristic topknot.

Roll the ball into a pear shape. Cut a cross in the top of the brioche. Insert the narrow end of the 'pear' into the cross cut. Leave to prove for another 25 minutes and then brush with well-beaten egg. Beware, do not brush over the join between the ball and the base or they will be unable to rise properly in the oven, welded together by a varnish of egg.

Bake at gas mark 6/400°F/200°F for about 50–60 minutes for a large brioche, covering with paper if getting too brown. Small brioches can be cooked in a slightly hotter oven for 10–15 minutes.

Hoe Cakes

The donor of the original recipe is not named. Use the same ingredients but cook in greased, preheated, sponge finger tins and call them corn pones.

1 lb/500 g cornmeal
8 fl oz/250 ml boiling water
¹/₄ tsp salt
knob of butter
4 fl oz/125 ml milk

Pour the boiling water onto the cornmeal, salt and butter. Stir and allow to stand for 2 hours. Beat in the milk. Heat a heavy frying pan or griddle. Keep greased with a little butter. Fry tablespoonfuls, flipping over when set to brown the other side. Serve at once.

Some finely chopped cooked spring onions can be beaten into the batter before frying for extra flavour.

Serve either type of cornbread with gumbo, ratatouille, soup or stew in place of rolls, potatoes or rice.

Hazelnut Tuiles

Use these very delicate biscuits to accompany creams, sorbets, ice creams or fruit soups. They are called 'tuiles' as their curved shape is reminiscent of roof pantiles. You can make them more cup-like if you drape them over clean, upended jars when removing them from the oven.

Removal is easier if you use greased silicon paper to line your baking trays, a bit 'belt and braces', but helpful.

The nuts can be varied; try walnuts, pecans, flaked almonds or flaked peanuts. Use lemon or lime instead of orange, or omit the rind and add spices – cinnamon, cardamom, cloves, ginger or nutmeg – or add the tiny vanilla beans scraped from the pod. A more subtle vanilla perfume can be obtained by using vanilla sugar.

2 oz/60 g plain flour
4 oz/125 g icing sugar
2 oz/60 g unsalted butter
1 orange
2 egg whites
2 oz/60 g shelled hazelnuts

Dry roast the hazelnuts in a frying pan until very lightly browned; cool. Finely chop or grate them.

Melt the butter and allow to cool. Grate the orange rind, ensuring there is no white pith. With a whisk, combine the egg whites, butter, orange rind, flour and sugar into a smooth batter. Carefully place teaspoonfuls of batter on the greased, lined baking sheet. Smooth them into circles and sprinkle with a little of the hazelnuts. They will spread, so do not put too many on each sheet, 4–6 maximum. Only cook one batch at a time. Bake at gas mark 6/400°F/200°C for 5 minutes. Remove from the tray immediately and leave to cool, draped over a rolling pin. Wipe the silicon paper, re-grease and cook another batch.

For the cup-shaped ones, use 2 teaspoons of batter and cook for 7 minutes.

Focaccia

Elizabeth David says that focaccia is Genoese pizza. Often flavoured with rosemary, focaccia of late has been very trendy, taking over where pitta breads left off. The following recipe makes two large flat loaves. I like the Maldon type of sea salt best here. If you do not want lavender try rosemary or garlic. A cheap pizza place surprised and delighted me with focaccia when I had ordered their advertised garlic bread expecting the usual baguette. Dried herbs could be crumbled into the dough, but it is more authentic to push them into the top.

1 lb/500 g strong plain flour
¼ oz/7 g fermipan dried yeast
good dark green fruity olive oil
  which has had lavender steeping
  in it
warm water
sea salt
lavender leaves

Sift together the flour, 1 tsp finely ground salt and the yeast. Make a well in the centre and add 2 tbs of the olive oil and about ½ pt/300 ml warm water. Do not add all the water at once, only enough to make a softish dough. Knead well until smooth and elastic. Place in a well oiled bowl and turn about so that the ball of dough is covered in a film of oil. Cover the bowl with a teatowel and leave in a warm place until doubled in size – this takes between 1–2 hours normally.

Push down sharply on the dough in the bowl, knocking it back. Turn it out and knead for a couple of minutes. Divide into two and roll or press each out into a circle almost ½ in/1 cm thick. Brush two thick baking sheets with oil and place the breads on them. Using your thumb press a couple of lavender leaves into the dough every 2 in/5 cm or so. Make a pattern with the indentations if liked, pinwheeling them into the centre. Drizzle with oil and scatter with some *uncrushed* salt flakes.

Prove for 15–20 minutes then bake at the top of a hot oven (gas mark 8/450°F/230°C) for 15–20 minutes. Drizzle more fragrant oil on before taking, warm, to the table.

A step further around the Mediterranean can be taken using sesame oil, dropping the herbs and sprinkling with sesame seeds. The final pre-table oil should be *toasted* sesame variety. Try it warm with hummus and a Greek salad.

Herbed Scones

The great joy of this recipe is the speed with which you can prepare it. Homemade accompaniments to soups or stews make people feel they are really being cherished. Either bake the scones separately on a baking sheet or lay on the top of a casserole, cobbler style. Choose the herbs to complement the soup, stew or cheese. Sage scones are particularly good over a ragoût of oyster mushrooms with Bramleys and cider. The detailing of size and shape matters. A hearty soup calls for ample scones, perhaps in rustic wedges. Delicate broths could be served with tiny crescents. Change the flour for variations in texture and taste – try wholemeal or a 75:25 ratio of plain flour to fine oatmeal or barley flour.

8 oz/250 g plain flour
1 tsp baking powder
½ tsp salt
pinch dry mustard
2 oz/60 g butter (and please use butter)
¼ pt/150 ml soured milk
1 egg
up to 1 tbs chopped fresh herbs of choice – use your discretion: rosemary and thyme, for example, would be far too overpowering if used indiscriminately; smaller quantities are required. Green garlic can also be used.

Sift together the flour, baking powder, salt and mustard powder. This is important to avoid pockets of air in the scone, caused by an uneven distribution of baking powder. Stir in the herbs. Beat the egg and milk. Rub the butter into the herbed flour and bind to soft dough with most of the egg and milk – adding it all if necessary. Knead very lightly on a floured surface and pat or roll lightly out to between ½–1 in/1–2.5 cm thickness, depending on the finished size you wish to achieve. Place on a floured baking sheet. If you use interlocking patterns for cutting (diamonds, squares) you can avoid rerolling, but if necessary, knead the scraps very lightly. Small crescents will take about 7–8 minutes in a hot oven (gas mark 6/400°F/200°C); 2 in/5 cm rounds between 10–15 minutes. The tops of the scones can be glazed with any surplus egg/milk mixture or plain milk or egg. They can also be topped with grated cheese. Any glaze on the sides of the scones will inhibit rising.

To cook as a cobbler, lay the cut scones directly into the stew mixture and place in a hot oven (gas mark 7/425°F/220°C) until well risen and browned (about 10–15 minutes).

Jenny's Yoghurt and Cinnamon Rolls

I have shamelessly redone my friend Jenny's Vancouver Sunday brunch favourites. I had to – I lost the recipe she gave me. I hope she approves the modifications. As they rise in the fridge during the night they are well suited to a late (children willing) lazy breakfast. Also good as a dinner roll, for soup, with scattered herbs instead of sugar and cinnamon. Make the dough first thing in the morning in that case.

1 lb/500 g wheatmeal flour or half wheatmeal and half plain
¼ pt/150 ml plain yoghurt
3 oz/90 g melted butter
2 eggs
¼ oz/7 g fermipan-type dried yeast
3–4 oz/90–120 g soft brown sugar
1 tsp salt
ground cinnamon
a little milk

Have everything at warm room temperature. Stand the yoghurt over hot water if it has been in the fridge. Sift the flour with the dried yeast. Stir 4 tablespoons of the melted butter into the yoghurt. Beat the eggs with the salt and 2 oz/60 g of the sugar. In a large bowl, combine the yoghurt and egg mixtures and stir in the flour. Beat well, with the side of your hand for best results or a K or paddle beater on a food mixer. By hand, for about 6 minutes or mechanically, half that. Cover with a plate and place in the refrigerator until the morning.

Blearily, turn on the oven to gas mark 6/400°F/200°C. Make tea. Knead the dough briefly and roll out on a lightly floured surface into a large oblong about 12 × 12 in/30 × 60 cm. Brush the surface with melted butter and sprinkle with cinnamon and brown sugar. Roll up, swiss roll or palmier fashion, and cut into 24 1 in/2.5 cm thick slices. Lay on greased baking trays and leave in a warm place to double in size while you return to bed, virtuous, with the tea.

Get up. Brush rolls with milk, sprinkle with sugar and place them in the oven for 12–15 minutes.

Nan Bread

Nearly fifteen years ago I bought a wonderful book – *Indian Vegetarian Cooking*, I believe it was called, by Jack Santa Maria. I was first attracted to it by its beautiful cover, a detail from a painting of the market at Benares. I have not seen the book for over five years. I had tried in vain to replace mine, lost in irretrievable breakdown circumstances, as I enjoyed Santa Maria's approach to vegetarian food, finding a like mind who sought to exploit the potential of vegetables and their richness rather than find substitutes for meat dishes. Recently the book has been republished, sadly minus the fabulous cover. Indian cuisine has a long history of meat-free cooking for religious and economic reasons. Not all vegetarians are from the disadvantaged classes. Brahmins, traditionally vegetarian, were not poor and their food is not subsistence fare.

Jack Santa Maria gave at least two recipes for nans – one of them, if memory serves, a Royal Nan – and I used them both. I think what follows is probably an amalgam of the two with a quirk or so of my own.

In the absence of a clay tandoor, a heavy-duty preheated baking sheet works well or, I have discovered, a well-seasoned cast-iron-lidded frying pan.

1 lb/500 g strong plain flour
½ oz/15 g dried yeast
¼ pt/150 ml plain yoghurt at room temperature
1 oz/30 g ghee (clarified butter), melted + a little for brushing
½ tsp salt
1 tsp sugar
warm water
a little sesame oil

optional extras: with these it becomes a Peshwari nan

1 tbs dessicated coconut
1 tbs slivered almonds
1 tbs raisins
1 tsp aniseed
good pinch crushed cardamom seeds

Sift the flour, yeast, sugar and salt. Combine the ghee and yoghurt and pour onto the flour. Work to a soft dough, adding a small amount of warm water if too dry. Knead well, until smooth and elastic. Cover the ball of dough in a thin film of oil and place in a warm, covered bowl. Allow to double in size.

Push down sharply on the dough in the bowl, knocking it back and knead briefly. Place a baking sheet in a hot oven (gas mark 7/425°F/220°C) to preheat. Divide the dough into 16 equal balls and roll out to ovals about 8–9 in/20–22 cm long. Lay as many breads on the sheet as will fit. Brush with ghee and put in the oven for 4–5 minutes, until a speckling of brown spots appears. Turn over, brush the other sides and return to the oven for a further 5 minutes. Keep warm while cooking the rest of the breads. If you need to reheat do it briefly under a very hot grill.

To make the Peshwari nan, mix together the filling ingredients and push a teaspoon of the mixture into the centre of each dough ball before rolling out.

German Sunflower Bread

My long time favourite baker's bread has been ousted. Delicious as the chewy malt-meal cob is, it is beaten by the rye and sunflower loaf, bought in York but baked by Germans in Lancashire. As a 46-mile round trip is a bit excessive for one's daily bread, I have worked out my own recipe for this wonderful bread. Rye flour does not contain much gluten so I include some plain strong flour. The bread is not very dark like Schwarzbrot and it keeps well for days. Good toasted, thick, for breakfast with marmalade and, thin, an excellent base for smorgasbord.

1½ lb/750 g rye flour – not wholemeal rye
1½ lb/750 g strong plain flour
½ oz/15 g dried yeast
2 tsp salt
3 tbs light muscovado sugar
¾ pt/450 ml warm water
2 oz/60 g butter or margarine
3 oz/90 g sunflower seeds
2 tsp caraway seeds (optional)
1 egg white

Sift the flours, yeast and salt. Stir in the caraway and sunflower seeds, reserving a few for the tops. Warm the water with the sugar and butter. Make sure it is no hotter than blood heat before pouring most of it onto the flour. Work to a soft dough, adding the rest of the water and more if necessary. Knead until no longer sticky. It should be smooth (seeds apart) and elastic. Place in a warm, floured bowl and leave to double in bulk.

Push down sharply on the dough in the bowl, knocking it back and knead for 3–4 minutes. Shape into two long loaves – you can put them in greased loaf tins, if liked, or just on a greased and floured sheet. Lightly whip the egg white and brush the loaves. Sprinkle with the reserved seeds and allow to prove for an hour.

Bake in a hot oven (gas mark 6/400°F/200°C) for about 25–30 minutes. The loaves should sound hollow when rapped on the base. Resist the temptation to eat hot as the bread is much better cold.

Index

chanterelles, 172

chard: sag bhagee, 147–8

cheese: avocado gratin, 174; calzone, 114; cauliflower cheese soup, 21; cauliflower or broccoli cheese, 178; cheese and onion plait, 299–300; cheese churros, 157; cheese fondue, 238; Christmas crackers, 86–7; Dolcelatte and pear pizzette, 118; fennel and Torta di Dolcelatte soup, 28; fondue Hollandaise, 230; Greek salad, 52; lasagne verdi, 110–11; moussaka, 151–2; mushroom fritters, 113; port and Stilton undercurrants, 77–8; Scándinavian omelette, 137; strawberry cheese streusel, 279; stuffed croissants, 291; stuffed mushrooms, 172–3; stuffed onions, 195; tarte au Chaume, 64; tomato and Stilton ice cream, 269

cheese, soft: avocado and Mozzarella loaf, 287; Brie fingers, 132; cannoli, 122–3; croquembouche, 84–5; fennel and ricotta ravioli, 119–20; filled cake, 272–3; fruit pizza, 116–17; lasagne Michael Gray, 112; Mascarpone and Amaretto baskets, 270; Mozzarella, 103–4; panir, 147–8; pineapple and cream cheese sorbet, 265; piroshki, 150–1; pizza Bianca, 113; ricotta pancakes, 135; sablé Italienne, 74–5; spanakopitas, 159; stuffed nasturtium salad, 51; torta di Torta, 62–3

cheesecakes: blackbottom, 274; Wensleydale, garlic and three herb, 261–2

cherries, 67

chestnuts: chestnut, mushroom and red wine soup, 37; Christmas Brussels sprouts, 179; double-ovened chestnut soufflés, 142–3; raised chestnut and mushroom Christmas pie, 75–6; red cabbage in cider, 177–8; soufflé aux marrons, 144

chick peas: hummus, 216

chicory: sunray salad, 47

chiffonade de printemps, 177

Chinese salad, 56

chives, 191; egg and chives, 167

chocolate: blackbottom cheesecake, 274; chocolate and hazelnut tortellini alla panna, 120–1; chocolate custard, 232; filled cake, 272–3; layered mousse, 258; marbled fondue, 228; Mexican chocolate cream, 255

choux pastry: brandied peach ring, 100–1; choux swans with walnut pâté, 92–3; croquembouche, 84–5

chowder, sweetcorn, 36

Christmas Brussels sprouts, 179

Christmas cake, 295–6

Christmas crackers, 86–7

Christmas pudding, 293–4

churros, cheese, 157

cider: fondue Hollandaise, 230; red cabbage in cider, 177–8; sage and cidery pudding, 65

clafoutis, greengage, 139–40

clementines, caramelised, 235

cobbler, fruit, 286–7

consommé, beetroot and cranberry, 19

cornmeal: cornbread, 292; hoe cakes, 301; spoonbread, 143

coulibiac, 94–5

coulis, 233; apricot and orange, 234; tomato and red pepper, 233–4

courgettes: carrots and courgettes, 186; gougère with ratatouille, 98–9

couscous and tajine, 160–1

cranberries: beetroot and cranberry consommé, 19; croquembouche, 84–5

cream: burnt cream with rhubarb, 268; crème Anglaise, 231; Mexican chocolate cream, 255; spiked cream, 224; *see also* soured cream

cream cheese *see* cheese, soft

cream of watercress soup, 32

crème Anglaise, 231

crème caramel, spiced, 141–2

croissants, 289–90; stuffed croissants, 291

croquembouche, 84–5

crumbles: apricot and banana, 89; redcurrant and raspberry, 90

cucumber, 169; buttered cucumber and dill, 170; cucumber and mint ice, 254; cucumber and strawberry salad, 55; cucumber raita, 229–30; stir-fried cucumber, 169

curries: almond curry, 155; banana korma, 154; channa dhall, 156; curried parsnip soup, 23; curried peach tartlets, 96–7

custard: baked savoury custard, 138–9; chocolate custard, 232; crème Anglaise, 231

dill slaw, 167

Dolcelatte and pear pizzette, 118

double-ovened chestnut soufflés, 142–3

dried fruit: bara brieth, 285; barmbrack, 284; Christmas cake, 295–6; Christmas pudding, 293–4

éclairs, asparagus, 101–2

eggs, 127–44; aubergine sandwiches, 131; baked savoury custard, 138–9; batter pudding, 129–30; egg and chives, 167; quails' eggs in a nest, 128; Scandinavian omelette, 137; spiced crème caramel, 141; timbale with truffled eggs, 134

elderberries: elderberry and port sauce, 237; glazed pear with elderberry and port, 54

English onion soup, 26

equipment, 5–8

fennel: fennel and ricotta ravioli, 119–20; fennel and Torta di Dolcelatte soup, 28; lasagne Michael Gray, 112; Mediterranean salad, 53

filled cake, 272–3

flageolet beans, 217

flaky pastry: jalousie of kohlrabi, 81–2

Florentine calzone, 115–16

focaccia, 303

fondue: cheese fondue, 238; fondue Hollandaise, 203; marbled fondue, 228

French garlic soup, 29

fritters: cheese churros, 157; mushroom fritters, 133; tempura, 162–3

fromage frais: raspberry brulée, 260; tomato mousseline, 259–60

fruit: autumn pudding, 280; fruit cobbler, 286–7; fruit vinegars, 248–9; fruits of the forest bombe, 256–7; marbled fondue, 228; summer fruit terrine, 277–8; summer pudding, 271; *see also* dried fruit *and individual types of fruit* garlic, 191; French garlic soup, 29; garlic and potato purée, 203; garlic risotto, 148–9; garlic vinegar, 247; Wensleydale, garlic and three herb cheesecake, 261–2

German sunflower bread, 307

ginger: caramelised pear and ginger pudding, 281; carrot, orange and ginger sorbet, 252; carrot, orange and ginger soup, 20; gingered broccoli, 181–2; peach and ginger sauce, 227; rhubarb and ginger sorbet, 266–7; sesame, ginger and soy vermicelli, 107

girolles, 172

glazed carrots, 185

glazed pear with elderberry and port, 54

glazed shallots, 192

globe artichokes, 196; artichokes à la Grecque, 199; pizza Bianca, 113; stuffed artichokes, 197–8

gnocchi verdi in zuppa di pomodoro, 33–4

gooseberry relish, 245

gougère with ratatouille, 98–9

goulash, 153

granita with melons, 276–7

gratin, avocado, 174

Greek salad, 52

green bananas, 189; banana chips, 189; banana patties, 190

green salads, 41–3

greengage clafoutis, 139–40

guacamole, 175

hazelnuts: chocolate and hazelnut tortellini alla panna, 120–1; hazelnut tuiles, 302; marbled fondue, 228

herbs: flavoured oils, 250; herb vinegars, 246–7; herbed scones, 304; in salads, 41; Wensleydale, garlic and three herb cheesecake, 261–2

hoe cakes, 301

Hollandaise sauce, 240–1

hot-water crust: raised plum pies, 69–70

hummus, 216

ices, 251; cucumber and mint ice, 254; fruits of the forest bombe, 256–7; Marsala and brown bread parfait, 275–6; peach parfait, 263; tomato and Stilton ice cream, 269; see also sorbets

ingredients, 9–14

jalousie of kohlrabi, 81–2

jellies, 251; petites terrines, 264; summer fruit terrine, 277–8

Jenny's yoghurt and cinnamon rolls, 305

Jerusalem artichokes, 196; artichoke purée, 197; roast artichokes with rosemary, 196

kashka (buckwheat grains): coulibiac, 94–5

kiwi fruit: kiwi and avocado salad, 58; kiwi sorbet, 262

kohlrabi: jalousie of kohlrabi, 81–2; roast kohlrabi cups, 183

kumquats: Sussex puddle pudding, 73

lasagne, 108–9; lasagne Michael Gray, 112; lasagne verdi, 110–11

lavender vinegar, 246

layered mousse, 258

leeks, 191; braised leeks, 193; Christmas crackers, 86–7; leek terrine, 194–5; leek vinaigrette, 192–3; stout pudding, 66

legumes, 214

lemony potatoes, 203–4

lentils: tourtière, 164–5

lettuce: lettuce soup, 30; mixed salad greens, 41–3; peas and lettuce, 215; see also salads

limequats: Sussex puddle pudding, 73

lovage, Worcester and walnut salad, 44

Madeira sauce, 223

mangetouts: stir-fried mangetouts and almonds, 215

mangoes: tropical strudel, 83–4

marbled fondue, 228

marigold and potato salad, 49

Marsala and brown bread parfait, 275–6

marzipan, 297–8

Mascarpone and Amaretto baskets, 270

mayonnaise: potato and marigold salad, 49

Mediterranean salad, 53

melons, granita with, 276–7

meringue, spiced apple, 87–8

a mess of greens, 184

Mexican chocolate cream, 255

mint and cucumber ice, 254

mixed salad greens, 41–3

morels, 171–2

moussaka, 151–2

mousse, layered, 258

mousseline, tomato, 259–60

Mozzarella, 103–4; avocado and Mozzarella loaf, 287

muffins, American, 288

mushrooms, 171–2; beurre Bourguignon, 239; calzone, 114; chestnut, mushroom and red wine soup, 37; clear mushroom soups, 24–5; goulash, 153; lasagne, 108–9; Madeira sauce, 223; moussaka, 151–2; mushroom fritters, 133; mushroom risotto, 149; mushroom salad, 173; mushrooms in soured cream, 167; oyster mushroom and soured cream tart, 68–9; raised chestnut and mushroom Christmas pie, 75–6; sablé Italienne, 74–5; sage and cidery pudding, 65; stout pudding, 66; stuffed croissants, 291; stuffed mushrooms, 172–3; stuffed onions, 195; torta di Torta, 62–3; won tons, 125–6

mustard-glazed turnips, 212

nan bread, 306–7

nasturtium salad, stuffed, 51

nectarines: fruit pizza, 116–17; grilled nectarines, 236

oils, flavoured, 250

okra: couscous and tajine, 160–1

olives: Greek salad, 52

omelette, Scandinavian, 137

onions, 191; cheese and onion plait, 299–300; English onion soup, 26; onion and apple tart renversée, 79–80; potatoes and onions in white wine, 205; stuffed onions, 195; tomato ragoût with polenta, 209–10

oranges: apricot and orange coulis, 234; avocado, tomato and orange salad, 59; baby beets in orange sauce, 176;

caramelised clementines, 235; carrot, orange and ginger sorbet, 252; carrot, orange and ginger soup, 20; Mediterranean salad, 53

oyster mushrooms: oyster mushroom and soured cream tart, 68–9; won tons, 126

pancakes, ricotta, 135

panir, 147–8

parfait: Marsala and brown bread, 275–6; peach, 263

parsnips, 200; curried parsnip soup, 23; parsnip and potato galettes, 200–1; quails' eggs in a nest, 128; sage and cidery pudding, 65

passionfruits: blackbottom cheesecake, 274

pasta, 103, 104–5; apricot and amaretti ravioli, 123–4; cannoli, 122–3; chocolate and hazelnut tortellini alla panna, 120–1; fennel and ricotta ravioli, 119–20; lasagne, 108–9; lasagne Michael Gray, 112; lasagne verdi, 110–11; sesame, ginger and soy vermicelli, 107; tagliatelle with avocado, 106; won tons, 125–6

pastries, 60–102

pâtés: choux swans with walnut pâté, 92–3; port and Stilton undercurrants, 77–8

patties, banana, 190

peaches: brandied peach ring, 100–1; curried peach tartlets, 96–7; peach and ginger sauce, 227; peach parfait, 263; peach vinegar, 249

pears: caramelised pear and ginger pudding, 281; Dolcelatte and pear pizzette, 118; glazed pear with elderberry and port, 54; pear sauce, 226; Williams salad, 50; winter salad, 45

peas: peas and lettuce, 215; samosas, 146–7

peas, yellow split: channa dhall, 156

peppers: gougère with ratatouille, 98–9; goulash, 153; lasagne, 108–9; tomato and red pepper coulis, 233–4; tomato ragout with polenta, 209–10

petites terrines, 264

pickled pineapple, 225

pickled samphire, 207

pies, 71–2; raised chestnut and mushroom Christmas pie, 75–6; raised plum pies, 69–70; tourtière, 164–5

pineapple: pickled pineapple, 225; pineapple and cream cheese sorbet, 265; tropical strudel, 83–4

pink fir apple and prunes, 202

piroshki, 150–1

pitahayas: black and white salad, 57

pizzas, 103–5; Dolcelatte and pear pizzette, 118; fruit pizza, 116–17; pizza Bianca, 113

plantains see green bananas

plums: Brie fingers, 132; plum and almond tart, 80; raised plum pies, 69–70

polenta, tomato ragoût with, 209–10

pomegranates: spiced rice, 221

porcini, 172; Florentine calzone, 115–16

port: elderberry and port sauce, 237; glazed pear with elderberry and port, 54; port and Stilton undercurrants, 77–8

potatoes, 202; garlic and potato purée, 203; lemony potatoes, 203–4; parsnip and potato galettes, 200–1; pink fir apple and prunes, 202; potato and marigold salad, 49; potatoes and onions in white wine, 205;

potatoes in red wine, 204; quails' eggs in a nest, 128; samosas, 146–7; tourtière, 164–5

potatoes, sweet see sweet potatoes

prunes: Carib prune pie, 91–2; pink fir apple and prunes, 202; stuffed croissants, 291

puffballs, 171

quails' eggs in a nest, 128

radicchio: sunray salad, 47

raised chestnut and mushroom Christmas pie, 75–6

raised plum pies, 69

raita, cucumber or banana, 229–30

raspberries: raspberry brulée, 206; raspberry soup, 35; redcurrant and raspberry crumble, 90

ratatouille, gougère with, 98–9

ravigote-sauced vegetables, 129–30

ravioli: apricot and amaretti, 123–4; fennel and ricotta, 119–20

red cabbage in cider, 177–8

redcurrants: port and Stilton undercurrants, 77–8; redcurrant and raspberry crumble, 90

relish, gooseberry, 245

rhubarb: burnt cream with rhubarb, 268; rhubarb and ginger sorbet, 266–7; rhubarb soup, 40

rice, 218; garlic risotto, 148–9; moussaka, 151–2; rice salad, 218; savoury rice pudding, 219; spiced rice, 221; tricolour rice, 220–1

ricotta: fennel and ricotta ravioli, 119–20; ricotta pancakes, 135

risotto, garlic, 148–9

rolls, Jenny's yoghurt and cinnamon, 305

rum butter, 243

sablé Italienne, 74–5

sag bhagee, 147–8

sage and cidery pudding, 65

salads, 41–59; avocado, tomato and orange, 59; black and white, 57; Chinese, 56; cucumber and strawberry, 55; Greek, 52; kiwi and avocado, 58; Mediterranean, 53; mixed salad greens, 41–3; mushroom, 173; potato and marigold, 49; rice, 218; strawberry and avocado, 48; stuffed nasturtium, 51; sunray, 47; tomato and sorrel, 46; turnip, 213; Williams, 50; winter, 45; Worcester, walnut and lovage, 44

salsify, 201; salsify pie, 71–2

samosas, 146–7

samphire, 206; boiled samphire, 206; pickled samphire, 207

satay, 158

sauces: almond curry, 155; apricot and orange coulis, 234; beurre blanc, 242; beurre Bourguignon, 239; blackcurrant reduction, 244; chocolate custard, 232; crème Anglaise, 231; elderberry and port, 237; Hollandaise, 240–1; Madeira, 223; peach and ginger, 227; pear, 226; tomato and red pepper coulis, 233–4

savoury rice pudding, 219

Scandinavian omelette, 137

scones, herbed, 304

sesame, ginger and soy vermicelli, 107

shallots, glazed, 192

soda bread, 283
sorbets: carrot, orange and ginger, 252; celery and apple, 253; kiwi, 262; pineapple and cream cheese, 265; rhubarb and ginger, 266–7; *see also* ices
sorrel: asparagus with sorrel butter, 188–9; tomato and sorrel salad, 46
soufflés: banana, 136; double-ovened chestnut, 142–3; soufflé aux marrons, 144
soups, 15–40; apricot, 18; avocado, 39; beetroot and cranberry consommé, 19; carrot, orange and ginger, 20; cauliflower cheese, 21; celeriac bouillon, 27; celery, apple and Calvados, 22; chestnut, mushroom and red wine, 37; clear mushroom, 24–5; clear tomato, 38; cream of watercress, 32; curried parsnip, 23; English onion, 26; fennel and Torta di Dolcelatte, 28; French garlic, 29; gnocchi verdi in zuppa di pomodoro, 33–4; lettuce, 30; raspberry, 35; rhubarb, 40; sweet potato, 31; sweetcorn chowder, 36; three green, 34
soured cream: broad beans in soured cream, 214; mushrooms in soured cream, 167; oyster mushroom and soured cream tart, 68–9; soured cream tart, 67; strawberry cheese streusel, 279
spanakopitas, 159
spiced apple meringue, 87–8
spiced crème caramel, 141–2
spiced rice, 221
spiked cream, 224
spinach: Florentine calzone, 115–16; lasagne verdi, 110–11; sag bhagee, 147–8; spanakopitas, 159; won tons, 126
spoonbread, 143
spring greens: chiffonade de printemps, 177
squashes: couscous and tajine, 160–1
Stilton: port and Stilton undercurrants, 77–8; tomato and Stilton ice cream, 269
stock, 15–16
stout pudding, 66
strawberries: blackbottom cheesecake, 274; cucumber and strawberry salad, 55; filled cake, 272–3; fruit cobbler, 286–7; strawberry and avocado salad, 48; strawberry cheese streusel, 279; strawberry vinegar, 248–9
streusel, strawberry cheese, 279
strudel, tropical, 83–4
stuffed artichokes, 197–8
stuffed croissants, 291
stuffed mushrooms, 172–3
stuffed nasturtium salad, 51
stuffed onions, 195
stuffed tomatoes, 208–9
suet pastry: sage and cidery pudding, 65; stout pudding, 66; Sussex puddle pudding, 73
summer fruit terrine, 277–8
summer pudding, 271
sunflower bread, German, 307
sunray salad, 47
Sussex puddle pudding, 73
sweet potato soup, 31
sweetcorn chowder, 36

tagliatelle with avocado, 106

tarts: Carib prune pie, 91–2; curried peach tartlets, 96–7; onion and apple tart renverseé, 79–80; oyster mushroom and soured cream tart, 68–9; plum and almond tart, 80; soured cream tart, 67; spiced apple meringue, 87–8; tarte au Chaume, 64
tempura, 162–3
terrines: leek, 194–5; petites, 264; summer fruit, 277–8
three green soup, 34
timbale with truffled eggs, 134
tomatoes, 208; avocado, tomato and orange salad, 59; baked tomatoes, 210; Brussels, Italy, 179–80; calzone, 114; clear tomato soup, 38; gnocchi verdi in zuppa di pomodoro, 33–4; gougère with ratatouille, 98–9; goulash, 153; Greek salad, 52; lasagne, 108–9; lasagne Michael Gray, 112; stewed green tomatoes, 211; stuffed tomatoes, 208–9; three green soup, 34; tomato and red pepper coulis, 233–4; tomato and sorrel salad, 46; tomato and Stilton ice cream, 269; tomato mousseline, 259–6; tomato ragoût with polenta, 209–10; torta di Torta, 62–3
Torta di Dolcelatte: torta di Torta, 62–3
tortellini: chocolate and hazelnut tortellini alla panna, 120–1
tourtière, 164–5
tricolour rice, 220–1
tropical strudel, 83–4
truffles, 171; petites terrines, 264; timbale with truffled eggs, 134
tuiles, hazelnut, 302
turnips, 212; mustard-glazed turnips, 212; turnip salad, 213

vegetables, 168–221; banana korma, 154; batter pudding and ravigote-sauced vegetables, 129–30; petites terrines, 264; tempura, 162–3; *see also individual types of vegetable*
vermicelli: sesame, ginger and soy vermicelli, 107
vinaigrette, leek, 192–3
vinegars, fruit, 248–9; peach, 249; strawberry, 248–9
vinegars, herb, 246–7; garlic, 246; lavender, 246
Virginia cornbread, 292

walnuts: Brussels sprouts and walnuts, 180–1; choux swans with walnut pâté, 92–3; stuffed mushrooms, 172–3; Worcester, walnut and lovage salad, 44
watercress soup, cream of, 32
Welsh onions, 191
Wensleydale, garlic and three herb cheesecake, 261–2
Williams salad, 50
wine: beurre Bourguignon, 239; chestnut, mushroom and red wine soup, 37; potatoes and onions in white wine, 205; potatoes in red wine, 204
winter salad, 45
won tons, 125–6
Worcester, walnut and lovage salad, 44

yoghurt: cucumber or banana raita, 229–30; home-made, 229; Jenny's yoghurt and cinnamon rolls, 305